HORSES, MULES, AND PONIES
AND HOW TO KEEP THEM

$\frac{1}{10}$

URAL OWL.
SYRNIUM URALENSE.

EX LIBRIS

A CLYDESDALE STALLION.

(*Drawn on Wood, by H. W. Herbert.*)

HORSES, MULES, AND PONIES

AND HOW TO KEEP THEM

Practical Hints for Horse-Keepers

HENRY WILLIAM HERBERT

THE LYONS PRESS

First Lyons Press Edition 2000

Originally published in 1859 by the Orange Judd Company, New York.

Printed in Canada

10 9 8 7 6 5 4 3 2 1

The Library of Congress Cataloging-in-Publication Data
is available on file.

HERBERT.

Henry William Herbert, more familiarly known as "Frank Forester," was born in London, on the 7th of April, 1807. His father, the Hon. and Rev. William Herbert, Dean of Manchester, and third son of the Earl of Carnarvon, was a profound scholar, and is well known to the American public as the author of "Attila." His mother, a most estimable lady, was the second daughter of Viscount Allyn, of Kildare, a representative peer of Ireland, and is still living in London.

Herbert was thus descended from some of the most aristocratic families of Great Britain and Ireland; and to the advantages of birth he joined those of a thorough education, which commenced under the auspices of private tutors in his father's house, and was continued at Eton and Cambridge, until he graduated from Caius College at the age of twenty-three. His tastes and occupations through life induced a habit of study, and it was recently remarked by a gentleman of New York, whose position brings him in contact with literary men and scholars, that Herbert was one of the best educated men of his acquaintance.

Our author's acquirements at Cambridge were not all of a scholastic nature; for he there contracted such habits of life, that before he attained the age of twenty-five, he had thrice been "whitewashed" for insolvency; had been sentenced to outlawry for debt; and had emigrated to

America, where he soon expended his little remaining money. It is now that his life, as a man, commenced; and the many difficulties and misfortunes which beset his way, are thus alluded to in his last letter to the press:—" I bear an honorable name; I have striven hard, in great trial, in great temptation, in a foreign country, in a false position, among men who did not, perhaps could not, sympathize with me, to keep it honorable." Again—" Remember also, when you judge me, that of all lives, mine has been almost the most unhappy. No counsellor, no friend, no country. have been mine, for six-and-twenty weary years. Every hope has broken down under my foot as soon as it has touched it. Every spark of happiness has been quenched as soon as it has been kindled."

For eight years Herbert was a teacher in a school in New York, where he gave the most perfect satis- faction. He was a frequent contributor to the best jour- nals of the day, and an editor of the " American Monthly Magazine." In " The Captains of the Old World," " The Roman Republic," "The Brothers, a tale of the Fronde," " Ringwood the Rover," " Warwick Woodlands," " Crom- well," &c., he has given pleasure and instruction to many readers. These facts concern Herbert's literary reputa- tion, which was good among distinguished literary men; but that which binds him to the hearts of true sportsmen, and lovers of nature, he has won under the *nom de plume* of " Frank Forester," in the " Field Sports," " Fish and Fishing," " The Deer Stalkers," " The Complete Manual for Young Sportsmen," etc. More recently, he wrote a very large work on " The Horse of America," and, last of all, these " Hints to Horse-Keepers."

Herbert was twice married;—first, in 1839, to a Miss Barker, of Bangor, whither he had accompanied a gentleman of New York, a literary friend, for the purpose of acting as groomsman at the marriage of his friend and the lady in question. With the variableness of a woman, Miss Barker made a bridegroom of the groomsman, and cast an enduring shadow over the life of her former suitor. The only child by this wife was a son, now living in England, at the age of eighteen. Mrs. Herbert died in 1846.

In February of 1858, Herbert married a lady from Providence, R. I., after a brief and romantic acquaintance. His affection for her seems to have been unbounded; but —whether on account of habits long ago contracted, or in consequence of the slanders of meddlesome neighbors, the world does not know, and has no right to inquire—she left him; and he, broken down by this last great sor ow of a life of sorrows, committed suicide at the Stevens House in New York, on the 17th day of April, 1858. He was buried in the cemetery adjoining his place, " the Cedars," near Newark, N. J.

The character of Herbert is a difficult one to criticize; but it is very certain that his intellectual attainments, his great love for everything in nature, and his power of communicating that love to his readers, by far outweigh in importance his faults, which were those of the head and not of the heart. In no line that he ever wrote is there an improper tendency, or the expression of an impure thought. Judged by his works, he appears preëminently a good man. Judged by what is known of his life, he appears to have been prevented only by faults which were the inheritance of a misspent youth, from becoming a bright example of combined greatness and goodness.

1*

CONTENTS.

CHAPTER I.

HOW TO BREED A HORSE—CHOICE OF STALLION.

CHAPTER II.

HOW TO BREED A HORSE—CHOICE OF THE MARE.

CHAPTER III.

HOW TO BREED A HORSE—MUTUAL ADAPTATION OF SIRE AND DAM.

CHAPTER IV.

HOW TO BREED A HORSE—CANADIAN BLOOD.

CHAPTER XI.

HOW TO STABLE AND GROOM A HORSE.

CHAPTER XII.

HOW TO BREAK, AND USE A HORSE.

CHAPTER XIII.

HOW TO PHYSIC A HORSE—SIMPLE REMEDIES FOR SIMPLE AILMENTS.

CHAPTER XIV.

FARRIERY, ETC.

CHAPTER XV.

HOW TO SHOE A HORSE.

CHAPTER XVI.

BAUCHER'S METHOD OF TRAINING HORSES.

CHAPTER XVII.

HOW TO RIDE A HORSE.

CHAPTER XVIII.

LADIES' RIDING—WRITTEN BY A LADY.

CHAPTER XIX.

HOW TO DRIVE A HORSE.

CHAPTER XX.

RAREY'S SYSTEM OF HORSE-TAMING.

CHAPTER XXI.

RACING.

CHAPTER XXII.

VETERINARY HOMŒOPATHY.

CHAPTER XXIII.

CARRIAGES.

CHAPTER XXIV.

HARNESS.

SATIRIST.

CHAPTER I.

HOW TO BREED A HORSE—CHOICE OF STALLION.

NATIONAL VALUE OF THE HORSE—THE BETTER CLASS OF HORSES THE
CHEAPEST FOR ALL PURPOSES—WHAT CONSTITUTES EXCELLENCE?—
"BLOOD;" WHAT IT GIVES—SHOULD BE ON THE SIDE OF THE SIRE—
BREED UP, NOT DOWN—DISEASES AND DEFECTS HEREDITARY—GENERAL
RULES,

To enter into an argument at this day of the nineteenth
century, to show that the horse stock of any country is a
material item in the account of the national wealth,
strength and greatness, would be to admit the arguer himself an ass, or at least to show that he believed himself to
be addressing an audience of asses. In no country in the
world, perhaps, is such an argument less needed than in
our own, where, certainly, the keeping of horses for the
purposes of pleasure as well as of utility is more largely
disseminated among persons of all classes than in any other,
and where the desire and ability both to keep and breed
horses of a high grade is daily gaining ground, both in
town and country. Among farmers the desire to raise valuable stock is, at least, increasing proportionally to the
increase of the profit to be derived from them, which is

advancing every day not in consequence of any casual or temporary caprice, but is attributable to the growing perception of the fact, among all horse-keepers, that it is not only *as* cheap, if one keeps a horse at all, to keep a good as to keep a bad one, but in reality much cheaper. The prime cost is the only difference to be considered: the price of stable-room, keep and care is identical; the wear and tear is infinitely less in the sound, able, useful animal than in the broken-down jade; the work which can be done and the value earned by the one is in no possible relation to those by the other; while, to conclude, the cash value of the superior animal, judiciously worked,—and by judiciously is meant profitably to the owner, as well as moderately and mercifully to the beast,—and properly tended, is actually increasing annually at a greater rate than that at which the inferior animal is deteriorating.

In other words, a four-year-old horse, well bought at a price of two or three hundred dollars or upward, will, when he has attained the age of seven or eight years, after having earned his meat and paid the interest of his prime cost by his services, be worth twice the money, either for working purposes or for sale, if the owner see fit to dispose of him; while an animal bought for half or a third of that price, at the same age, will probably, at the same increased age, be wholly worn out, valueless and useless; and the greater the excellence of the animal in the first instance, the greater and more rapid will be the increase in value; the lower his qualities, to begin, the speedier and more complete the deterioration.

Now, as to what constitutes value or excellence in all horses.—It is indisputably quickness of working; power to move or carry weight, and ability to endure for a length of time; to travel for a distance with the least decrease of pace ; to come again to work day after day, week after week, and year after year, with undiminished vigor. And it is scarcely needful to say that, under all ordinary circum- stances these conditions are only compatible with the highest form and highest physical health of the animal. Mal- formation must necessarily detract from speed and power ; hereditary disease or constitutional derangement must nec- essarily detract from all powers whatsoever. Under usual circumstances it would hardly be necessary to undertake to show that quickness of working, or, in other words, speed, is necessary to a high degree of excellence in a horse of any stamp or style, and not one iota less for the animal which draws the load or breaks the glebe, than for the riding horse or the pleasure traveller before light vehicles. But it has of late become the fashion with some parties to undervalue the advantages of speed, and to deny its utility for other purposes than for those of mere amusement; and, as a corollary from this assumption, to disparage the effect and deny the advantage of *blood*, by which is meant descent, through the American or English race-horse, from the oriental blood of the desert, whether Arabian, Barb, Turk, Persian or Syrian, or a combination of two or more, or all of the five.

The horse which can plough an acre while another is ploughing half an acre, or that which can carry a load of passengers ten miles while another is going five, indepen- dent of all considerations of amusement, taste, or what is generally called fancy, is absolutely worth twice as much to his owner as the other.

Now the question for the breeder is simply this : By what means is this result to be obtained ? The reply is, by getting the greatest possible amount of pure blood com- patible with size, weight and power, according to the pur-

pose for which he intends to raise stock, into the animal
bred. For not only is it not true that speed alone is the
only good thing derivable from blood, but something very
nearly the reverse is true. It is very nearly the *least* good
thing. That which the blood-horse does possess is a degree of strength in his bones, sinews, and frame at large,
utterly out of proportion to the size or apparent strength
of that frame. The texture, the form and the symmetry
of the bones,—all, in the same bulk and volume,—possess
double, or nearer four-fold, the elements of resistance and
endurance in the blood-horse that they do in the cold-
blooded cart-horse. The difference in the form and texture of the sinews and muscles, and in the inferior tendency
to form flabby, useless flesh, is still more in favor of the
blood-horse. Beyond this, the internal anatomical construction of his respiratory organs, of his arterial and
venous system, of his nervous system, in a word, of his
constitution generally,—is calculated to give him what
he possesses, greater vital power, greater recuperatory
power, greater physical power, in proportion to his bulk and
weight, than any other known animal—added to greater
quickness of movement, and to greater courage, greater
endurance of labor, hardship, suffering—in a word, greater
(what is called vulgarly) game or pluck than will be
found in any other of the horse family.

But it is not to be said, or supposed, that all blood-horses
will give these qualities in an equal degree ; for there is as
much or more choice in the blood-horse than in any other
of the family. Since, as in the blood of the thorough-bred
horse all faults, all vices, all diseases are directly hereditary,
as well as all virtues, all soundness, all good qualities, it
is more necessary to look, in the blood-horse, to his antecedents, his history, his performances, and, above all, to his

shape, temper, soundness and constitution, than it is in any other of the horse family.

To breed from a small horse with the hope of getting a large colt; from a long-backed, leggy horse, with the hope of getting a short, compact, powerful one; from a broken-winded, or blind, or flat-footed, or spavined, or ringboned or navicular-joint-diseased horse, with the hope of getting a sound one; from a vicious horse, a cowardly horse,—what is technically called a dunghill,—with the hope of getting a kind-tempered and brave one; all or any of these would be the height of folly. The blood sire (and the blood should always be on the sire's side) should be, for the farmer-breeder's purposes, of medium height, say 15½ hands high, short-backed, well-ribbed up, short in the saddle-place, long below. He should have high withers, broad loins, broad chest, a straight rump,—the converse of what is often seen in trotters, and known as the *goose rump;* a high and muscular, but not beefy crest; a lean, bony, well-set-on head; a clear, bright, smallish, well-placed eye; broad nostrils and small ears. His fore legs should be as long and as muscular as possible above the knee, and his hind legs above the hock, and as lean, short and bony as possible below those joints. The bones cannot by any means be too flat, too clear of excrescences, or *too large.* The sinews should be clear, straight, firm, and hard to the touch. From such a horse, where the breeder can find one, and from a well-chosen mare (she may be a little larger, more bony, more roomy, and in every way coarser than the horse, to the advantage of the stock), sound, healthy and well-limbed, he may be certain, accidents and contingencies set aside, of raising an animal that will be creditable to him as a scientific stock breeder, and profitable to him in a pecuniary sense.

The great point then to be aimed at is, the combining in the same animal the maximum of speed compatible with sufficient size, bone, strength, and solid power to carry heavy weights or draw large loads, and at the same time to secure the stock from the probability, if not certainty, of inheriting structural deformity or constitutional disease from either of the parents. The first point is only to be attained, first, by breeding as much as possible to pure blood of the right kind ; and, second, by breeding what is technically called among sportsmen and breeders, *up*, not *down :* that is to say, by breeding the mare to a male of superior (not inferior) blood to herself,—except where it is desired to breed like to like, as Canadian to Canadian, or Norman to Norman, for the purpose of perpetuating a pure strain of any particular variety, which may be useful for the production of brood mares.

By superior blood we mean that which approaches nearer to thorough blood. Thus, a half-bred mare should never be put to a half-bred stallion, as in that case the produce will, in nine cases out of ten, degenerate below the dam; whereas, if she be bred to a thorough-bred the pro duce will be superior, and will continually improve *ad infinitum*, by adhering to the same process of breeding up. In the second place, a reasonable probability of raising sound and healthy stock can only be attained by carefully selecting parents free from disease, which is either hereditary, or apt to become so.

It is idle for persons at this time of the world, to sneer at the idea of disease or other qualities being hereditary, or transmissible in the blood : it is known, both medically and physiologically, that they are so. All diseases of the lungs and windpipe, known as the heaves, as broken wind, as roaring, whistling thick wind, and the like, are, incon testably, transmissible. Blindness is, if possible, yet more so; and even when one eye is destroyed by accident, if the other eye, through a sympathetic affection, follow it, we should consider it by no means safe to breed from a horse so injured. Lameness, arising from pure accident, is of course not transmissible; but where a race-horse has broken down, as it is termed, in running,—that is to say, where the sinews, or smaller metacarpal bones, commonly known as the splint bones, have given way from want of strength sufficient to endure the strain laid upon them,—it will be well to observe whether there be not some visible defect of the conformation of those parts, tending to undue weakness: such as disproportionate length of the lower or cannon bone of the fore leg, which can scarcely be too short; or the defect which is generally called *tying in*, consisting of an improper contraction of the volume of the leg, immediately below the fore knee, and indicating an insufficiency of the splint bone. These malformations are distinctly hereditary. If a horse, therefore, break down in his fore legs, having such a malformation, the breaking down itself may be said to have been hereditary; and one would, therefore, eschew breeding from such a horse. Now, to give two cases in point: there is probably not a horse in America which a good judge would sooner select, in regard to size, strength, power, and all other qualifications, to which to put country mares, than Boston. He is in every respect the beau-ideal of what, in England, would be considered a hunter getter. And the English hunter is precisely the stamp and style of horse which is the most profitable for the farmer to raise, for all general purposes. No one in England would drive before his carriage, or ride on the road, anything but English hunters, if he could afford the price; and, as to their powers for draught or burden, it is only necessary to say that men weighing twenty horseman's stone, or 280 pounds, find no difficulty, being willing to pay the price, in getting hunters nearly tho-rough-bred—none others than such could do it—capable of carrying them across country, over hedges, brooks and timber, as fast as fox-hounds can run. But—for there is a *but*—Boston went blind, and his best son, Lexington, has gone blind also, first of one eye, and then completely; and this fatal fact sets Boston aside forever as a country breeder's horse.

From the foregoing, then, may be deduced the following GENERAL RULES:

First. The more valuable horses are the most econom-ical for all purposes.

Second. The more "blood" compatible with the size required, the better,—the high-bred animal having greater *quickness, strength, bottom, health and vigor* of constitution, as well as *courage and pluck.*

Third. The "blood" should be on the side of the *sire;* that is, the stallion should be thorough-bred, or at least of purer blood than the mare.

Fourth. Choose a stallion in every respect sound, short backed, well ribbed up, short in the saddle-place and long below, with high withers, broad loins, broad chest, straight rump, a high and muscular but not *beefy* crest, a lean, bony, well-set-on head, a bright, clear, smallish, well-placed eye, broad nostrils and small ears. His fore legs above the knee, and the hind legs above the hock, should be long and muscular, and below these joints short and bony. The bones of the legs should be large, flat, and free from excrescences—the sinews clear, straight, and hard to the touch.

CHAPTER II.

HOW TO BREED A HORSE.—CHOICE OF THE MARE.

WE now come to another and by no means secondary part of the business; that is to say, to the choice of the mares. And here we say that the first thing to be looked for is, not blood nor performances, but size and symmetry, accompanied, as a matter of course, by constitutional and structural soundness. Blood from the sire, beauty from the dam, is the golden rule of the breeder. We know it is commonly said by farmers, concerning some miserable, undersized, ewe-necked, cat-hammed wretch of a mare, broken-winded, ring-boned and spavined, "Oh, she will do to raise a colt out of!" So she will! But what will the colt be? The breeder had better, for all purposes, especially for his own pecuniary benefit, have shot her at once; for the colt will not be worth the mare's grass, let alone the price of the stallion's services. When we say that blood is not to be looked for, we mean not as a primary necessity. Of course, it is to be looked for, thus,—that a fine mare, having the breeding points finely developed, got by a prime thorough-bred horse, is a preferable animal for a dam, to an equally fine mare who has no thorough

2

blood at all. But, on the contrary, a mare with all the best bloods in the world in her veins, if she has not good shapes, good size, and good points, is not fit for a stud mare. We do not merely mean as to the absence of actual deformities, or constitutional disease, such as spavin, ringbone or navicular disease, but as to lack of structural excellence and beauty. We go so far as to say that a farmer had far better let alone breeding from a mare which he knows to be herself a good and true one, if she be cross made, unsightly, and deficient in points of strength or in action; for excellence will sometimes be found, accidentally and exceptionally, in all shapes, even the most unlikely. But it will be found, in ninety-nine cases out of a hundred, that the ill shapes will be transmitted, while the excellence will not. Therefore, say we, when a good old mare, however good she may have been, if she want size, bone, muscular development and form, has done her work, it is better to let her go, her duties done, than to seek to turn her to farther profit by breeding from her, since the profit is extremely likely to prove a loss. An unproved mare, of fine form and good temper, with plenty of bone, good constitution, and free from unsoundness or vice, is a better animal from which to raise stock than the toughest bit of mare's flesh that ever stood on iron, if she materially lack any one of those conditions.

"In choosing the brood mare," says an excellent modern writer on the horse, though he is speaking of thorough-breds, "four things must be considered : First, her blood; secondly, her frame; thirdly, her state of health ; and fourthly, her temper.

"In frame, the mare should be so formed as to be capable of carrying and well nourishing her off-spring; that is, she should be what is called roomy.' There is a formation of the hips which is particularly unfit for breeding purposes, and yet which is sometimes carefully selected, because it is considered elegant; this is the level and straight hip, in which the tail is set on very high, and the end of the haunch bone is nearly on a level with the projection of the hip bone. Nearly the opposite form is the more desirable, where, on examining the pelvis, it will be seen that the haunch bone forms a considerable angle with the sacrum, and that there is, as a consequence, plenty of room, not only for carrying the foal, but for allowing it to pass into the world. Both of these points are important, the former evidently so, and the latter no less so on consid· eration; because, if the foal is injured in the birth, either of necessity or from ignorance, it will often fail to recover its powers, and will remain permanently injured. The pelvis, then, should be wide and deep,—that is to say, large and roomy; and there should also be a little *more* than the average length, from hip to the shoulder, so as to give plenty of bed for the foal, as well as a good depth of back ribs, which are necessary to give the strength to support this increased length. This gives to the whole frame-work of the trunk a larger proportion than is always desira· ble in the race-horse, which is easily overtopped in race-horses,"—that is to say, they may easily have more body than their legs can properly carry,—"and hence many good runners have failed as brood mares, while a great number of bad runners have been dams of good horses. Beyond this roomy frame, necessary as the egg-shell of the foal, the mare only requires such a shape and make as is well adapted for the purpose she is intended for," that is to say, for producing colts of the style and form she is in· tended to produce. We will add, that she must have four good legs under her, and those legs standing as a foun· dation on four good, well-shaped, *large* feet, open-heeled, and by no means flat-soled. That she should have a good, lean, bony head, small-eared, broad-fronted, well set on, upon a high, well-carried neck, thin at its junction with the head; high withers, thin, and, above all, long, sloping shoulders. A straight shoulder is an abomination; it renders speed impossible, and gives a rigid, inflexible motion, often producing the bad fault of stumbling. She should be wide-chested, and deep in the heart-place. Her quarters should be strong, well let down, long and sickle-shaped above the hocks. It is better that she go with her hocks somewhat too wide apart than too near together—the former point indicating power, the latter, weakness of a bad kind. It has been shown that a brood mare may, nay, *should*, be considerably longer in the back than one would choose a working horse to be; but if she be particularly so, it is desirable to put her to a short-backed and close-coupled horse.

"In health," says the same writer who has been quoted above, "the brood mare should be as near perfection as the artificial state of the animal will allow; at all events, it is the most important point of all; and in every case the mare should be very carefully examined with a view to discover what deviations from a natural state have been entailed upon her by her own labors, and what she has inherited from her ancestors. Independently of the consequence of accidents, all deviations from a state of health in the mare may be considered as more or less transmitted to her, because, in a thoroughly sound constitution, no ordinary treatment, such as training consists of, will produce disease; and it is only hereditary predisposition which, under this process, entails its appearance. Still there are positive, comparative and superlative degrees of objectionable diseases incidental to the brood-mare, which should be accepted or refused accordingly. All accidental defects, such as broken knees, dislocated hips, or even breaks-down,' may be passed over; the latter, however, only when the stock from which the mare is descended are famous for standing their work without this frailty of sinew and ligament. Spavins, ringbones, large splents, side-bones, and, in fact, all bony enlargements, are constitutional defects, and will be almost sure to be perpetuated, more or less, according to the degree in which they exist in the particular case. Curby hocks are also hereditary, and should be avoided; though many a one, much bent at the junction of the *os calcis* and *astragalus*, is not at all liable to curbs. It is the defective condition of the ligaments there, not the angular junction, which leads to curbs; and the breeder should carefully investigate the individual case before accepting or rejecting a mare with suspicious hocks. Bad feet, whether from contraction or from too flat and thin a sole, should be avoided; but when they have obviously arisen from bad shoeing, the defect may be passed over. Such are the general considerations bearing upon soundness of limb.

" Broken-winded mares seldom breed, and they are therefore out of the question, if for no other reason; but no one would risk the recurrence, even if he could get such a mare stinted. Roaring is a much-vexed question, which is by no means theoretically settled among our chief veterinary authorities, nor practically by our breeders. Every year, however, it becomes more and more frequent and important, and the risk of reproduction is too great for any person wilfully to run, by breeding from a roarer. As far as I can learn, it appears to be much more hereditary on the side of the mare than on that of the horse; and not even the offer of a " Virago" should tempt me to use her as a brood-mare. There are so many conditions of what is termed "roaring," that it is difficult to form any opinion that shall apply to all cases. In some

instances, where it has arisen from neglected strangles,—
generally known in the United States as colt distemper,—
or from a simple inflammation of the larynx, the result of
a cold, it will probably never reäppear; but when the genuine ideopathic roaring has made its appearance, apparently depending upon a disease of the nerves of the larynx,
it is ten to one that the offspring will suffer in the same
way.

"Blindness, again, may or may not be hereditary; but in
all cases it should be viewed with suspicion as great as that
due to roaring. Simple cataract, without inflammation, undoubtedly runs in families; and when a horse or mare has
both eyes suffering with this disease without any other derangement of the eye, I should eschew them carefully.
When blindness is the result of violent inflammation brought
on by mismanagement, or by influenza, or by any similar
cause, the eye itself is more or less disorganized; and
though this is of itself objectionable, as showing a weakness of the organ, it is not so bad as the regular cataract."

The writer quoted is one of much and standard authority, yet it is questionable whether, in his desire to put the
question fairly in all its lights, he has not laid too little
rather than too much stress on both these perilous affections.
We should say, under no possible circumstances breed from
a stallion which has any affection of any kind, of the respiratory organs, whether seated in the lungs or in the
windpipe, or from one which has any affection of the eyes,
unless it be the direct result of an accident, such as a blow
or a puncture,—nor even then if the accident having occurred to one eye, the other has sympathetically followed
suit; and, on the other side, we should say, on no account
breed from a mare affected in either way, unless she be
possessed of some excellencies so extraordinary and coun-
tervailing that for the sake of preserving the stock, one

would be willing to run some risk of having a worthless animal for his own use, in the hope of possibly having one free from the dreaded defect and of superlative excellence. In any event, however, the practice is to be eschewed and the risk to be considered excessive.

Previous to sending the mare to the horse she should be got into the most perfect state of health and condition, by moderate exercise, abundance of good nutritious food, and warm stabling. It is not desirable that she should be in a pampered state produced by hot stables or extraordinary clothing, that she should have the short fine coat, or the blooming and glowing condition of the skin, for which one would look in a race-horse about to contend for a four mile heat—not that she should be in that wiry form of sinew and steel-like hardness of muscle, which is only the result of training. Still less desirable is it that she should be overloaded with fat, especially of that soft fat generated by artificial feeding.

While the mare is carrying her foal, during the first three or four months of her gestation, she will be much the better, not the worse, for doing her ordinary work,—not of course galloping long distances at her speed, nor trotting matches, nor doing extraordinary distances on the road; but, if she be a carriage mare or a hackney, doing her regular day's work at her ordinary pace before a carriage or under the saddle; or, if she be a farm mare, going through the usual routine of light ploughing, harrowing, or road-work, never being put to any sudden or extreme exertion, such as being made to pull at excessive loads, or to any efforts likely to produce sudden jerks or strains, which are, of all things, the most likely to cause a mare to slip her foal. At a later period her work should be lighter and slower, but none the less regular, nor should her exercise ever be wholly intermitted. If she be let to run at grass, she should be in a small inclosure, in which she may trot indeed, and even canter, or gallop at half speed, but in which she cannot well get to her racing speed, or she will be likely to overdo herself, besides running the chance of getting falls and other accidents, which may produce consequences the most disastrous. Such enclosures should be divided by fences sufficiently high and solid that they shall not present to the animals the idea of being easily surmounted or broken through,—for if they seem to be so, even if they be not so in reality, the mares will be constantly trying to leap them, or force their way through them, and bad, perhaps fatal, accidents will be occurring. It is a far better plan to have the fences made, at least at the upper part, of open work, so that the animals in two adjacent lots may be able to see one another and communicate, without being able to get at each other,—as when so situated they will be constantly gently trotting to and fro in order to find a method of getting together, which will keep them in proper exercise,—than to confine two or more mares in the same lot or enclosure, as in that case they will be apt, in play and rivalry, to extend themselves too much in their speed, and over-exert themselves. An acre is ample space for such an enclosure, and it should be provided with a good comfortable hut or porch for shade in summer and warmth in winter, the doorway of which ought not to be less than five feet in width and eight in height, with the angles of the door-posts and lintels rounded off in order to prevent the hips from being injured as the animal passes rapidly and impetuously in and out, or from the poll being injured by the throwing up the head suddenly and striking the sharp edge of the lintel.

The food of the mare during her gestation should be liberal, generous and nutritious, without heating; for it is to be remembered that during this time the female has to generate blood for the nourishment of her fœtus as well as of herself. Green succulent grasses and roots are excellent at this time, as clover, lucerne, green corn sowed broadcast and cut young for the purpose; ruta baga turnips and, best of all, carrots. Large quantities of oats or of corn should not be given—if the latter be used at all, it should be *old* and thoroughly dried—though it is not advisable to cut them off entirely; from four to eight quarts of oats may be given daily with advantage, and bran mashes, with the oats added to them, steamed or moistened with hot water, will be found the best method of administering them. There is no more certain method of insuring the production of a poor, under-sized, starveling and weak-constitutioned foal, than to starve the mother, or to feed her on ill-suited or improper food during her gestation, or to keep her cold, or wet, or exposed to violent changes of temperature. Equal care should be taken of both mother and foal, after the birth of the young animal; and it will be found well to repay the extra expense if both are furnished with a little oats and with nutritious food of the descriptions named above, so long as the young animal is sucking the dam.

"Lastly, the temper," says the same authority on whom we have already drawn so largely, "is of the greatest importance, by which must be understood, not that gentleness at grass which may lead the breeder's family to pet the mare, but such a temper as will serve the purposes of the rider, and will answer to the stimulus of the voice, whip or spur. A craven or a rogue is not to be thought of as the mother of a family; and if the mare belong to a breed which is remarkable for refusing to answer the call of the rider, she should be consigned to any task rather than the stud farm. Neither should a mare be used for this purpose which had been too irritable to train, unless she happen to

2*

be an exceptional case; but if of an irritable family, she would be worse than even a roarer or a blind one."

Sulkiness and savageness, and even the liability to start and shy violently, are likewise to some degree hereditary; but as these are capable of being modified and affected in the highest degree, if not absolutely cured, by judicious and humane treatment in young animals, they are not so essential to be guarded against.

GENERAL RULES.

First. Size, symmetry and soundness are mostly to be regarded in the mare;—blood from the sire, beauty from the dam, is the Golden Rule.

Second. She should have a roomy frame, hips somewhat sloping, a little more than the average length, wide-chested, deep in the girth, quarters strong and well let down, hocks wide apart, wide and deep in the pelvis.

Third. In temper she should be gentle, courageous, free from all irritability and viciousness.

Fourth. Previous to putting her to the horse she should be brought into the most perfect state of health, not over-fed, or loaded with fat, or in a pampered state, but by ju· dicious exercise and an abundance of nutritious food and proper grooming she should be in the very best condition

Fifth. During gestation she should have generous and nourishing, but not heating diet. For the first three or four months she may be worked moderately, and even to within a few weeks of her foaling she may do light work with advantage to her system.

CHAPTER III.

FIRST CONSIDERATION IN IMPROVEMENT OF THE "COLD" BLOOD—RELATIVE
SIZE OF SIRE AND DAM—DEFECTS IN EITHER PARENT, HOW REMEDIED IN
PROGENY—BLOODS WHICH "HIT"—GENERAL RULES.

In the preceding chapters we have shown a few of the
general principles of horse breeding; the advantages arising from breeding to pure blood on the sire's side, whatever the quality of the dam; the points of symmetry and
strength most desirable, the necessity for perfect structural
and constitutional soundness and health, on both sides, and
for the absence of hereditary vice of temper; and, lastly,
the state of health to be aimed at in the dam, as well previous to her being taken to the horse as during the period
of her gestation, and the means to be taken to attain and
preserve that condition of health, or, as it is usually termed
among horsemen, *condition*, emphatically. We shall now
proceed to show, a little more particularly, what are the improvements to be obtained in different varieties, and how
this improvement is to be produced; for it is very certain that
the same horse will not answer for every kind of mare, but
that, on the contrary, for very different styles of dams very
different styles of sires will be required to produce equal
results in the progeny. Now, it may be stated generally,
that the ordinary objects of breeding up are twofold. One,
the most common and most feasible, is, from an entirely
cold stock,—we will say, for example, the Cleveland Bay,
or, the nearest approaches to be found to it in this country,

the Conestoga cart mare, or the larger Vermont draught mare—we do not speak in this connection of the Morgan, or the Canadian, or the Norman, some mares of which last stock have been recently imported into this country; since all of these have some strains, more or less distant, of thorough blood—to raise a progeny improved in spirit, speed, lightness of action, endurance of fatigue and courage, by stinting mares of that stock to blood-horses. This is the simplest of all the ends to be attained, and can be almost certainly accomplished, by sending the mare—taking it for granted that she is sound and generally well formed—to any thorough-bred horse, provided he also is sound, well-shaped and free from vice. Any such horse will, more or less, improve the progeny, both in blood and in form, structure and strength of bones, both in frame and spirit, without any especial reference to the particular strain of thorough blood from which he himself comes.

In the second and third, and yet more in later gene-rations, when blood has been introduced, and the dams as well as the sires have some mixture of a pure lineage, it is more requisite to look to families; since some families no-toriously cross well with others, and some as notoriously ill. Of course, it is better that the sire, where it is possible, should be of a racing stock that is famous for courage and stoutness, such as any of the stocks which trace remotely to Herod, Cade, Regulus, Eclipse, or others of known fame; but thus far it is not essential, or a *sine qua non*, since every blood-horse, even if, as Sir John Fenwick said, in the reign of Charles II., he be the meanest hack that ever came out of Barbary, is so infinitely superior in courage, stoutness and quality, both of bone and sinew, as well as blood, to the best cold-blooded mare that ever went on a shodden hoof, that he cannot fail to improve her stock, whatever may be his comparative standing among racers.

All, therefore, that the breeder has to do in this instance is, to satisfy himself that the horse is *really thorough-bred*—that is to say, traceable on both sides of his pedigree to English stud-book race-horses—and that he has the virtues and has not the defects of form which have been previously subjects of discussion. Next to this, there must be a harmony in the size, and, to some extent, in the forms of the animals. The putting small mares to gigantic horses, or colossal mares to ponies, in order to give size to the offspring, will never answer, but, on the contrary, will result in the production of rickety, mal-formed produce. The mare, as it has been said, may be with advantage something larger, longer, and more roomy than the horse, but not too much so.

We should say, a mare of sixteen hands, and proportionate strength, should never be put to a stallion under fifteen hands, and from thence up to fifteen and two inches; nor a mare over sixteen hands to one short of fifteen and a half, up to fifteen, three, hands. Still less should little mares be put to tall horses, or low mares to leggy horses, in order to give height. If the brood mare be low, but long and roomy, it is no bad fault; but the way to give size to the progeny is to select, not a tall or leggy horse for the stallion, but one of singularly perfect symmetry, not much higher than the dam,—though an inch or two inches will do no harm, provided he be not long in the legs especially from the knee downward,—short-backed, close-coupled, and generally strong built—particularly so in those points where the mare is the most defective.

We stated above that there is no greater blunder than to breed an animal rickety and defective in one point, to another imperfect in that point, or even unduly developed in it, with the expectation of curing both defects in the progeny. One often, however, sees both mares and horses,

with some one or more faults in symmetry, which are positive defects, although only in a secondary degree, and
which are, at the same time, counterbalanced by so great a
number of positive advantages, excellences and beauties,
that he is wise to waive the one defect, striving to remedy
it, in view of the other good to be hoped for from the
strain. The transmission of external shapes is as yet a
mystery, and probably ever will continue so. No one can
say whether the stallion or the mare has the greater share
in giving structural form or constitutional disposition to
the young animal.

Indeed, there seems reason to believe that there is not
any invariable rule on the subject; but that some dams
and some sires possess an extraordinary power of impress-
ing their own forms and stamping their own images, in
the greater degree, on the young. The general rule,
however, and that which it is wise to observe is, that *like
begets like*. Therefore the practice should be always,
where one decides to breed from a mare slightly defective
in one point of symmetry, to select a stallion as excellent
as possible in that point ; and if one be resolved for any
cause to breed from a stallion of whose blood, or beauty,
or performances he is particularly enamored, and that
horse be weak in any point or points, to put to him whatever mare one may have in his stud most excellent where
he is weakest; but in no case, even if it prohibit one from
breeding from that horse at all, to put him to a mare
which is faulty in the same part.

The second ordinary object of breeding-up is, where
mares of some highly valued strain, possessing some degree
of pure blood engrafted on an inferior stock, have degenerated in size, in height, strength and size of bone, to breed
them to such horses as shall, without deteriorating their
blood, improve them in size and bone. This is a far more

difficult question in breeding, and, before it can be answered, it will be necessary to know of what blood is the impure portion constituted, and in what proportion does it exist. If it be distinctly of cold blood, as of Cleveland bay, Suffolk Punch, Conestoga, or common cart-horse, and if the proportion of thorough blood mixed with it be inconsiderable, it may, at once, be pronounced useless to take any pains about it, as the results will not repay the trouble or expense. If the proportion of pure blood be considerable, but remote, and the stock have been long *in bred*—as, for example, is the case with the Morgans—the only possible way to breed them up is to stint the mares to the very best and most powerfully made, short-coupled, broad-chested, strong-loined, short-legged, thorough-bred stallions that can be found, of a totally distinct recent strain of blood, if the blood of the mares can be ascertained; although it will not be the worse if, some ten or more generations back, they both run into the same line. In this case, the stallion, in the first cross, should not be taller or larger than the mare, but may exceed her in strength, size of bone, and muscular development. The fillies in the second generation will be larger in all ways than their dams—since improvement of strength, health, symmetry, and development implies improvement in size. These fillies may be again put to horses of exactly the same stamp as that last described, but just so much larger than the filly as the filly is larger than her dam. This will, in all probability, achieve the desired end. This is, in fact, what is known among breeders as breeding *up*, in the true sense of the word. If, on the other hand, the mares, degenerated, have been crossed with pure English blood, but remotely and not recently, on Canadian or imported Norman stock, there will be no objection to crossing them back once to Canadian or Norman stallions; since in Canadian or Norman blood there is a remote, dormant strain of pure blood, probably Andalusian Arab, which assimilates well with modern thorough blood ; and the breeding back will often, in that case, so far reinvigorate the race, that the fillies produced by that union will often reproduce animals of astonishing excellence by a farther cross with well-chosen thorough blood of the present day.

We have touched slightly on the effect produced by the intermingling, or crossing and re-crossing of various distinct or cognate strains of blood, and the result on the character of the stock. When a cross of this sort is eminently successful in any particular line, for a number of years and in a majority of instances, we are accustomed to say that such or such a blood has "hit" or "nicked" with another; and this effect is not dependent solely on the intrinsic excellence of either blood, but on some unknown and mysterious influence produced, in one or more generations, by the cross. For instance, Priam, the son of Emilius, son of Orville, out of Emily, and Cressida, daughter of Whiskey, out of Sorcerer's dam by Diomed, was not only one of the most successful runners, if not the most successful, of his day, but in England was nearly as successful a stallion, having begot, previous to his exportation, an unusual number of winners. He was subsequently purchased and brought to this country, where the most sanguine expectations were formed of the great advantage which would accrue from the infusion of his singularly rich and noble blood. The result, however, was diametrically opposite to that which was expected.

Scarcely a horse of any repute has been begotten by this stallion in the United States, although his high reputation for blood, beauty, and performances, procured for him more than his proportion of the best blooded and otherwise best mares in the country. Many persons--

some of them excellent judges—entertain the opinion that the Priam cross has done permanent mischief to the horse stock of America, as it is alleged that nearly all, if not all his get, although they have large, flat, bony knees, are *tied in*, as it is technically termed, immediately below the knee, at the origin of the splint bone. This malformation is one of the most serious that can exist in a race or family of horses, as it renders them liable, and, in fact, almost certainly so, to break down, when put to any severe stress of work. At all events, it is indisputable that the blood of Priam has not "hit" or "nicked" with the best racing blood of America.

To take another instance, Glencoe, another distinguished English runner, of equally distinguished blood, though of a distinct strain, being the son of Sultan, son of Selim, and of Trampoline, daughter of Tramp out of Web by Waxy, was imported into this country a few years later than Priam, with equally high expectations of success, which have in his instance been fully realized, if not exceeded; for his stock are of the very best now running in the country. Therefore, we say emphatically, that the Glencoe stock has "hit" most eminently with the old blood of America, which, it must always, however, be remembered, is, in no respect, so far as it is pure blood, American or of American origin, but only descended from the earlier importations of the old English blood of the days of Janus, Eclipse, Highflyer, and the sons of Childers, and the Godolphin. Now, why one blood should "hit" and another "miss," when each strain is equally rich and pure, and when each has produced an equal number of distinguished performers, no one can say positively; no distinct reasons have ever been assigned, nor, theoretically, can any principle be laid down on the subject. The blood of Priam, as it has been shown, above, "hit" with the fashionable blood of England, and signally "missed" with that of America. On the contrary, the blood of Glencoe "hit" with the most fashionable blood of both countries; and although he has got more fine stock in America, owing to his having served here during a much longer period, and of course, covered more fine mares, is scarcely more famous as a stock getter in this than in the mother country. In like manner, Leviathan, Sovereign and Sarpedon have all "hit" more or less decidedly, with the older English blood of America; and Trustee must not be forgotten, both as the sire of the incomparable Fashion, and as a horse who has been extraordinarily fortunate in getting roadsters of high quality out of common mares.

Now, although there is no possibility of predicting, absolutely, what bloods will and will not hit, there are at least some facts established which will enable us to venture a conjecture on the subject. It is well known to be the habit of gregarious and polygamous animals, such as horses, oxen, and some others, which are not long-lived— but of which the largest and most powerful males enjoy the company of the females of their own troop or band, of which they are the lords and Sultans, and from which they beat off and banish the younger and inferior animals of their own sex—to copulate, for at least two or three generations, with their own female descendants, while in a state of nature. As they decline in strength, vigor and courage with the increase of years, they are in their turn beaten off, and compelled to give way to some more powerful rival, in the pride and maturity of equine manhood, perhaps from a different horde of animals, and almost certainly from a distinct strain of blood. Hence we come to the conclusion that horses in a wild state are accustomed to breed into the same family and blood; that is to say, with their own daughters and grand-daughters, for about two generations—this is what is known to horse-men as *in-breeding*—and then for many after generations to breed with strangers, or very remote connections. And it is worthy of remark that, although there are two distinct theories, exactly opposite to each other, one in favor of in-breeding, the other of out-crossing, several of the best strains of blood on the English turf are directly traceable to an original incestuous connexion.

Some of the most distinguished families, for instance, of English racers, trace to Spanker, a very high-bred horse, and very close to Arab stock on both sides, and his own dam: and where no near connexion has existed for many years in the blood of any peculiar family, it is on the whole the most approved method, to breed *in*, that is, between close blood relations, for two, or perhaps three generations, and then to seek for some strain of blood as remote as possible by which to vary and reinvigorate the strain. This plan of breeding has been of late years very fashionable in England, and the result has been shown very beneficially in several families famous for their qualities of speed, endurance, and recuperation, at present on the turf. It is certain, on the other hand, that to persist too long in breeding, generation after generation, *in and in*, is the most prejudicial of all modes; and that animals so unnaturally connected in blood, degenerate in bone, in size, in stature, and ultimately in all qualities.

Whenever, therefore, it is known, or strongly suspected, that in any family too long and persistent an adherence has been had to one and the same blood, and still more, wherever the present generation is seen to have greatly degenerated in size, recourse should be had to a strain of blood as widely different as possible, in order to freshen and strengthen the stock.

We may deduce, then, the following summary of GENE-RAL RULES.

First. There should be a mutual adaptation in form and size, and indeed, in all important characteristics between the sire and the dam.

Second. If the mare be defective in any particular, do not breed her to a stallion having a similar, or even an opposite fault; but rather choose one perfect in that point.

Third. Avoid breeding exceedingly small mares with enormously large horses: distortions will generally be the result. For a mare of 16 hands, select a horse of not less than 15 hands; if she be too low or small, the horse may be an inch or two higher, but not of the tall or leggy kind.

Fourth. It is frequently the case that without any known cause, the blood of a certain strain of horses will not cross well with that of another. Such instances, when ascertained should be avoided.

Fifth. If the mare is of a good strain of horses but one which has degenerated in size from "in-breeding," the only remedy is to breed to the purest stallion that can be found, but of a different strain from hers, unless some ten or more generations removed.

Sixth. After breeding for several generations from males and females of one strain, it will generally be found beneficial to change to another entirely different. Degeneracy in size will generally result from a neglect of this rule.

CHAPTER IV.

HOW TO BREED A HORSE—CANADIAN BLOOD.

THE CANADIAN ORIGINALLY THE FRENCH NORMAN—CHARACTERISTICS—HARDI HOOD—SPEED—MODE OF IMPROVING THEM—CROSSING WITH THOROUGH BREDS.

THERE is one breed or stock of horses to which, thus far, we have but casually alluded. We mean the Canadian. It deserves, probably, a more extended notice, as being in itself, in the first place, a perfectly distinct family, where pure; and in the second, as being very widely extended, both in its mixed and unmixed form, in the Northern and Eastern States; and, moreover, as being itself an exceedingly valuable animal as a working horse, and a progenitor, or progenitrix. The Canadian horse where he is yet to be found in his pure state,—that is to say, uncrossed with either the English thorough-bred, or the English high-bred stallion of the hunter caste,—is originally, beyond doubt, the French Norman horse; and even where the crosses mentioned still exist, the French Norman blood vastly preponderates. The present characteristics of the Canadian are—a head rather large than otherwise, but lean, bony, and well formed, with an unusually broad forehead, with the ears far apart, carried loftily, a small clear eye, and a courageous aspect; a bold upstanding, but thick crest; a broad, full chest and a strong shoulder, a little apt to be too straight, as well as to be low and heavy at the withers; a stout, strongly-framed barrel, the characteristic fault of which is, to be somewhat flatsided, and not unfrequently too long; excellent loins; a round, fleshy croup; muscular thighs; and, above all, the soundest, most undeniable, flat-boned legs that are to be found in any race of horses not thorough-bred, and the toughest, hardest and most iron-like feet that are to be found in any race whatsoever. In fact, immunity from disease of the legs and feet, under the most unfavorable circumstances,— when ill-groomed, ill-shod, and subject to every trial and hardship,—appears to be the distinguishing mark of the French Canadian horse. There is no horse, probably, in the known world, to which all ordinary diseases of the foot, and especially that which is known as foot-founders, are so nearly unknown; and it has been well stated by an intelligent writer, well versed in the peculiarities of this particular race, that "there are numbers of horses in Canada that, under a mass of shaggy hair, never trimmed, and rarely cleaned or dried, possess dry, sinewy legs, on which the severest service never raises a wind-gall."

In addition to these characteristics, the Canadians are generally distinguishable by their colors, of which the prevailing one is black; and, probably the second, rich dark brown, often dappled with lighter brown on the shoulders and quarters. After these colors come chestnuts of different shades, but generally running to the sorrels and duns, with manes, tails and legs of lighter color than the body; and lastly, dark iron-greys with black legs. The last, however, which in Normandy is at the present day, with the single exception of black, the commonest color, is, in Canada and the United States, the least common. The true Canadians are remarkable for the great volumes of their manes and tails, which are also distinguished by the peculiar wavy and almost curly texture of the hairs composing them, and for the shaggy coating of their back sinews nearly to the knee, and of their fetlocks. In height the Canadian rarely exceeds fifteen hands, and in fact seldom attains to that standard; from fourteen to fourteen hands and a half being their usual size. They are not generally speedy, even at ordinary road speed; still less often are they fleet, or what would be called *fast;* though there are exceptions, as for instance the celebrated trotting stallion St. Lawrence, who has gone fast among fast horses, and has been so long on the trotting turf as to show that he possesses in a high degree the hardy endurance of his race. Their best rate of going, for fair, ordinary travellers,—not select specimens,—does not, perhaps, exceed six or seven miles the hour; but at whatever rate they can go at all, at that rate they can go before or under a heavy load, and for a long, continuous distance. Many Canadians will do fifty miles a day for several successive days; and not a few can be found which will accomplish sixty, seventy, eighty, and even ninety, for one day; and the lesser rates for a proportionate length of time.

It seems remarkable that such should be the case, but we are strongly disposed to believe that, even in these days of horse improvement, horse fairs and agricultural progress, no systematical attempts have ever been made to improve the Canadians themselves in their pure form; although many have been made, with great success, to create improved crosses by the intermixture of them with other races. No race, probably, is more susceptible of direct improvement than this; and, as their excellence is universally acknowledged, both as the small poor farmer's working and draught horse, for which they are adapted above all American breeds, and as brood mares, from which to raise a highly improved and useful general working roadster, by breeding them to thorough-breds, according to the rules heretofore laid down, it is evident that this is an end most devoutly to be wished.

It would seem that, after the first importation of the Norman horse by the early French settlers, there were few importations of fresh strains of Norman blood from the mother country, in which continual systematic improvements have been made ; and that, certainly, from the date of the English conquest of Canada, no efforts whatever have been made to procure the breed in its purity, or to raise its standard in height, to lighten its heavier and worse points, or to increase its speed and beauty, all of which might unquestionably be effected by judicious management. The effect of this continued breeding into the same exact strain, generation ofter generation, has been the same as it was with the Virginia race-horse prior to the recommencement of the importation of thorough blood, subsequent to the American Revolution. The strength, the courage, the *blood*, in a word, was there, but the size had deteriorated.

The first and simplest mode of improving the Canadians as Canadians—that is to say, without endeavoring to raise them to a higher degree of blood—is, to select the largest and most shapely mares of that breed, and more particularly such as are the most free from the characteristic faults of the Canadians, viz., the thick neck, low, heavy withers, straight shoulder and flat side ; then to select the best stallions of that breed, having regard to the very same points named above,—and to see that the mare is in fine breeding condition when put to the horse. Care being had to follow up this plan judiciously, and to keep the mare during her pregnancy and the nourishment of her foal liberally and comfortably fed and sheltered, though not to force either mother or offspring, as is done with thoroughbreds, by hot lodging and over stimulating provender, there cannot be a doubt but that, in course of two or three generations, at farthest, an inch, or perhaps even a couple of inches, might be added to the stature of the Canadians, without deteriorating—we should rather say while improving upon—their original merits of bone and sinew, and amending the more defective points of their shape. Apart from their natural good qualities as farming horses, teamsters and animals of moderately quick draft, the Canadians, with the single exception of the Percheron Normans, which are,—after all is said, nothing but Canadians in their best form,—are the only horses of cold blood from which we believe it advisable to breed on both sides; that is, both from the stallions and mares; either each to each, for the maintenance of their own blood, or each to others, for the improvement of various foreign strains. By carefully breeding Canadian mares to Canadian stallions. according to the directions above stated, or still more to imported Normans, an improved Canadian can be produced, taller, more shapely, and perhaps lighter in the neck and shoulders, and speedier. This will be, of course, a better animal both for work and for breeding than the present race. By breeding the present Canadian mare, or still better, improved progeny, to well-selected thorough-bred horses, a very good roadster and highly improved light carriage-horse will be the result; and by breeding the female offspring of this cross again to the thorough-bred, of sufficient bone and size, we do not doubt that the finest saddle-horses, phaëton horses or light carriage horses in the world can be produced, nearly of the same style as the Morgans, but superior to what the Morgans ever were, in their best day.

The male offspring of all crosses or half-breeds—we do not include imported Norman into Canadian in the cate-

gory of crosses—should invariably be castrated. For our
own part, we should consider it a most desirable thing, if
possible, that there should not be such a thing as a half-bred
stallion in the world; but that all the distinct breeds, as
Canadians, Vermonters, *quasi* identical with Cleveland
bays, and Conestogas, *quasi* identical with the English im
proved dray-horses, should be preserved distinct by breeding the mares to stallions of their own families, unless
when it is desirable to lighten the stock; and then to
lighten it by breeding to thorough-breds. Canadian or
Norman stallions are the only male horses which we would
ever put to any *lighter* mares of American blood; but we
are strongly of opinion that both the Morgan mares and
the ordinary better class American farming mares, which
have some indefinably remote cross of better blood than
the cart-horse, can be made to produce a progeny highly
improved, hardened in bone, bettered in legs, feet, and constitution, and more adapted for being the mothers of fine,
large carriage-horses, by breeding them to Normans,
whether native or imported. It is a remarkable quality
of the Normans, that though small themselves, when
crossed,—either males to other races, or females to thorough-breds,—they almost invariably breed larger instead
of breeding smaller than themselves.

CHAPTER V.

ORIGIN AND HISTORY OF THE PERCHERON NORMAN—A PURE RACE—CHA-
RACTERISTICS AND POINTS—IMPORTATION INTO THIS COUNTRY.

In the preceding chapters on this subject, we have had
occasion to speak of the Percheron Norman horse, some of
which breed have been within a few years, comparatively
speaking, introduced into this country ; and, believing that
the knowledge of this race at all, and still more of its existence in the United States, is confined to a small number
of persons, and for the most part to a single locality, we
have thought it would be not uninteresting to our agricultural readers to give a brief account of the animal, its
derivation, its importation into this country, and of the
benefits which are, we fully believe, to be derived from its
employment. In the first place, then, Le Perche is a district of that portion of France which was formerly known
as Normandy, in which the breed of the Norman horses
has been most highly cultivated, and exists in its most
perfect form and improved condition. Indeed, by some
means somewhat anomalous, and at variance with the general experience and principles of breeding, this breed,
which must in its origin have been a cross, has, in the
process of many ages, become a family perfect in itself,
capable of transmitting its qualities and reproducing itself,
like to like, without any loss of energies or characteristics
by breeding mares and stallions of the same race together.
The remarkable purity of the race is attested by the cer-

tainty with which the stallions transmit to their progeny, begotten on mares of a different race, their own characteristics, and the high degree in which the offspring of the mares, bred to horses of superior class, retain the better qualities of their dams. For it appears to be a certain rule in breeding, that the purer the blood, and the higher the vital energy and vigor of either parent, in the greater degree does that parent transmit its properties to the young—although, as before insisted upon, the certain transmissions of the larger portion of those energies is always on the stallion's side, and it is only in the longer retention of an inferior proportion of her qualities by the progeny that the better blood of the dam can be traced when bred to an inferior sire. When bred to a purer blooded stallion than herself, the more pure blood the mare herself has the more strongly will her own marks descend to her progeny, and the less will they be altered or modified by those of the sire.

Now, the Percheron Normans are clearly a pure race *per se;* we do not mean by the words, a thorough-bred race, but a race capable of producing and reproducing themselves *ad infinitum,* unaltered, and without deterioration of qualities, by breeding like sires to like dams, without infusion of any other blood, just as is done by Durham, Ayrshire, or Alderney cattle, by setters, pointers, greyhounds, and, in a word, by any and all animals of distinct and perfect varieties of the same species. The only remarkable thing in this case is, that such should be the facts, under the circumstances, of the Percheron Normans, being originally—as they are beyond a doubt—the produce of a cross, although a most remote cross in point of time. The original Norman horse now nearly extinct, which was the war-horse of the iron-clad chivalry of the earliest ages—of William the Conqueror, and Richard

Cœur de Lion, is thus accurately described by the im-
porter of the Percherons into New Jersey: "They average," he says, and we are personally cognizant of his
accuracy, "full sixteen hands in height, with head short,
thick; wide and hollow between the eyes; jaws heavy;
ears short, and pointed well forward; neck very short and
thick; mane heavy; shoulder well inclined backward;
back extremely short; rump steep; quarters very broad;
chest wide and deep; tendons large; muscles excessively
developed; legs short, particularly from the knee and hock
to the fetlock, and thence to the coronet, which is covered
with long hair, covering half the hoof; much hair on the
legs." It was soon found even while complete armor was
in use, that these enormous, bony Normans, which are still
though deteriorated the ordinary, heavy draught horses
of France, had not sufficient speed to render the cavalry
charge effective, or sufficient blood to give spirit adequate
to the endurance of long-continued toil. The Andalusian
horse, which in its highest form, was a pure barb of Mo-
rocco, imported into Spain by the Saracen Moors under
Tarik, who has left his name to the rock of Gibraltar, and
in its secondary form, a half-bred horse, between the
African barbs and the old Spanish horse, which had long
before received a large tincture of Oriental blood from the
Numidian chargers of the Carthagenians, who so long occupied that country, proved, in its unmixed state, too light
for the enormous weight of a caparisoned man-at-arms, or,
if occasionally equal to that weight, too costly to be within
the means of any but crowned heads. "The bone and
muscle," observes the same writer we have before quoted,
"and much of the form of the Percheron, come from this
horse"—that is, from the old Norman war-horse previously
described; "and he gets his spirit and action from the
Andalusian. Docility comes from both sides. On the

expulsion of the Spaniards from the Northern Provinces, the supply of Arabian stallions was cut off, and, since that time, in the Perche district of Normandy, their progeny has, doubtless, been bred in and in; hence the remarkable uniformity of the breed, and the disposition to impart their form to their progeny beyond any breed of domestic animals within my knowledge. Another circumstance which, I think, has tended to perpetuate the good qualities of these horses, is the fact of their males being kept entire; a gelding is, I believe, unknown among the rural horses of France. You may be startled at this notion of mine, but, if you reflect a moment, you must perceive that in such a state of things—so contrary to our practice and that of the English—the farmer will always breed from the best horse, and he will have an opportunity of judging, because the horse has been broken to harness, and his qualities known, before he could command business as a stallion." There can be no possible question that the writer is correct in this view of the advantage, so far as breeding is concerned, of preserving *all* horses entire and ungelded; as it must naturally and necessarily follow, where a great majority of the males of any breed are gelded when young colts, and a few only are selected to some extent by chance to serve as stallions, that many of the very best, and perhaps actually the best, of every year, are deprived of the means of perpetuating their excellence. This, undoubtedly, is one of the causes of the constant preservation, if not improvement, of the race-horse; that, inasmuch as thorough-bred colts are never, unless from some peculiar cause, such as indomitable vice, deprived of their virility, the breeder has *all* the males of the race from which to select a stallion at his pleasure, instead of having only a small number from which to select. Yet even in the thorough-breds the breeder sometimes has cause to regret the caprice or error of an owner, which has allowed a colt to be deprived of his sex, whose after qualities proved him to be eminently worthy and preëminently adapted to become the father of a noble line. Who, for instance, but must regret that St. Nicholas, that noble specimen of a race-horse, perhaps the best now running on American soil, should be a gelding, and incapable of transmitting his blood and his honors to posterity ?

Now, the points of the peculiar breed known as the Percheron Normans are these: First, they are considerably taller than the Canadian horses, among which, it is believed, the Percheron blood is still to be found, though degenerated in stature, from cold, exposure, and ill-usage. Their standard is probably from fourteen and a half to fifteen and a half hands, the latter height, however, being as much above the average, perhaps, as sixteen hands is above that of ordinary horses. Secondly, they are very short in the saddle-place, and comparatively long below ; they are well ribbed-up and round-barreled, instead of having the flat sides and sway backs which are the most defective points of many of the Canadians ; they have not the heavy head and extremely short, thick neck of the old Norman horse, and many of his descendants on this side of the ocean ; but, on the contrary, have the head short, with the genuine Arabian breadth of brow and hollow of the profile between the eyes and nostrils, which is often called the basin face ; nor are their heads thicker, especially at the setting-on place, nor the necks, which are well arched and sufficiently long, heavier or more massive than corresponds well with the general stoutness of their frame. Their legs are particularly short from the knees and hocks downward; nor, though heavily haired, have they such shaggy fetlocks and feet as the larger Normans or Canadians, while they have the unyielding, iron-like sinews and feet, apparently unconscious of disease, for which the latter race are famous

An English writer in *The British Quarterly Journal of Agriculture*, speaking of the general working-horse of Normandy, says : " The horses of Normandy are a capital race for hard work and scanty fare. I have never seen such horses at the collar, under the diligence, the post-carriage, the cumbrous and heavy voiture or cabriolet for one or two horses, or the farm cart. They are enduring and energetic beyond description; with their necks cut to the bone, they flinch not; they put forth all their efforts at the voice of the brutal driver or at the dreaded sound of his never-ceasing whip; they keep their condition when other horses would die of neglect and hard treatment. A better cross for some of our horses cannot be imagined than those of Normandy, provided they have not the ordinary failing of two much length from the hock downward, and a heavy head." The two points last named are precisely those which are entirely got rid of in the best style of Percheron Normans, which are, as we have stated, those of the Normans most deeply and thoroughly imbued with the Arabian, or, to speak more correctly, Barb blood of Andalusia. It is not easy to procure the best and fastest *stallions* of this breed, as they are bought up by the French Government for the diligence and mail service, for which they are highly prized, and in which they are constantly kept at a pace varying from five to nine miles an hour, over roads and behind loads which would speedily kill an English or American horse, without loss of health or condition. But there is no difficulty in obtaining the choicest mares at comparatively low rates—mares being little valued *for work* in France.   Mr. Edward Harris, of Moorestown, N. J, who has been at much pains to import fine horses and mares of this breed, asserts of his horse "Diligence," that he has produced above four hundred foals—that he has never heard of one fetching less than one hundred dollars, and many much higher prices, and that he has never heard of his having produced one worthless colt, or one that is spavined, curbed, ringboned, or has any of those defects which render utterly useless so large a number of fine-bred colts of the present day.

We cannot close this chapter without stating our belief that, in the present state of American breeding, more good can be attained, though the process is slower, by importing the best Norman and Cleveland-bay *mares*, and breeding them and their progeny—gelding all the males—for two or more generations to select thorough-bred horses, than by importing stallions of these very breeds in an endeavor to work a regeneration on our weedy country mares, or to raise valuable stock out of thorough-bred mares, which is hopeless. We fully believe that a breeding farm started with a dozen such mares, six of each breed, well chosen, and bred year after year to the best and best selected thorough-breds, would in a very few years realize a large fortune to the breeder.

3*

CHAPTER VI.

HOW TO BREED A HORSE—MODERN ARAB BLOOD.

ENGLISH AND AMERICAN THOROUGH-BREDS DERIVED FROM ORIENTAL BLOOD —ARE NOW SUPERIOR TO THE MODERN ARABS—NOLAN ARAB.

IT is an indisputable fact, that all the excellence of the English and American thorough-bred horse is derived from Oriental blood of the desert, and originates, it is believed, in the admixture of the various breeds of the several countries to which the horse in its purest and highest form, has from remote ages been indigenous. These countries are Arabia, Syria, Persia, Turkistan, the Barbary States, Nubia and Abyssinia, all of which have races nearly connected with each other, but all possessing distinct characteristics. There would appear, of these races, to be in the English thorough-bred horse—with which the American is identical—a larger proportion of Barb than of pure Arabian blood. The celebrated Godolphin is generally considered by the most competent judges to have been a Barb. Fairfax's celebrated horse was a Barb ; the royal mares imported by King Charles II., to which nine-tenths of our modern thorough-bred horses trace, were Tunisian or Tangier Barbs. The other most famous progenitors have been Turks, as the Byerly Turk, the Lyster, or straddling Turk, the D'Arcy yellow Turk, Plaice's white Turk, and many others. The most noted of the pure Arabians was the Darley Ara-

bian. And it is, perhaps, the most considerable opinion
that the great and unrivalled excellence of the English
horse arises from the fact that he is the offspring of a judicious cross of all the best oriental races, and not the
produce of a system of close in-breeding.

It is worthy of remark, however, that although the fact
is universally admitted that the whole original excellence
of the English thorough blood is attributable to the blood
of the desert, and although no horse is to be held as thorough-bred unless he can trace in both lines, paternal and
maternal, to that blood, and although many horses of various Eastern and African breeds have been constantly imported both into England and America during the last two
hundred years, no one of them has improved the breed of
race-horses within the last century, or perhaps two centuries. So low at present does modern Arabian blood stand
in the estimate of English turfmen, that a horse begotten
by a Turkish, Arab, Barb or Persian stallion, on an English thorough-bred mare, receives in the Goodwood Cup
and other races in which allowances are given, 24 lbs. from
all English bred racers; and a horse begotten by such a
stallion on a mare of any one of the same races, receives
an enormous advantage of 48 lbs. The fact that even with
this enormous advantage, no horse so bred ever wins any
plate or race of consideration, shows that the distaste
to the blood is not a prejudice, but is founded on valid
reasons. Why this should be so is not so clear. It
appears, however, to be a certain and fixed rule of breeding, that in order to improve any race the higher and purer
blood must be on the sire's side, not on the dam's; and
that he must be the superior animal. It is, we think, now
an indisputable and undeniable fact, that the English
thorough-bred horse is, in all respects, but especially in
size, bone, power and beauty, a superior animal to any

of the Oriental races, and consequently that his blood cannot be improved by any further admixture of that strain. Why this should be so, cannot clearly be shown; but it arises probably from two causes: first, that as the Mohammedan race has degenerated in intellectual energy, in civilization and in power, the breed of horses used by that race has suffered a corresponding deterioration, owing to the want of intelligent breeding, of care, of management, and to the inferiority of their food, stabling and nurture; and, second, that the English and American descendants of the same horses have, by the vast attention given to breeding them only from the best and most choice parents, to their more generous nutriment, better housing and clothing, and to the enlightened and scientific culture which they have long received, been improved in proportion to the deterioration of their ancestors.

No intelligent sportsman doubts that the English or American thorough-bred horse can beat the Oriental horse anywhere and everywhere, and in all respects. In Hindostan at the European races, the whole-bred and even the half-bred English horses invariably beat the Indian Arabs; and very recently an Irish mare, named Fair Nell, disgracefully beat all the Egyptian Barbs of Ali Pasha, who had challenged the English Jockey Club to a trial match between English and Oriental horses for a prize of £10,000. The Jockey Club declined to take up the match collectively, because, as a body, they do not own race-horses, and individually, because the risk of running the best horses in a race of eight miles, which was proposed, over the rough and stony or sandy desert, was held rightly to be too great to justify the sending of animals of great value to a distant and barbarous country. The English residents of Alexandria and Cairo, however, excited by national spirit, and provoked by the triumphant tone of the Orientals, resolved to test the question. The Irish mare "Fair Nell" was selected, which was not a racer of any note or distinction, and about which there is now some dispute, whether she is or is not actually thorough-bred, though she is known to be very highly and very well bred; and the result was, that vastly to the disgust and disappointment of the Egyptians, she defeated all the best Arabs of the Pasha's stud with perfect ease. It has been asserted and is constantly urged by the favorers and defenders of Oriental blood, that no horses of really superior qualities or decided excellencies, as Arabs or Barbs, have recently been imported; and that to this, and to no natural or general inferiority of the Arab or Oriental horse, is the want of success in breeding from him to be attributed; and, as a matter of course, every one who imports an Arab or a Barb, asserts that his horse, and his only, is a real and superior-blooded animal. The plea is not, however, a valid one; for it is not likely, when a great majority of the horses imported from the East into both England and America have been gifts of Oriental potentates to crowned heads or presidents, that no one of them should have been a valuable creature.

It is clearly the sounder opinion that the modern thorough-bred horse of Oriental origin is a superior creature to the modern Arab; and consequently it is clearly unwise to attempt to breed thorough-bred mares to Oriental stallions, or to breed any highly bred mares to such stallions, in preference to the best thorough-breds. Still it appears not improbable that the general trotting stock and country stock of America might be improved by crossing with good Arabian or Barb blood, where the best thorough-blood, combined with fine form and power, is not to be attained. We are even impressed with the idea, that with some half-blooded breeds, such as the Canadians and Normans, both of which have a large, although a very remote cross of the African Barbs of Andalusian breed, a recurrence to the original, undiluted Barb or Arabian blood might be preferable even to breeding from modern thorough-breds, on the principle, before referred to, of having, after many years or centuries of out-crossing, recourse to the original strain of blood, which is often found to "*hit*," as it is technically termed, when it succeeds highly. It is worthy of remark that some distinguished trotting horses trace to Black Bashaw, who was a pure Barb of Tripoli, and who is said to be a horse of great beauty and power. The Canadians and Normans both show far more similitude of structure and form to the Arab and Barb, than do the modern thorough-bred horses; and that is a strong reason for believing that such a cross might prove successful.

We should like to hear of the experiment being tried, and although we should not care to predict perfect success we should rather anticipate a good than an evil result; we would, however, on no account put a thorough-bred mare to any Eastern horse, nor any very highly bred mare, where a thorough-bred stallion is within reach. Of course the boniest, most compact and strongest Arabs should be selected; an Arab *weed* of inferior strain is a very poor creature for any purpose, and worst of all from which to breed. From what we have heard of the Nolan Arab, and from the consummate knowledge in horse-flesh of his gallant owner, we should augur as well of him as of any recent importation from the East. We should not be surprised if in future days material improvement in the horse-flesh of the West, where there has been until very recently a great want of thorough blood, may be traced, hereafter, to that horse.

CHAPTER VII.

UNKNOWN TO THE ANCIENTS—ORIGIN—DIFFERENT BREEDS—SHETLAND AND
SCOTS—GALLOWAYS AND NARRAGANSETTS—MUSTANGS AND INDIANS—
PROFIT OF RAISING PONIES.

It is very remarkable that these hardy, active, and, in many cases, beautiful little animals appear to have been either absolutely unknown to the ancients, or so much neglected and undervalued by them, as to have obtained not only no special description, but not so much even as a distinctive name in the principal languages of antiquity. In the Hebrew this may be accounted for by the fact, that the soil and surface of Judea were so ill adapted for the employment of the horse, that its use was superseded by that of the ass; which animal, with its strong, hard hoofs and inflexible pastern joints, was better suited to the rocky nature of the ground and the hill fastnesses of Idumea than the nobler horse.

This reason, however, in no respect explains why the Greeks and Romans, both of whom most sedulously cultivated the horse, and who, by their writings still extant on the subject of equestrianism, were well informed on all matters connected with that animal, and were good judges of its points according to the received modern ideas, should have no definite word, if indeed any word at all, signifying a pony. In both tongues there is a diminutive of the word horse: in Latin, from *equus*, *equuleus;* as also, from *man-*

nus, a nag or pad, *mannulus;* and in Greek, from *hippos,*
hipparion; and to all these diminutives, the primary meaning of which is, a foal or young, and, because young,
small horse, the lexicographers have attached the inter-
pretation *pony.* It is, at least, doubtful whether the diminutives mentioned ever bore that sense; the immature
young of the horse and the adult pony, which, properly
speaking, cannot even be termed a little or small horse,
since it is not in its nature ever to become, or to produce
by generation, a large horse, but to produce and reproduce itself, like to like, as is the case with any other distinct species of the same family. In corroboration of which
view, it is well to remark, that there are several races or
varieties of ponies, peculiar to various parts of Europe,
Asia, and, more recently, of America, in all respects as
distinct and peculiar as any of the families of the horse,
such as the Norman, Flemish, Cleveland Bay, Suffolk
Punch or thorough-bred, and which will no more, when
bred like dam to like sire, produce a young one of any
other family, still less of the full-sized horse, than will any
of the horse families named above. The pony, therefore,
is by no means to be regarded as a dwarf horse—since full-
sized and healthy horses never produce ponies, although
they may produce rickety, small-sized and defective colts
or fillies; nor do ponies, as above stated, ever produce
full sized horses, which would occasionally be the case, especially in the former instance, were they accidental monstrosities, and not a distinct race.

In what manner the pony was originally produced, in
its primary form, or subsequently established in all, or any
one, of its self-reproducing varieties, is impossible to de-
cide, and useless to speculate. It is evident and certain
that once, at a vastly remote period, they all arose from a
single type of each species; but that, at periods still exceed-

ingly remote, though comparatively recent, divers varieties have branched off accidentally from the primary species, which, by accident or design, by circumstances of climate, or by care and cultivation, have been first rendered permanent.

It is remarkable and significant that all the most distinct breeds of ponies, with which we are acquainted, are still to be found, and appear to have been originated in extreme latitudes either of heat or cold; latitudes to which the horse does not seem to be indigenous; to which he has, according to all natural probabilities, been imported; and in which one would naturally expect him to degenerate, at least in size. It follows, if this view be correct, that at the time when the Greek and Latin languages prevailed, ponies, which were then possibly in progress of formation in regions beyond the ken of early civilization, in the lands which are laid down on the maps of "the world known to the ancients" as countries uninhabitable on account of heat or of cold, and in which distinct ponies do now exist, had not yet been brought at all to the knowledge of the civilized world, or, if at all, so rarely as to be regarded as accidental dwarfs and monstrosities, rather than a distinct breed.

Now, of European ponies, the most clearly distinct types are those of the Shetland Isles, of Scotland, in the northern parts of Iceland, and of Sweden. There are also ponies, somewhat similar to those of Scotland, in Wales, and others in the New Forest, on the south-western coast of England, which seem referable to a cross of the same pony with some horse of higher blood. On the whole, it seems likely that the Shetland, Scottish, Welch, Swedish and Icelandic pony is one and the same animal, as to its origin or original mode of production, slightly influenced perhaps by the original type of the horse of which it is a pattern, diminished in size, but undeteriorated in spirit by years, nay, centuries, of habituation to cold and scanty fare. In Spain there existed from an early date in the middle ages a peculiar breed of very small, high-bred horses, scarcely to be called ponies, known as the Andalusian jennet, the descendants of which are said still to exist in the Connemara horse, peculiar to Galway in Ireland, and to have existed in the Scottish Galloway, on the shores of the Solway Frith, in the south of Scotland, and probably in the Narragansett pacer, both of which families are now unfortunately extinct. These Spanish ponies, or ponies of Spanish descent, are referable to another and entirely different mode of production, by breeding, and not by deterioration in size, or dwarfing. In Asiatic and European Russia, again, the Cossack horse, which is little more than a large pony with good Turkish blood, is evidently the result of modified dwarfing by hardship and severity of climate. It is remarkable, however, of all these European and Asiatic ponies, as also of the American varieties, of which we shall speak hereafter, that, unlike most animals which have degenerated in size, owing to severity of climate and scanty fare, they have lost nothing of their spirit, and — what is yet more singular— have gained rather than lost in their capability to endure toil, hardship, and spare diet, in which particulars the tiny Shetlander and the rugged Cossack will probably surpass any other horses in existence.

Of the Southern Asiatic races comparatively little is known; but it is certain that in Ceylon there is a pygmy race of ponies not exceeding twenty-seven inches in height. A little mare was exhibited in London, in 1765, brought from the East Indies, only twenty-seven inches in height, well-formed, and between four and five years old.

In Persia and among the mountains of Afghanistan, there is found a useful breed of large ponies, called *Yauboos,* which is probably merely the Turkoman horse stunted by the hard fare and severe winters of the hill country. And lastly, in America we have the Indian Pony of the north, of the Canadian type, the Mustang of the south-west, and in South America a very singular-looking breed of horses, of very diminutive size, which is found in the mountains of Venezuela.

On these various families of ponies we shall touch more at length, and on the qualities for which they are famous and worthy to be more generally cultivated in our own country.

We admit that we wish we were more a race of horsemen, and less a race of sulky, buggy or wagon-drivers. The saddle is the true use of the horse; and riding is the manliest, freest, boldest of exercises. We can hardly fancy a good rider to be a fool or a fribble; a coward he cannot be by any possibility. It is for this reason that we would gladly see ponies more largely introduced, and even bred in this country; nor would it be amiss to introduce premiums for the encouragement of this breed at agricultural fairs.

SHETLANDS AND SCOTS.

Unquestionably, the most remarkable of all the European pony races, and the best adapted for one of the principal uses to which ponies are applicable, are, the little Shetlanders, which are natives of all the northern Scottish isles, but which are found of the smallest size and of the most perfect form in the extreme northern isles of Yell and Unst. None of the Shetlanders exceed in the average nine or ten hands—that is to say, from three feet to three feet four inches in height; and none are considered truly bred which exceed eleven hands, or three feet eight inches. Many are found which do not exceed thirty or thirty-two inches, and which are consequently inferior in size to some of the largest dogs of the Newfoundland and Labrador, or Great St. Bernard breeds. Their characteristic form is a round, closely ribbed-up barrel; a well-laid, sloping shoulder, but thick rather than fine, and with little elevation of the withers; a short, thick neck, covered with redundant masses of coarse mane, scarcely inferior to that of the lion; a well-shaped, lean and bony head, wide in the brow and not seldom showing something of the characteristic basin-face of the Arab. The ears are unusually small, erect and well-placed; the eyes large, clear and intelligent. Their loins are superb so that their breadth bears no small proportion to the entire height of the animal. Sway backs and flat sides are unknown to the race. Their quarters are scarcely large in proportion to their other muscular developments, but their legs and feet, which are not so densely matted with hair as would be expected from their flowing tails and abundant manes, are, like those of the Canadians and Normans, to which they have many strong points of similitude, literally made of iron. Splints, curbs, spavins, windgalls, thorough-pins, ringbones and navicular disease seem to be things utterly foreign to the Shetlander. Out of many hundreds which we have seen,—sometimes in droves of fifty or sixty at a time travelling down from their native moors and mountains, the raggedest, rustiest, most comical-looking little quadrupeds eye ever dwelt upon, driven by a gigantic six-foot Highlander, perched on the back perhaps of the smallest of the number,—we never saw a lame Shetlander. Their hardihood and spirit is wonderful. In their native isles they run wild on the hills as the ragged, black-faced sheep, with which they keep company, never herded, sheltered nor fed, but picking up a hardy livelihood from the tender shoots of the heather, and the coarse, innutritious grass which grows among it. In very severe winters, when in that high northern latitude the mountains are buried deep in frozen snow, they resort to the sea beaches and feed on the kelp and sea ware. Even when taken into domestication their fare is but little improved. Oats is a luxury unknown, and a few bundles of wild meadow hay or barley straw furnish a dainty banquet to the wee Shetlander. His speed is of course not great, but he will go along at a sort of waddling run under a weight which it would bother some horses to carry,—that is to say, from 150 to 200 pounds,—at the rate of four or five miles an hour; and will accomplish his fifty miles between sunrise and sunset with a great hulking Highlander on his back, who seems fitter to carry the pony than the pony to carry him.

For little boys and girls learning to ride, the Shetlander is perfection; for though he has sometimes a will of his own, and has always a very sufficient share of spirit, which sometimes leads him to play queer, grotesque tricks and to make uncouth gambols more resembling those of a big dog than of a small horse, he is very docile, intelligent, affectionate and gentle. He readily becomes extremely fond of his small rider; and if, as will sometimes happen, he kicks him over his head for fun, he will generally stop by his side until he gets up again, and will suffer himself to be remounted without opposition; and then, which is a great consideration, it is not far to fall from his back to the ground. The colors of the Shetlanders are generally black, dark brown, and a sort of rust-colored sorrel. Whites and greys are exceedingly rare, and blacks are considered the best of the race. There is a race of very small ponies, analagous to the Shetlanders, in Terie, one of the Hebrides or Western isles, belonging to the Duke of Argyle.

Next in size to the Shetlanders is a small white race of ponies, generally supposed to be of Hanoverian origin, which were some years ago much the fashion for ladies' pony carriages. They ran from ten to eleven hands high with softer and finer coats than the Shetlanders, and with manes and tails which, though full and flowing, were not so abundant and massive as those of their little congeners. They were not unfrequently *albinoes*, having blood-red pupils to their eyes, which tends to confirm suspicion of their Hanoverian origin. Persons who remember the drive in Hyde Park and the corner of Rotten Row in the days when George IV. was King, will not easily forget the beautiful turn-out of the beautiful Lady Foley, a four-in-hand of snow-white ponies, scarcely bigger than the rats which furnished Cinderella's carriage-horses, and two little ten-year-old outriders mounted on two others of the same stamp, in full uniform of top boots, leather breeches, and miniature hunting whips. These pretty Hanoverians are, however, only pretty playthings for pretty women, for they have none of the stamina of the Shetlanders. Shetland ponies of the true breed are not often imported into America, although of late years a good many of the larger Scottish and Welsh ponies are being introduced, and, if black, are often erroneously called Shetlanders. At the State Fair of New Jersey, held at Newark, in 1857, we noticed a very neat, very small dark grey pony, not above ten hands high, but finer coated and less shaggy than the ordinary run of Shetlanders. He was in the care of a very large, very green Hibernian, between whom and ourselves passed the following colloquy.

"That's a very nice pony, my man ; who owns him ?" "He *is*. Gin'ral Moore, of Belleville." "Is he a native pony, or imported ?" "He *is*." "He is *what* ?" "He *is that !*" "Yes, I see—where did he come from ?" "He come from New York; the Gin'ral got him there !" "Ah, I understand. But did he come from across the sea, or

how ?" " Across the *say !* Is it foolin' me yez is? Arrah,
don't I tell yiz he cum from New York, and then ye ax
me, is New York across the say? Be off wid yiz!"
Before we could obey our irate friend's mandate, however, a long, slab-sided, upland Jerseyman came up, and,
after eyeing the pony for some time, broke out as follows: " Waal, now, that's about the littlest kind of
horse I ever did see. What on airth's the use of that
critter, I'd like to know? I reckon you keeps him on
account of the milk." Meaning evidently for the purpose
of driving a churning machine. If our Hibernian was
wroth before, he was now furious. " Milk!" shouted he.
" Is it milk yiz said? He's a horse—can't you see? He
niver gave no milk, not a drop on't." " Nary!" replied
our Jersey compatriot, and we dissolved in laughter. We
afterward learned that the little animal is a pure Shetlander; and we may add, that he is the most beautiful
specimen of the breed, though by no means the most characteristic, we have ever seen. He had, though very
small, more of the horse than of the pony in his shape
and movement; was slenderer and finer limbed, and had
not the heavy tail and shaggy mane.

The larger Scottish pony is little more than an enlarged
pattern of the Shetlander. He preserves the general form,
the close barrel, strong loins and general stocky air and
build, but he has a somewhat longer neck, higher withers,
and finer hair in the mane and tail. His ordinary height
is from eleven to thirteen hands, above the latter of which
standards the animal is rated in England as a horse, no
longer as a pony. These larger Scottish ponies, which
are usually the second step by which a boy ascends toward
the top of the noble art of horsemanship, have often a fair
turn of speed, can leap cleverly enough, and have all the

endurance, with greater strength, greater quickness, and more showy action, of their smaller countrymen.

GALLOWAYS AND NARRAGANSETTS.

After the various descriptions of ponies which have been enumerated and described, there is none more worthy of notice than the peculiar race of small horses, rather than what can be exactly classed as ponies, which formerly existed, nearly identical in all their characteristics, in two small districts of Great Britain, wholly unconnected the one with the other, yet, singularly enough, with names so similar as to justify a first idea of their being in some sort similar or identical. The one of these is the small district of *Galloway*, on the shores of the Solway Frith, in the south-west of Scotland. The other is a portion of the county of *Galway*, in the west of Ireland. The whole width of the Irish Sea and of the island itself lies between the two districts, which have, in spite of their similar names, no connection, whether of origin or of population; yet, strange to say, in each locality there is, or rather was— for they have recently become nearly extinct—a peculiar breed of horses wholly different and distinct from the native stock, whether of Scotland or Ireland, yet so similar in all their characteristics and qualifications that their identity of origin cannot be doubted. These are the animals which, from the Scottish district on the border of the counties of Wigton and Kirkcudbright, received the name of GALLOWAYS, a word which afterward came to be misapplied to small horses of all descriptions.

In that district they were long famous for their endurance, speed, docility and easiness of gait, as well as for their high and courageous spirit; and so long as the country roads and, indeed, the great national thorough-fares of England and Scotland were such as to render the saddle the only rapid and agreeable, and by far the most certain mode of travel, these beautiful and excellent little animals were preserved in their purity, were carefully propagated from the best mares and stallions of their own race, and commanded large prices for the use both of gentlemen and ladies, as road hackneys. Their power of carrying weight, and of travelling at an easy and moderate gait for an almost unlimited number of consecutive hours, was really wonderful. But when the progress of improvement covered England and her provinces with a network of excellent roads, it became unnecessary to keep up a particular breed of horses, too small for agricultural use, too light for draft, without sufficient speed or length for hunters, and from which no class of horses for general utility could be raised by any system of cross-breeding. Consequently the beautiful and enduring little Galloways fell gradually into disrepute, and were either not bred at all, or merely bred for fancy purposes. In Galloway, the breed is now entirely extinct; although of late years attempts have been made to produce its counterpart by breeding large-sized pony mares of the Scotch and Shetland breeds to small, low-built, close-coupled, bony, thorough-bred stallions, for the purpose of becoming children's riding horses and boys' hunters.

In Galway, the existence of the animal was not known until a comparatively recent period ; and, as in that wild, remote and semi-civilized district, the same reasons still exist which originally caused them to be prized so highly in the sister kingdom,—the want of good roads for wheeled carriages,—they are believed still to exist there in their purity; although the rudeness of the district an the extremed poverty of the farmers have led to their deterioration. It is not, however, to be doubted, that if an intelligent system were adopted, the Galway-Galloways might be bred up to their original high standard.

4

It is claimed that they are descended from horses cast on the shores of the two districts from the ship-wrecked galleons of the Spanish Armada. In both districts it is a matter of historical notoriety that Spanish war-ships were wrecked at the period in question; and as they doubtless had cavalry on board, there is no cause for disputing the tradition, the rather that the Galloways of both districts have many of the peculiarities of the Andalusian jennets, and show a large tincture of Moorish blood.

"The pure Galloway," says Youatt, "was said to be nearly fourteen hands high and sometimes more, of a bright bay or brown, with black legs, and small head and neck, and peculiarly deep, clean legs. Its qualities were speed, stoutness and sure-footedness over a very rugged and mountainous country." From other authorities, better acquainted, perhaps, than Mr. Youatt, with the race in question, we find that they more often exceeded fourteen hands by half a hand than fell short of that height; that they were quite as often or oftener of a rich, deep, glossy chestnut—a peculiarly Andalusian color—as either brown or bay; that they were conspicuous for their breadth between the eyes, for their basin faces, for their thin, silky manes and tails, and for the total absence of hair on their fetlocks. They were, also, many of them, natural pacers, or amblers, as that pace is called in England, and were all of them easily trained to take and hold it for many hours together. A distinguished Scottish divine thus describes the animal in question: "There was once a breed of small, elegant horses in Scotland, similar to those of Iceland and Sweden, which were known by the name of Galloways, the best of which sometimes reached the height of fourteen hands and a half. One of this description I possessed, it having been bought for my use when I was a boy. In point of elegance of shape it was a perfect picture, and in disposition it was gentle and compliant. It moved almost to a wish, and never tired. I rode this little creature for 25 years, and twice in that time I rode 150 miles at a stretch without stopping, except to bait, and that not for above an hour at a time. It came in at the last stage with as much ease and alacrity as it travelled the first. I could have undertaken to have performed on this beast, when it was in its prime, 60 miles a day for a twelvemonth running, without any extraordinary exertion."

It is a matter of real regret that so excellent a breed of creatures should have been allowed to become extinct in both hemispheres, if it be not preserved by chance in the degenerated race of Galway. We say in both hemispheres —for although it is not generally known, it is yet certain that we once possessed in the far-famed Narraganset pacer the actual Spanish pacing jennet of Andalusia, and the exact counterpart of the Scottish Galloway. The color, pace, docility, size, endurance, all the characteristics, indeed, would almost establish this fact without direct evidence. But direct evidence is not wanting, as will be discovered by reference to "Updyke's History of the Episcopal Church in Narraganset," where will be found a curious letter from a Mr. Hazard, who was intimately acquainted with the race while it was at its highest perfection and held at its highest value; and who distinctly states it to be of Spanish origin, the ancestors having been brought from Cuba, where the breed was in such demand for ladies' saddle-horses that he attributes the extinction of the race in Rhode Island to the exportation of them in undue numbers to the Havana. We suspect, however, that the cause was rather the same which led to its extirpation in England—the improvement of roads and the introduction of wheeled carriages as the means of private conveyance, which rendered a larger and stronger horse necessary, and

for which trotters are preferable to pacers. To whatever
cause it is due, the decline of the breed must be regretted.
It is doubtful whether it can ever be renewed or replaced,
and it was undoubtedly a pure race of rare powers.

THE MEXICAN MUSTANG AND NORTHERN INDIAN PONY.

We have treated of the principal races of ponies peculiar
to the Old World, and to those more particularly which
are remarkable for good qualities and are worthy of cultivation. We now come to the ponies of our own continent.
For although it is not to be denied that the horses of
America are all, in the beginning,· traceable to a foreign
origin, and although we have no distinct breed or family
of the full-sized horse which is not distinctly to be traced
back to some one particular European family, of which it
still preserves the principal characteristics, we have certainly two families of ponies which, thoughthey are probably to be discovered originally in two European breeds
of larger size, differ from the original type so widely that
they may now be set down as distinct. These are the
Mexican Mustang and the Indian pony of the north,
which are in themselves distinct breeds, although there is
undoubtedly growing up a hybrid race between the two.

The Mustang of the Mexican and Texan prairies, where
it has spread over much of the western country beyond
the Mississippi, is clearly of Spanish origin, and both has
and shows a considerable share of Moorish blood. It is
under-sized, very slight-limbed, and often ill and dispro-
portionately made, with the neck or the back, or both, far
too long for either symmetry or strength. Their hoofs are
often very badly formed, and their posteriors are generally
weak, long and slender. On the other hand, they show
blood in the shape and setting on of their lean, long heads,

in their wide nostrils and fine manes and tails. They have considerable spirit and fire, and are sometimes vicious at first, but when resolutely combated lack persevering pluck, and easily give up the contest. It is said, also, that although when first mounted they display much life, vigor and showy action, they lack hardihood and endurance. It is well proved that, in a wild state, they can be ridden down and captured without much difficulty by good trained domestic horses, even carrying the weight of a rider, whenever they can be approached sufficiently close to allow anything approaching to an equality in the start. They are, however, the cavalry horses of the Camanche and Apache Indians; and although they are confessedly unable to stand the shock of a charge of American troop-horses, it does not appear to us, from the facility with which they evade or frustrate the pursuit of our mounted regiments, and the extreme difficulty of bringing them to engagement, that they can be so deficient in endurance or power of sustaining fatigue as they have been represented. It is clear, however, that they are in all respects so far inferior to the American horse that they can never sustain any comparison with him. Nothing is to be gained by crossing them with our horses, and the only utility which they can ever subserve is as the riding animals of children or very young ladies. They do not generally run, so far as we can judge from the specimens which we have seen in the Northern States, to above 13½ or 14 hands; and, though some of them are certainly pretty, graceful, elegant creatures, and some of them easy and light-going natural pacers, they have not impressed us favorably, as compared either with any of the imported European ponies, or with that of the northern Indians. It is, however, not only probable, but nearly certain, that we have not seen the best specimens of the breed, as they are not in very high

repute or in general use in the North. They are of all
colors,—browns, bays, blacks, sorrels, duns, and, by no
means unfrequently, piebalds, which is an extremely ple-
beian color, and which most certainly implies a deterioration of blood from the Oriental or desert type. When it
is seen in domestication, it is held to imply a cross of the
Hanoverian or Pomeranian horse, both of which run to
fancy colors, spots and piebalds.

The pony of the northern Indians, prevailing from Canada downward, west of the lakes, over the Upper Mississippi country, is a totally distinct animal. He rarely exceeds
thirteen, never fourteen hands, and is a veritable pony—
short-barreled, round-ribbed, strong-limbed, short and thick-
necked, with legs, fetlocks and feet literally of iron. His
legs are covered with thick hair, his mane is almost as
voluminous as that of a lion, often falling on both sides of
his neck, while the forelock covers his eyes, and his tail is
heavy and waved like that of the Canadian. In one word,
he is the pure Norman war-horse of the largest, oldest,
coarsest and most massive type, *razeed* into a pony. We
are not aware that there is any history or tradition as to his
origin, but we cannot doubt that he is nothing more or
less than the original Norman horse of the Canadas, degenerated in size but in no other respect, by ages of neglect,
misuse, scanty sustenance, want of shelter, and cruel usage,
generation after generation. We doubt not they could be
bred up in size by judicious treatment. As it is, however,
they are in every respect but size and great speed all that
can be desired. They are as sure-footed and as easily fed
as mules, and, fifty to one, more enduring of cold. At
their own pace, from five to seven miles an hour, they will
jog along, perfectly unwearied, for fifty miles a day, week
after week, with a load of one hundred and sixty pounds
on their saddle, or three hundred in a wagon behind them.

They are very docile, apparently as intelligent as dogs, good-tempered when not stallions, and extraordinarily high-couraged. We once saw, some five-and-twenty years ago, large herds of these ponies running half wild in the great meadows of the Mohawk Reservation, on the banks of the Grand River, near Brantford, in Upper Canada; and afterward travelled many days in succession in a light wagon, drawn by a pair of these little shaggy brutes not much bigger than Newfoundland dogs, both thorough stallions, hardly able to see out of their little fierce eyes through their thick shag of hair; and we were singularly impressed with their qualities. They were driven with the least possible quantity of harness, and that chiefly made of rope, without breechings, bearing-reins or blinders. The driver had no whip, and said he dared not use one to them if he had, but ruled them perfectly, when he chose to do so, by his voice. Chiefly, however, he left them to themselves, and admirably did they perform. The roads, if they could be called roads, were atrocious; often axle-deep in mud; often over corduroy tracks, made of un-hewn logs, through deep, shaking morasses, full of holes that would have engulfed a big horse and his rider, and, at times, passing over large, deep, boggy streams and rivers, on a species of bridge which we never saw before or elsewhere, and trust we may never see again. Whenever they doubted their ground, the ponies lowered their noses, snorted, snuffed at the doubtful place, and seemed to examine it with more than human intelligence, and always in the end scrambled over the difficulty, and brought us through or over it in safety. At the end of the trip we parted with our small equine friends with real regret, and never have forgotten them. This stamp of Canadian pony, we think, by all odds, the best animal of the sort on this continent for teaching boys to ride; and we should feel confident that by breeding the largest mares of this race to short, compact, stocky-bred blood stallions, one would obtain a most hardy, serviceable and beautiful small horse, partaking in many of the best qualities of the lost race of Galloways. The mares could be easily obtained, for a merely nominal sum, from the upper province of Canada; and we verily believe that it would prove a good specula-tion to an intelligent breeding farmer, to attempt to raise some of this stock, so rapidly and regularly is the demand increasing in our large cities for horses suitable for the young people of the wealthier classes; and so desirable is it that the taste itself, and the demand to which it gives rise, should be encouraged.

CHAPTER VIII.

HOW TO BREED MULES.

How important this branch of rural economy is becoming in the United States may be seen by the following notice of *The Columbus Inquirer*, copied into the veterinary department of *Porter's Spirit*, and the comment accompanying it: " A few days ago one hundred mules were sold in Scott county, Kentucky, at an average of $177 each. Our Southern planters have here another illustration of the fact, that they can never fully realize the high price for cotton until they raise their own stock and provisions; for the high price of one is always attended by a corresponding rise of the other." In view of this fact, we propose to devote a little space to the examination of the history and natural history of the mule; the advantages which he possesses,—as he does possess advantages of some kinds and for some purposes over both the horse and the ox; his qualities, and the best and most profitable mode of raising him for the market, and for producing his best qualities and characteristics.

To tell persons now-a-days that the mule is the hybrid between the horse and the ass would appear to be so absolute a truism that the recipients of the information would be very apt to laugh at the informant, and yet,

4* [81]

strange to say, few persons, comparatively speaking, know precisely, if indeed at all, what is or is not a mule—much less that there are two distinct animals, both the offspring of the horse and ass, one of which is, and the other is not a mule; much less, again, what are the distinctions between the two.

The offspring of the male ass and the female horse—mare—is truly the mule—in Latin, *hemionus*, or half ass. The offspring of the male horse—stallion—and the female ass is the hinny—in Latin, *hinnus;* a word which conveys, as does the former word *hemionus*, a distinct sense, lost in the corresponding English synonyms, for *hinnus* is a derivative of the verb *hinnire*, to neigh; and in fact the hinny neighs, while the mule brays. Nor is this all: for while the mule has the greater external resemblance to the ass, so has the hinny the greater external resemblance to the horse; and a more minute examination carries us yet farther, and shows us that the mule, not only in outward form but in temper and characteristics, has more of the ass in his nature—the hinny more of the horse. It is in a considerable degree by the knowledge of these facts, which are positive, that the breeder is led, when he insists that, in order to produce the greatest advantage on the offspring, the excess of blood and vital energy must be on the side of the sire, and not on that of the dam; since he finds invariably that from the jackass and the mare, whether the latter be the merest dunghill or as thorough-bred as Spiletta, the mother of Eclipse, springs the mule of the ass type.

The mule has long ears, slightly modified and shortened by the intermixture of the horse; the, comparatively, hairless tail; the narrow quarters and thin thighs; the erect mane, the elongated head, the slender legs and narrow, erect hoofs, and the voice of the ass. The hinny has a smaller, better-formed head, the flowing mane and full tail, the general form, the finer coat, larger legs, broader feet, and the voice of the horse. What would at first appear remarkable is, that the mule, or offspring of the male ass and mare, is a far larger animal than that of the stallion and female ass; and not only that, but frequently larger than either of his parents. In proof of which may be cited an advertisement from *Porter's Spirit of the Times*, of Jan. 8, of this year, offering for sale "a splendid pair of jet-black mules, *seventeen hands three inches high*, beautifully matched, three years old. They were got," it is added, "by the finest Maltese jack in Kentucky, out of thorough-bred mares, got by Wagner and Grey Eagle," &c. Now these prodigious animals, fully equal in height to the largest London dray-horse, which would probably weigh nearly two thousand pounds, if their height be correctly stated—which one may presume to be the case, since no benefit could arise to the advertiser from a deception which must instantly be discovered on examination by a purchaser—are the produce of a sire, the largest specimens of which never exceed the stature of a small horse. and dams which, in the absence of any knowledge on the subject, we may set down as probably not exceeding fifteen hands and two inches, and certainly not exceeding sixteen hands, inasmuch as the latter is, ordinarily speaking, the maximum height of the race-horse. Here, therefore, we have the hybrid offspring overtopping the sire in height by at least three hands, or twelve inches, and the dams by two hands, or eight inches:—a convincing proof, by the way, of the absurdity and hopelessness of expecting to produce an enlarged progeny by breeding small, weak, undersized mares to large, powerful stallions; and a strong argument in favor of having the size, length and room to contain the fœtus on the side of the female parent.

The mule, again, which is the offspring of the male ass, has the great excess of his qualities,—the incomparable endurance, the patience, the faculty of subsisting and keeping himself in good condition where the horse would starve, and the extraordinary sure-footedness of the ass, and it must be added, in a great degree, his temper, his obstinacy, stubbornness and passive vice; although it is believed that, both in the ass and mule, these bad qualities have been greatly fostered and increased by the cruelty and neglect of ages—no such qualities being observed in the beautiful, docile and tractable asses of the East, where they have. been from the most remote ages used as the saddle animals of the superior classes—and that they may, by kind and judicious treatment, be greatly modified, if not eradicated.

The hinny, on the contrary, although hardier, more patient, more enduring of privation and scanty fare than the horse, is infinitely inferior, in all these qualities, both to the ass and the mule; while he is at the same time gentler, more tractable, and nearer to the horse in temper, —strong arguments, it will be observed, for seeking invariably to have the qualities of the blood, temper, courage, spirit, on the side of the sire, those of form and size on that of the dam.

Both the mule and hinny are clearly modified asses,— that is to say, they have both more in their composition of the ass than of the horse, but the proportion of that *more* depends on the male. and not on the female parent. It appears that the vital energy and power of transmitting organization is stronger in the ass than in the horse, prob- ably because he is entirely in-bred, less changed by domes- tication, and nearer to his natural condition than the more cultivated and more highly favored animal. The zebra and quagga are yet more potent in this strange power of transmitting properties than even the ass; for it is an established fact, on well authenticated record, that a thorough-bred mare having once produced a striped foal to a quagga, continued for several successive generations, when bred to thorough-bred horses and having no further connection with the quagga, to produce striped offspring, the stripes becoming fainter and fainter in each successive foal; a fact which has led, in connection with other circumstances, some of the best French Physiologists to the conclusion that a female, which has once borne a hybrid, becomes herself a hybrid, and can never again bear a perfect animal of her own race; a fact certainly worthy the consideration of persons who, like the breeder of the mules in the advertisement quoted above, stint mares of such blood as Grey Eagle and Wagner to Maltese jacks. Only imagine their faces, should they after this breed the same mares to a Lexington, a Monarch or a Revenue, and find the progeny, on its appearance, long-eared, with a stripe along its back and a bar across its shoulders.

It is clear, then, that while in all hybrids of the horse and ass, the latter gives the greater proportion both of external and internal characteristics, it is determined by the sire, not by the dam, in what degree that excess shall exist; and this principle will lead to a full understanding of how mules may be bred to the best advantage.

Thus, if we are breeding mules, on the spirit, courage, temper and characteristics of the male ass, everything will depend in the production of the like qualities in the progeny: while so long as the mare is sound, strong enough, bony enough, and roomy, it will matter very little, so far as the characteristics of the young are concerned, whether she be a Suffolk Punch. or as pure a thorough-bred as

Spiletta, the mother of Eclipse. But not only is it very certain that the Grey Eagle and Wagner blood is wasted to no purpose by this prostitution to vile uses, in giving the qualities of blood to the mules, but it is even questionable whether two stout, sound, active Canadians, or Normans, would not have thrown better foals to the same jack than these noble mares, thus sadly misapplied.

On the other hand, if we are breeding hinnies, we want the very best stallion we can find, in blood and bone, so that he be not disproportionably large; while in the female ass, we only require soundness, and sufficient size to render her roomy enough to contain a fœtus so much larger than her own natural progeny, as the hinny foal is like to be. But as no one breeds hinnies or is likely to do so, this side of the question is worthy of no farther consideration, and with a few words more we quit it altogether. It is generally asserted that the hinny has been tried and found nearly a worthless animal, though admitted to be a beautiful one. He has only been bred occasionally in Spain, since the great decline in the number and quality of the male asses, and of mules, generally, from the want of male asses,— arising from the frightful consumption of those animals during the Peninsular war,—and the subsequent incessant civil wars which have convulsed that unhappy country, has rendered it necessary to supply their want. We are not inclined to adopt this assertion. We believe that the hinny, so far from being a worthless animal, is as good as he is handsome, and superior to the mule for the uses for which he is fitted,—that is, for a saddle animal. But being inferior to the horse as a saddle animal, and inferior to the mule as a beast of draft or burden, in which respect alone the latter can compete with the horse, he has no special place of his own; and, therefore, it having been worth no one's while to cultivate hinnies, they have fallen into disuse and got a bad name. It may, however, well be doubted whether, in the great demand and inadequate supply of handsome, clever ponies suited for carrying boys, young ladies, and timid, or valetudinarian, or aged persons, who require horse exercise, it might not prove an exceedingly paying speculation to import a few of the very finest and largest-sized Maltese or Arabian female asses,—which, by the way, command no price as compared with the jacks, and to breed from them to the best and highest bred, undersized thorough-bred stallions. We have seen abroad in past years one or two hinnies, with ears but little larger than those of a coarse pony, with long thin manes, full tails, sleek, shining coats, which were altogether beautiful animals. They have a good deal of spirit, and the patience, without the stubbornness, of the ass. If, however, it has not been a matter of profit heretofore to raise hinnies, it has been far otherwise in the case of mules. So highly were they esteemed by the Romans, that we are informed by Pliny, that Quintus Axius, a Roman Senator, paid four hundred thousand sesterces, equivalent to thirteen thousand dollars, for a male ass, peculiarly qualified by size, beauty and spirit for the propagation of mules.

They are now, probably, more largely bred and more highly prized in the United States than in any other country in the world, unless it be South America. As draught beasts, beasts of burden, and for field labor, they surpass any other animal in the world; and the use of them allows the noble horse to be applied to his own proper uses,—the saddle or speedy light carriage draught,—and not to field labor or the rude and sordid drudgery to which he is too often degraded, and to which he is wholly unfitted. It is claimed for the mule, and rightly, that he can do his own work, that is to say, field work, heavy teaming, and carrying pack-burdens, all, as well as the horse,—the last item better than the horse,—and twice as much of each one of them as the horse, provided he be not hurried; keeping himself in perfect condition, where the horse would knock up and starve; that he can do all this on half the food and with half the care that the horse requires, although the more food and the more care both have the better they will do their work; and lastly, the mule being an animal of great longevity and great retention, or conservation, of both his vital energies and his physical powers, is able to work to the advantage of his owners, twice, if not thrice as many years as the average of horses. These are the inducements to breed the mule, and to apply it strictly to the purposes for which it is best fitted, and for which nature seems to have intended it.

We propose now to treat of the difference between the mule of Europe and that now generally raised in the United States; the error, as we believe it to be, in the present American system of breeding, and the best plan to be adopted for raising the most valuable mules.

Inasmuch as asses are not bred to any extent in the United States, it is of the first consequence for breeding to import fine jacks from their native countries, of the breed and description most suitable to the purposes for which they are intended; and of the second, to cross them with properly-selected mares, so as to raise mules of the best type, size and substance for general work.

And it will be well here to observe that in the United States generally the work of the mule is and ever will continue to be,—unless some radical change takes place— which is not to be expected—in the tastes and habits of the people,—field-work, agricultural labor and team-draught on the roads, as opposed to use under the saddle or in pleasure vehicles. In the prairies, plains and mountains of the extreme west, on the Mexican frontier and on the

California route, they are and will be used as pack animals, and in a minor degree as beasts for the saddle, both for travellers and for the trappers of those wild solitudes; but this is the exception and not the rule.

Now, any person who has travelled on the continent of Europe, in those countries where mules are in use, especially Spain and Portugal—for the mules of Italy and Switzerland are of an inferior kind—cannot have failed to observe that it is the medium and even the small-sized mules, which are the most highly esteemed; that the great majority of the race do not exceed fourteen hands in height, so that one of fifteen is a rarity; and that those nearest to the standard first named, are most prized for their hardiness, while they consume far less provender, in proportion to the amount of labor which they are capable of performing, than the loftier animals of the same breed. In the United States, the ratio of value in the mule is exactly the reverse of the above in general estimation— the largest mules being the most highly prized; and, as a matter of course, all pains are taken to raise the standard, and to breed them of the greatest possible height. In this aim the breeders in the United States have been eminently successful,—if that can properly be called a success, the effect of which is to produce what one aims at producing, though in fact he had done better to produce something else. And it may be said that the average size of the mule of the United States is not inferior to that of the ordinary working horse, while that of many is vastly superior.

We have at present within our own knowledge many teams of working mules, employed in drawing iron from the New Jersey foundries and in carting coal and ore, which vary from sixteen to seventeen hands in height, while some exceed by half a hand the latter standard, which, it may be said, is never attained by any horse, unless it be the huge London dray-horse, an animal incapable of working faster than at a foot's pace, and only bred in fact for show and ostentation, not for utility. How it is that an animal sprung from the cross of two species, the sire of which is always greatly smaller than the dam, should be larger than either parent, is one of the unexplained mysteries of breeding; but the mode in which it has been accomplished is no mystery. It is by selecting the very largest and loftiest jacks of the breeds used, in Europe generally, for the saddle, and, in Spain, for the draught of public conveyances and private pleasure carriages, and breeding from them out of the tallest, largest and most roomy mares that can be procured. That such dams should produce hybrids larger than their sires is in the natural course of things, since—as we have pointed out in our previous papers on horse-breeding—it is the mare, furnishing the matrix of the foal, that gives the size and bone to the progeny. But why such mares should produce a much larger offspring, to a male infinitely smaller than themselves in stature, than they would bear to a stallion of their own race, equal or even superior to themselves in height, is not to be accounted for by any known principles of physiology. The fact is, however, as stated, and the result is not desirable. For the mule of increased size appears to approach somewhat nearer to the horse in organization, whereas it is desirable that he should approach nearer to the ass. He is a slower and more sluggish animal, than the smaller breed, is less enduring of labor, less capable of toiling under extraordinary temperatures of heat—which is one of the admitted points of superiority in the mule over the horse—and, being much heavier in proportion, is apt to sink his small, narrow, compressed hoofs far deeper into the ground, where the soil is deep and the roads are sticky and tenacious, while he will consume from one-fifth to one-third more provender. Yet even at this he will consume so much less, while doing more constant, though somewhat slower, work than the horse, that three of the large-sized mules may be kept in perfect condition on the same amount of food which is required for the support of a pair of the nobler animals.

It is evident, therefore, that where mules are not required for show or speed, as saddle or carriage animals, as they are not, and probably never will be, in this country, the smaller-sized animals are the more profitable both to raise and to keep, for the purposes of labor.

Now, it should be understood, that there are at least three different varieties of asses—beside the small, common jack, supposed to be of African origin, generally of a light-grey color, with a black stripe along his back and a transverse list or bar across his shoulders—all of which, are more or less used for breeding in this country. Although the African jack above mentioned, is rarely used in this country for breeding purposes, the mules bred from him are infinitely the most hardy of all, though the lowest in stature. The other breeds are these: first, the large, coarse, heavy Spanish jack, with slouching ears and a dull, plodding gait, from which the mules for agricultural purposes are ordinarily raised on the Peninsula. It is this breed which has been so much exhausted by the consumption of the Peninsular war, and subsequent internal commotions, that it is in some districts all but extinct. Second, the Andalusian jack, with shorter and more erect ears, more active, spirited, and sprightly than the foregoing species, yet sufficiently strong and well provided with bone. This animal is probably no other than a slightly degenerated descendant of the Arabian species, which has become somewhat coarser and larger boned, as well as less spirited, in consequence of his long residence in a colder climate—

though still warm—than his native land, and perhaps of crossing with the species first described. The third is the Arabian jack, which is to the ass what the thorough-bred is to the horse,—taller in height, lighter in limb, slenderer in bone, with a high-carried head, shorter and always erect ears, and a higher and more sprightly spirit, than any other of the ass species. It is said by those who have seen and examined this animal in its native land, and who are competent to judge, that it bears so close a resemblance to the wild ass, Dziggtai, *Equus Hemionus*, of Persia and Mongolia, as described by Pallas, the naturalist, that it is not to be doubted that it is descended from that swift and beautiful creature. Were the saddle, or harness before pleasure vehicles, the object of mule-raising, this jack or his representative, the Maltese jack, which is evidently directly sprung from him, with little or no degeneracy or deterioration, would, unquestionably, be the best sire. But for draft mules for heavy work, these jacks are too slender in the limbs, and especially too long in the pasterns to make eligible sires.

In our opinion the Maltese jack should never be chosen as a sire for working mules in this country; but if he be, he should be bred to close-ribbed, strong-boned, stocky mares; Canadians we should prefer to any other form. It is our belief, however, that the Andalusian jack, if it can be procured, is the most eligible sire for the United States; but as it is understood to be difficult to procure this race, it would be perhaps advisable to commence from the commencement, and proceed to breed our own jacks for the purpose of breeding our own mules, instead of having recourse to the constant importation of male asses. This, in the end, would prove to be not only the surest but the cheapest method; and it is confidently believed that a superior jack to any now existing, for American breeding purposes, might thus be produced. In the islands of Majorca and Minorca, to which the ravages of foreign and civil war have not so far extended, it is well ascertained that the large, coarse, slouch-eared Spanish breed still exists in perfection; and thence it would be easy to procure jennies—as the females of the ass are technically termed—by breeding which to the finest Maltese jacks, there can be no doubt that stallions might be reared superior in the combination of bone with beauty and spirit to any breed of original jacks now in existence. The choice of mares from which to breed mules by such jacks is an easy matter. They should on no account be blood mares, or highly-bred mares, or tall mares. Fifteen hands in height is abundant stature, and fifteen two is too large, but they should be rather long-bodied, roomy, and, above all, bony. They should have long shoulders, as oblique as possible, since those of the ass are very straight, a peculiarity which it is desirable to correct; and, for analogous reasons, they should *not* have the pasterns too stiff and erect; and they *should* have the hoofs large, round and well opened. The better their necks, withers and heads, the neater, in all probability, will be the produce. On the whole, we have little doubt that fine, well-selected Canadian or Norman mares will prove to be the best mule mothers—as thorough-breds will prove to be the worst—while Andalusian jacks or half-breeds, between the Maltese and great Majorca race of asses, will prove the best possible sires. It only remains to be stated that, in order to have mules docile and gentle, they should be handled as young as possible, and invariably gelded before they are six month old. The longer that operation is deferred, the more indocile, obstinate, and, perhaps, vicious they will become, which is the greatest defect in the character of the mule, and that against which it behooves the breeder most to be on his guard.

CHAPTER IX.

HOW TO BUY A HORSE.

IT is not, of course, to be imagined, that any person entirely
unacquainted with horses, the points of their anatomical
structure, their constitution and their qualities, can be by
the mere perusal of any one or more books on the subject,
at once created into a good judge of the animal, and a competent purchaser beyond the risk of being deceived or of
deceiving himself. To become a perfect judge of a horse
requires the observation and attention of half a life-time;
nor with every man will these be sufficient; for a certain
degree of natural tact and talent, or adaptability to the
study, is clearly indispensable; and there are some men
who, if they were born in a manger and brought up in a
stable, would never become horsemen or judges of a horse.
Still, there is no doubt that a person desiring to purchase,
and desiring to exercise in some degree his own choice in
the matter rather than submit wholly to the guidance of a
friend, may, by carefully studying what has been written
on the subject, qualify himself so far as in a great measure,
using proper precautions and profiting by some advice, to
secure himself against the probability of being very grossly

deceived, and to obtain an animal which will please him better than one selected for him by a person employed as intermediate between himself and the dealer.

The first rule to be laid down, then, for the buyer who wishes to obtain a superior animal for his own use, and who is neither a first-rate judge of horse-flesh, nor a first-rate horseman himself, is, not to attempt to buy out of the farmer's or breeder's hands; least of all at a horse fair or agricultural show,—but from some large, well-known and respectable dealer, one who has a character to lose and who is, therefore, not likely grossly and outrageously to deceive, although he will probably not fail to do what he can in extracting as large a price as the verdancy or eagerness of the purchaser may give him the hope of obtaining. The reasons for this advice are as follows:

First: Breeders and farmers do not often themselves know what their horses really are as to actual soundness, much less as to speed,—which probably has never been cultivated; or endurance,—which has almost certainly never been tested. So that a farmer or breeder will often honestly guarantee an unsound horse to be sound, from not knowing enough to have discovered the contrary. The writer saw a curious point of this kind, when, in 1837, the authorities of the Canadian government were purchasing fine Vermont horses for the use of the Royal Artillery. The dismay of the farmers who came in to sell, in compliance with advertisements, was extreme, and their disgust yet greater, at finding that not above one in three animals, which they believed to be perfectly unimpeachable, could pass muster as sound in wind and limb under the scrutiny of experienced veterinary surgeons, who at once detected the germs of incipient diseases which had not even been suspected by the breeder. By buying of the dealer you are tolerably well assured that when he bought he believed the horse to be right, and, therefore, you have one intelligent opinion in your favor.

Secondly: Breeders' and farmers' horses are usually so overloaded with flesh and fat, especially at agricultural shows and horse fairs—having been prepared, in order to make the best show, by feeding them on hot mashes, boiled grain, boiled potatoes and the like, and by keeping them in hot stables—that it is difficult, if not impossible, to come to any true judgment as to the horse's real points; and that, even if the horse be bought rightly—which means well and wisely—for exactly what he is, and about what he is worth, there will be great risk of ruining him utterly if he be put to hard work in his present condition; and if he be judiciously prepared by his buyer before putting him to work, much time, much pains, and much expense will have to be laid out on him before he can be of any real utility.

Lastly: Horses in the hands of the farmer or breeder are never properly bitted, broken, or trained to going; and unless the buyer be able to break him in these respects, to form and finish him himself—which is to presuppose him to be a perfect horseman—it will cost him half as much more to have him trained and rendered fit for use, by a horse jockey or trainer, as it did to become his owner in the first instance. Therefore, it is ever the better and wiser way to buy at first, of a reputable dealer, a horse which is in working order, whose faults and excellences are both known to the seller, if he choose to let them out, and which can be both critically examined, owing to his being in working condition, and tried on the road, under saddle or in harness, if desirable.

The second great rule is, not to imagine that perfection can be bought for a song, or that great excellence is compatible with great cheapness. A remarkable bargain in horse-flesh is always suspicious, and the greater the bargain the more suspicious he becomes. If in appearance, show, beauty, style of going and action, the animal offered for sale be very superior, and the price at which he is offered very inferior, one may be perfectly certain that the horse has some very bad secret fault, whether of temper or constitution, of vice or of unsoundness, which time will be sure to discover. It is never safe to take it for granted that the seller of a horse is an ass, or is not aware of the worth of his merchandise. If he err, nine times out of ten it will be in overrating, not underrating its value. To get a good horse, ordinarily, one must expect and be content, to pay a good price—the more, the greater the number of excellencies one may desire to obtain.

These rules premised, it is necessary for the buyer to make up his mind exactly as to what he wants, which, of course, must be in a measure regulated by what he has got to pay. If he merely wants a stout, serviceable, sound, active, useful brute, without caring about speed, action, beauty, or blood, he will be readily and easily accommodated for a moderate sum, say from $75 to $125; with each of the other additions the figure advances in arithmetical progression, until, if one require a highly-bred, beautiful, fine-stepping, fast, gentle and perfectly broke horse, the price becomes a fancy one, and, according to the degree of each attribute, ascends higher and higher, and may become anything.

Of course it is not with animals of this kind that we are dealing; nor is it to this that we require our purchaser to make up his mind—but as to the use for which he requires his horse; whether for heavy draft, for a carriage-horse, a light harness horse, an agricultural horse, or a saddle-horse, all of which have different points of excellence and distinct qualifications. The heavy draft-horse and agricul-

5

tural horse are the least difficult to select, and the lowest priced; the carriage-horses next; then the light harness horse, and, lastly, the saddle-horse, which is the most difficult of all to find nearly perfect, as requiring the greatest union of rare qualities. The heavy draft-horse requires only great power and weight, with a fast-walking action, or a moderate trot, and the power of going easily to himself The agricultural horse requires strength, quickness, activity, hardihood and courage. The carriage-horses are to be estimated very differently; size, fine figure, great show, stylish action and a moderate stroke of speed are all that is needed. With none of these animals is the manner of going, of being bitted, mouthed, or broken, of so great consequence.

For the light harness horse more is needed—more style, more speed, generally at a slashing trot, which may be as rough and difficult to sit as it may ; plenty of endurance, and above all a good mouth and a pleasant style of driving; since it is our own hands, not John's or Thomas's, which are to be excoriated, and our own shoulders which are to be lugged out of the sockets if he be an inveterate bearer. For the saddle-horse most of all is needed. He must be handsome ; he must have safe, showy, stylish action ; he must be sure-footed ; must have a fine mouth, a fine temper, lots of courage, and perfect docility. Above all, he must be an easy mover, both to himself and to his rider, or else grievous will be the loss of temper and the loss of leather to the latter. The best saddle-horses, unless one prefer to ride gallopers, are horses with not less than three, and as many more crosses as possible, of thorough blood on any good common stock. Three crosses from Canadians, or two from Morgans, make capital roadsters. Thorough-breds are not often great trotters, since their action is apt to be too straight and near the ground. When, however, they do take to trotting, they make the best trotters in the world; as they invariably, and they only, make the best gallopers.

The points of the physical structure of a horse on which the most, indeed the whole of his utility depends, are his legs. Without his locomoters, all the rest, however beautiful it may be, is nothing worth. Therefore, to these we look the first. The fore shoulder should be long, obliquely set, with a considerable slope, high in the withers and their above. The upper arm should be very long and muscular; the knee broad, flat and bony; the shank or cannon bone, as short as may be, flat, not round, with clean, firm sinews; the pastern joints moderately long and oblique, but not too much so, as the excess produces springyness and weakness; the hoofs firm, erect, or deep, as opposed to flat; and the feet generally large and round. In the hind legs, the quarters should be large, powerful, broad, when looked at in profile, and square and solid from behind. The hams should be sickle-shaped, not straight, and well let down, so as to bring the houghs well toward the ground. The houghs should be large and bony, straight, not angular or convexly curved in their posterior outlines; the shanks corresponding to the cannon bones, short and flat; and the hind feet similar in form to the front. The back should be short above, from the point of the withers and shoulder-blade, which ought to run well back to the croup. The barrel should be round, and for a horse in which strength and quickness are looked to more than great speed and stride, closely ribbed up. A horse can scarcely be too deep from the top of his shoulder to the intersection of his fore leg—which is called the heart-place—or too wide in the chest, as room in these parts gives free play to the most important vitals. The form of the neck and setting on of the head are essential not only to the beauty of the animal, but to the facility and pleasure of riding or driving him; hence, a horse with an ill-shaped, short, stubborn neck, or an ill-set-on head, cannot, by any possibility be a pleasant-mouthed horse, or an easy one to manage. The neck should be moderately long, convexly arched above from the shoulders to the crest, thin where it joins the head, and so set on that, when yielding to the pressure of the bit, it forms a semi-circle, like a bended bow, and brings the chin downward and inward until it nearly touches the chest. Horses so made are always manageable to the hand. The converse of this neck, which is concave above and struts out at the windpipe like a cock's thrapple, is the worst possible form; and horses so made almost invariably throw up their heads at a pull, and are those most exceptionable of brutes, *regular star-gazers*. The head should be rather small, lean, bony, not beefy, in the jowl; broad between the eyes; and rather concave, or what is called basin-faced, than Roman-nosed between the eyes and nostrils. The ears should be fine, small and pointed; the eyes large, clear and prominent, and the nostrils wide and well opened. A horse so framed cannot fail, if free from physical defects, constitutional disease and vice, to be a good one for any purpose—degrees of strength, lightness and speed being weighed in accordance with the purpose for which he is desired.

We shall proceed to point out some of those more prominent defects and ailments to be found in horses commonly offered for sale, and a few simple plans for detecting them, under ordinary circumstances, which, where resort is had to no villainous jockeying, will be found, in most cases, sufficient to an ordinarily acute observer.

DEFECTS TO BE DETECTED IN THE AGE AND EYES.

As to the age of horses, we would observe, that the number of years which the animal has lived is indicated, up to his seventh year, by marks in the teeth of both jaws, but principally of the lower jaw, which vary every year until the eighth, when they become obliterated; they are difficult to learn, and impossible to explain without the aid of diagrams, which will be furnished in this chapter, with more minute directions for ascertaining the age. There is a system of jockey rascality by which false marks are forged on the teeth of aged horses, making them to appear to be six or seven years old, which may deceive, and often do deceive, novices, but are thrown away on judges and old hands. This system is called *Bishoping*, and is executed by the use of a file and the usual cautery. There are, however, some signs of extreme age in the horse which can easily be recognized by any one, some of which are infallible. One of these is the fact that in a young horse the crown of the tooth is oblong or rather obovate in form, *lengthwise*, or in the line of the jaw-bone; but that in very old horses the crowns change their shape and become oblong or obovate *across* the jaw-bone. When, therefore, the tooth has assumed this form, or has even become much modified from the longitudinal shape, it is certain that the horse is too old to be a desirable acquisition. A second sign is the length of the teeth from the root to the crown, and their angular protrusion like those of the hare or rabbit; in both which particulars the increase is regular with the increase of age. Indeed, the degree of this protrusion is said to be so certain and infallible, that a machine has been invented by the French veterinarians for measuring the angle of protrusion, by which it is alleged that the exact age can be ascertained up to any known period of equine life. Without undertaking to answer for this, we should advise a buyer always to look to the points mentioned; as it is extreme age which one seeks to avoid, with reason, not maturity, or even the commencement of decline. Except to a racing man, it matters little whether the horse he buys be four, six, eight or nine years old, provided that he be sound, suitable in other respects, and free from the effects and marks of hard labor and wear and tear; remembering always that if the buyer requires a horse for immediate hard use, he should not purchase one under six; and if the animal be perfectly sound, and fresh and clean in his legs, will be wiser to buy at eight or nine than younger.

We now come to the eyes, which of all the parts of the horse are, except the legs, of the most vital importance, and in which it is often the most difficult to detect imperfection. There are some species of blindness, which to a common observer give no sign, and in many instances the writer has known the eye of a horse nearly stone-blind to be looked at casually by a purchaser, and passed as needing no further scrutiny.

"There is nothing," says Youatt, "which deserves so much attention from the purchaser of a horse as the perfect transparency of the *cornea* (or glassy and transparent portion of the eye), over the whole of its surface. The eye should be examined for this purpose both in front, and with the face of the examiner close to the cheek of the horse, under and behind the eye. The latter method of looking through the cornea is the most satisfactory, so far as the transparency of that part of the eye is concerned. During this examination the horse should not be in the open air, but in the stable, standing in the doorway, and a little within the door. If any small, faint, whitish lines appear to cross the cornea, or any part of it, they are assuredly signs of previous inflammation; or, although the centre and bulk of the cornea should be perfectly clear, yet if around the edge of it, where it unites with the *sclerotica* (or hard interior covering of the back of the eye), there should be a narrow ring or circle of haziness, the conclusion is equally true, but the inflammation occurred at a more distant period. Whether, however, the inflammation has lately existed, or several weeks or months have elapsed since it was subdued, there is every probability that it will return. There is one little caution to be added. The cornea, in its natural state, is not only a beautifully transparent body, but it reflects even in proportion to its transparency many of the rays which fall upon it; and if there be a white object immediately before the eye, as a very light waistcoat or much display of a white neckcloth, the reflection may puzzle an experienced observer, and has misled a careless one." It is hardly necessary to observe that the existence of a white filmy spot on any portion of the cornea, or, still worse, an opaque filmy condition of the whole of that beautiful and delicate membrane, is a fatal defect, the latter indicating a total loss of sight, the result either of specific ophthalmia, or of cataract. But it may be well to mention a very practical and simple mode of ascertaining how far the powers of sight in a horse are or are not effected. Holding him gently by the head-stall, let the observer place himself in front of the animal, and, after caressing him and rubbing his nose, so as to avoid giving him sudden alarm, let him move his fingers rapidly toward and across his eyes, carefully noting how far he starts back, or winks his eyelids. Care must be had, in this experiment, not to move the hand with so much violence as to cause a current of air; for that, striking on the delicate surface of the organ, even when it is totally bereft of vision, will sometimes cause the animal to wink and even to start back, as if he saw the motion which produced it.

DEFECTS TO BE DETECTED IN THE WIND.

Next to the eyes, the wind, as it is commonly called, or the condition of the lungs of the animal, is to be examined; and this is liable to so many modifications, and affects the animal so fatally as to his utility, when required for even moderately rapid work, that too much care cannot be had in the examination. It is needless to say that a horse, with the slightest imperfection of his lungs, windpipe, or breathing apparatus, ought at once to be rejected; as there is no hope of its ever decreasing, being cured, or palliated, either by rest or by work; but on the contrary, an absolute certainty of its growing worse, day by day, and the more so the faster and more regularly the animal is worked, until it becomes absolutely broken-winded and useless.

In this stage of the disease it needs no examination to detect it: when at work, the loud, sobbing breath, and the laborious heaving and jerking collapse of the flanks, show it too plainly to be mistaken. It is caused by a rupture of some of the air-cells of the lungs, and the inspiration of the air is readily effected by the animal at a single effort, as usual; but the expiration of the air, from the ruptured and ragged cavities into which it has been admitted, requires a double effort; and when the disease is in its worse form, even two efforts are insufficient fully to expel it.

BROKEN WIND is accompanied with a hard, husky cough, which is not easily described, but cannot be mistaken by any one who is used to horses. Broken-winded horses can never be cured, since it is not in the power of human art to build up and restore a broken-down and dis-

5*

organized structure; but there are jocky tricks by which they can be so far palliated as to be made to disappear, for two or three days' time, under any moderate observation. But let the horse be galloped a hundred yards, at his best, up hill; let his rider spring quickly to the ground, and apply his ear to the chest, and the double expiration will be clearly heard, even if the flanks do not show—as, however, in ninety cases out of a hundred, they will, by their jerking and laborious collapse—the extent of the affection. The minor and secondary modifications of this disease are, thick wind, roaring, wheezing, and whistling—all of which, more or less certainly, degenerate into broken wind, and are to be carefully looked for, and when detected, resolutely avoided. They all arise from a diseased or obstructed condition of some of the air passages, whether of the lungs themselves, the windpipe, the bronchial tubes, or the nostrils.

THICK WIND is produced by insufficient space for the play of the lungs, or for the issue of the air through the bronchial tubes, owing to the thickening of their mucous lining consequent on previous inflammation. It produces laborious breathing, only effected by prodigious exertion of the lungs; often extends almost to suffocation, and nearly always leads to broken wind, or total disorganization of the structure of the lungs—of some portion or ramification of which it indicates either an orignally faulty formation, or a diseased condition.

ROARING is a modification of thick wind, produced by the existence of a ring of coagulated matter, or a thickening of a portion of the mucous membrane, within the windpipe, which produces a contraction of that passage, and, preventing the regular issue of the breadth, renders some exertion necessary to expel it, and causes a loud puffing or roaring sound, similar to that of strong and hoarse exhalations, the inhalation being noiseless. Roaring occurs on sudden motion.

WHEEZING is a modification of roaring, and is produced, it would seem, by the lodgment of mucous matter in the bronchial tubes. It differs from roaring, in that it exists even when the animal is wholly at rest, and in his stable.

WHISTLING is a second modification of roaring, from which it differs in that the noise produced is shriller, and that it does not occur on sudden, but only after continuous motion. It is supposed to be caused by some contraction of the larynx.

Animals subject to any of these diseases speedily become exhausted by exertion, even while the disease is in its original state, apart from the distressing sound which they produce. All the forms are liable to degenerate into the worst form of broken wind, and all constitute an unsoundness for which a horse warranted sound is returnable. The modes of detecting these diseases are various, but simple and easy of execution. The first is by grasping the horse's throat from the front, and forcibly compressing the mouth of the larynx, so as to compel him to cough A sound horse will cough *once* and recover his wind, with a clear, sonorous inhalation and exhalation. The diseased horse will utter a broken, ragged, rattling cough, and recover his breath with a long, wheezing and laborious *râle.* This sign is infallible; and the degree of labor and diffi culty will certainly indicate the degree of the affection. A roarer may be detected even in the stable, by approaching him suddenly and hitting him an unexpected slap on the belly, when he will utter a loud grunt, not unfrequently accompanied by a flatulent crepitus. When the affection is confirmed roaring, it will manifest itself when he is put to his speed; but if he is merely a whistler, the noise is often drowned, particularly when the disease is only in its

incipient state, by the clatter of the hoofs. It may, however, always be detected by the rider suddenly pulling
him up, after a long, sharp gallop, and listening with his
ear inclined forward and downward, and brought close to
the windpipe; or, if he be not readily able to accomplish
this position while mounted, which he may not be able to
do if not a practised rider, by dismounting quickly and
listening with his ear applied to the neck, near its junction
with the head. If the whistling be bad it will be heard
even without this precaution, and will continue for some
seconds, or even minutes, after the motion of the animal
has ceased; but this method of auscultation will detect it
in its smallest and most incipient stage. There is no point
in which a tyro in horse purchasing is so likely to be deceived as in the wind. It requires, therefore, the utmost
precaution to detect it; and the most positive determination when it is detected, even in the slightest modification,
to reject the animal, however otherwise irreproachable.

DEFECTS TO BE DETECTED IN THE LEGS AND FEET.

We now come to the diseases and affections, or malformations, of the legs and feet, which are, of course,
most fatal of all to the horse, for any useful purpose
whatever; inasmuch as an animal, whose only utility lies
in his powers of locomotion, if deprived or seriously
curtailed of those very powers, is nearly valueless; quite
so, unless he be an entire horse or a mare capable of pro-
pagating its species, and even then of little worth, since
no one with judgment cares to propagate animals likely to
inherit lameness in their blood.

It is not necessary, of course, to speak of horses which
are absolutely lame at the moment when they are offered
for sale, since such cripples cannot avoid showing the ailment in their gait the moment they are put in motion,

especially on a hard road, so palpably that no tyro can fail to discover it. For this reason, it is well that the purchaser should always insist on seeing the animal which is offered for his inspection put through all its paces rapidly. for a short distance, on a hard surface ; since many cripples are able to make a good show enough on a soft ride, laid several inches deep with tan-bark or sawdust, or on a piece of nice turf, which if put in motion on a macadamized road will flinch and show the weak point immediately. It is rather, therefore, the points which indicate past lameness, likely to return, or the incipient traces of what will probably produce future lameness, for which the purchaser should be on the look-out, than for actual lameness which displays itself on the spot.

In the first place, we will observe, that white hairs in small spots on bay, brown, black or chestnut horses, un-less on the face and feet, indicate wounds or abrasures, where the roots of the hair have been injured so far as to weaken the subsequent growth ; bare spots indicate wounds of greater depth, where the roots of the hair have been entirely destroyed.

BROKEN KNEES. White spots on the knees show that the horse has broken his knees at some time or other, and ninety-nine times out of a hundred by falling—although the owner will always have a good reason for the blemish, that the horse was trying to leap a stone wall out of the pasture and grazed his knees on the coping ; or that he reared up in the stable and barked them against the under side of the manger ; or something else equally likely to have happened. Now, a broken knee from a fall, if it be healed, is no defect in itself, and produces no unsoundness ; still, as it is fifty to one that a horse which has once fallen will, under the like circumstances, fall again, a broken-kneed horse is to be eschewed even more than a runaway or a kicker. And as it is fifty to one that every broken-kneed horse is a stumbler, and that every horse with white or bare patches on his knees is both a broken-kneed horse and a stumbler, no one should buy a horse with bare or white patches on his knees.

IN EXAMINING THE LEGS OF A HORSE, the purchaser should first stand with his face to the broadside of the horse as he stands on flat ground, and observe whether he rests perpendicularly on all his legs, having the natural proportion of his weight on each leg straightly, squarely and directly; or whether he stands with all his legs straddled outside of their true aplomb; or with all drawn together under the centre of his belly, as if he were trying to stick them all into a hat; or lastly, whether he favors one or more of his legs, either by pointing it forward or by placing it in any position in which no weight at all or a very small stress of weight is thrown upon it. A horse may apparently favor one foot accidentally, from a casual impatience or restlessness. He is not, therefore, to be rejected because he points a toe once or twice. But if he seem to do so, he should be constantly brought back to the original position, in which he must bear equally on each foot; when, if he be found constantly to favor the same foot in the same manner, something serious must be suspected, which gives the horse uneasiness and pain, though not perhaps sufficient in degree to produce present lameness. If the toe of a fore foot be persistently pointed forward, disease of the navicular, commonly known as the coffin bone, is to be suspected, than which no worse or less curable disease exists. If both the fore feet are protruded and the hind feet thrown back, as if the horse were about to stale, he has probably been at some time foundered. If he stand with all his feet drawn together under him, he is generally entirely used up, and what is called groggy. If he stand with one or both his knees bent forward and his legs tremulous, or with both his fetlock joints knuckled forward over his pasterns, one may be sure that however good he may once have been, he has been knocked to pieces or injured by hard driving and hard work. Supposing the horse now to stand square and true on all his legs, leaning his weight on each and all indifferently, with one glance at the horse in profile the side examination may be held as complete and satisfactory. That glance will ascertain whether the posterior outline of the hock joint is nearly perpendicular, or whether it is angular or has a convex curvilinear protuberance immediately above the commencement of the shank bone. This curvilinear protuberance, if large, is a curb which will produce lameness, though not of an incurable sort; if not large, it is either the trace of a curb which has been cured, but may at any time return, or an indication of tendency to throw out curbs, on being put to hard work, especially in heavy ground. Horses which have been curbed, or which have curbed-shaped hocks, are generally to be avoided; but, as it is generally colts which throw out curbs, when first put to hard work, an old horse which has done his share of work without having been actually curbed, is not to be absolutely rejected because he has what are commonly called curby hocks; for, that he has not yet thrown them out, under the stress of his early hard work, is, to a certain extent, security that he will not do so now. Had the tendency been strong it would probably have developed itself already.

The side examination finished, the observer should station himself opposite to the head of the horse, and see that in this point of view also the horse, standing or moving, stands and moves with all his legs perpendicularly under him. Not to do so does not, it is true, indicate disease, but it indicates malformation, inducing awkwardness and sometimes weakness. A knock-kneed or bow-kneed horse, before, is like a knock-kneed or bow-kneed man : if the former, weak and shaky on his legs; if the latter, a clumsy mover, and, in the case of the horse, almost sure to interfere, or strike one leg with the inner edge of the hoof of the other—a very bad and, in some cases, very dangerous fault. If, behind, the hocks are drawn in and the shanks diverge outwardly, the horse is said to be cat-hammed or cow-hocked; and this is a serious malformation, an ungainly defect, and a cause and sign of weakness. If, on the contrary, the hocks and legs are unusually wide apart, so that the animal straddles in going, while it is a decided point of strength, and consequently no defect in a mere draft horse, it is yet ungainly and against a high degree of speed, especially in a galloper. Some trotters of great speed have been straddlers behind; and when this is the case and the animal is needed for harness only, as it is a sure mark of strength, it is not to be avoided, although ungainly ; for a saddle-horse it is decidedly objectionable, since it produces a style of action which is extremely disagreeable to the rider.

His examination concluded, the purchaser must examine the several legs, for distinct marks of structural unsoundness. The chief of these are, in the fore legs, *splents, damaged back sinews*, and *ringbones* or *side bones*—in the hind legs, *bone, blood*, or *bog spavins ; curbs*, which have been described above ; *thorough pins*, and, as in the fore legs, *ringbones* or *side bones*.

SPLENTS are small excrescences of the bone, extruding laterally from the canon bones, or shanks ; they sometimes produce lameness, if so near to the knee as to interfere with the action of the joint, or so far back as to interfere with the play of the back sinews. If on the middle of the bone, and nearly midway between the knee and fetlock, they are of little consequence. In fact, if a horse be not lame of them, they are of less importance than is generally considered to be the case. They will generally yield to blistering and acupuncturing. Still, a splenty horse is, *cœteris paribus*, to be avoided ; rather, however, in our opinion, because it shows a tendency to form bony excrescences, than from the actual evil that they do.

DAMAGED BACK SINEWS arise from the giving way of those most important motors, in consequence of wrench, or strain, or over-exertion. However momentarily cured, or relieved, a horse whose back sinews have once yielded, is never again to be depended upon. These sinews run down the back of the leg, immediately in the rear of the canon bone, from the hock to the fetlock, and in their proper condition, should be as round, as tense and as firm as a harp-string, and connected to the bone by a sheath of firm yet elastic ligaments. The state of these is ascertained by grasping the leg, from before backward, and running the hand downward from the knee to the fetlock, with the nails of the thumb and middle finger in the groove formed by the connection of the canon bone and sinew. If the sheath be even, free from loose cells or flexures, and if the sinew be firm, round, straight and cord-like, all is right. But if it be in places detached partially from the bone, flexed inward or outward, or if it feel spongy or knotty, it is certain that something has gone wrong, and will, or at least may, be wrong again. If pinched at the places where the flexures, detachments, sponginess or knottiness occur, the horse will often evince pain and wince manifestly from the pressure. Damaged back sinews, if they do not produce present lameness, do not constitute unsoundness, but they do constitute a serious blemish, and are, in our judgment, an all-sufficient obstacle to purchasing.

RINGBONE is a circular excresence of the bone, as its name indicates, encircling the coronet, or part of the foot immediately above the junction of the hair and hoof. It produces one of the worst and the most incurable of all foot lamenesses.

Side-bone is the same affection when it is only partial—not forming a complete ring round the foot. It produces the same lameness, and is equally incurable. It is common to both fore and hind feet, although far more frequent before. It can easily be detected by the hand passed carefully over the part.

Of *navicular disease* and other deep-seated lamenesses, there are no exterior signs, and, if the animal do not go lame, they are undiscoverable and beyond suspicion; it needs not, therefore, to allude to them.

Clean legs are those free from all splents, bony excrescences and protuberances, the effect of accident or knocking about.

Fresh legs are those in which there are no windgalls or puffy excrescences of the skin, but in which the bones, sinews, ligaments and cuticle are all in their normal and proper condition.

In the hind legs the joint most to be looked to is the hock, and the ailment most to be dreaded, the spavin.

THE SPAVIN is either bone, blood or bog, all equally producing a desperate and dangerous lameness; but the first curable, the last two utterly incurable. The first is a bony excrescence of the inward and lower anterior portion of the hock joint. It is discoverable by the eye, looking from before backward, or by the hand. It sometimes produces total lameness; sometimes severe lameness on first starting, which passes entirely away as soon as the animal gets warm to his work; and sometimes, though rarely, exists without producing any lameness at all.   It is sometimes curable by firing and blistering; sometimes utterly incurable.   It is always an absolute cause for not purchasing any horse; but not always an absolute cause for selling an otherwise good horse.   We once drove a grey grandson of Messenger, for five years, who had a very large bone spavin in the very worst place. He invariably took his three first steps from a stationary position, however momentary the duration of the time he had been at rest, like a dead-lame horse, but then went as sound as any other horse in the world, until he again stood still.   No day was too long for him, nor was every day in a month too often.   But, after all, he was not the rule, but the exception which proves the rule.

Bog spavin is the extravasation of the synovial fluid, which lubricates the joint, and its collection in a sac in the inward and lower anterior portion of the hock joint, somewhat within and before the point at which the bone spavin occurs.   It may be seen partially in profile, but can be felt readily by pressure of the hand, under which it fluctuates.

Blood spavin is a similar extravasation of arterial blood and formation, nearly in the same place, of a sort of aneurismal sac.   It is detected as before, and may be distinguished from the bog spavin by the fact that it pulsates. Both these spavins are incurable under any ordinary treatment; the former absolutely so.   It is possible that tying the artery might reduce the latter, but we are not aware that the operation has ever been tried.

Thoroughpin is a similar extravasation of the synovial fluid, and the formation of a sac, running between the bones of the hock joint, not from the front backward, but across the joint, from side to side.   It can be easily detected by the fingers, under the pressure of which the fluid can be felt to ebb and flow from side to side. Thoroughpin, like the kindred spavins, is incurable.   It is needless to say that every horse with determined bone, bog or blood spavin, or with thoroughpin, must be summarily rejected, but not needless to say that every one with any tendency to irregular bony enlargement, or to puffiness in the places indicated, should be peremptorily refused as something more than suspicious.

These are the points which it is most necessary for the purchaser to look to; still, even if he be a really good amateur judge of a horse, he will be wise not to buy except of a person of whom he knows something—not to buy without a guaranty of soundness; and above all, not without the opinion of a reputable veterinary surgeon, whom he *knows* to have no interest in the sale, or friendship with the seller. Even so, he will never be perfectly sure that he will not himself be *sold;* for, as a distinguished novelist has well observed, although there is no honester beast in the whole range of creation than a horse, no other has so singular a faculty for making men dishonest.

HOW TO TELL THE AGE OF A HORSE.—The age of the horse is usually determined by the appearance of the teeth; of these there are two sets: first the milk teeth, which come before the age of one year; second, the " permanent set" which come soon after the falling out of the former : this change is completed at the age of five years.

The teeth which are most uniform in their progression are the nippers or *incisors*, those on the lower jaw being ordinarily referred to. Of these nippers there are six,— those farthest from the centre are called " corner teeth."

These corner teeth, and, indeed, all of the nippers, are composed of a bony substance which is inclosed in the enamel, which gives hardness to the teeth. Their form is somewhat conical, though irregularly so (fig. 1). The top of the newly-formed tooth, say the corner tooth of a five-

years-old horse, is long from side to side, while, a little farther down, the form becomes more triangular; and near
the bottom—that part of the tooth which is below the gums

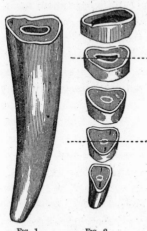

in early life—it is long from
front to rear, and narrow from
side to side. This is shown in
fig. 2, which represents a tooth
cut across at various distances
from the top of the crown,
and in which the different
forms of the different parts of
the tooth are plainly represented. Now sup-
pose the tooth
to be split down
the middle, from
one end to the
other, on a line

FIG. 1.   FIG. 2.

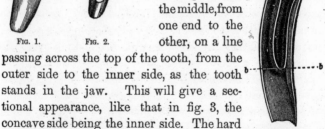

FIG. 3.

passing across the top of the tooth, from the
outer side to the inner side, as the tooth
stands in the jaw. This will give a sec-
tional appearance, like that in fig. 3, the
concave side being the inner side. The hard
enamel which coats the outer portion of the
tooth folds inward and passes down, forming a cavity,
nearly to the bottom of the tooth, and then returns near
the inner edge, until it joins the exterior coating of enamel on that side. The cavity thus formed is filled with
a dark-colored matter, and it is closed, or nearly closed,
at the top by a dishing cover of enamel. We are now
prepared to understand how the appearance of the teeth
becomes changed with age. The corner tooth, at five
years of age, is long from side to side, and has, at its
summit, a deep cavity, called a "mark," which is

FIG. 4.

represented at the tops of figures 2 and 3, the six nippers together forming nearly a semicircle; and their general appearance is similar to that represented in figure 4.

As the horse becomes older his teeth are worn away by use, and it is to this cause only are due the changes by which we determine his age. The effect of this wearing down is the same as would be that of cutting or sawing off a portion of the teeth. They are supposed to be worn down about one twelfth of an inch per year, though the precise amount must depend very much on circumstances, such as crib-biting, vigorous feeding, etc. If we look at the mouth of a horse eight or nine years old, we shall see that his corner teeth have been so worn down that the mark, or superficial cavity, is entirely destroyed, and that the surface has descended to the point marked by the lines *a. a.*, figures 2 and 3; still later the upper

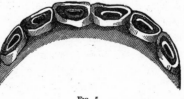

FIG. 5.

surface of the tooth descends to the point marked by the lines *b. b.*, figures 2 and 3. The folding in of the enamel has now almost entirely disappeared, leaving very little discoloration on the teeth, while the upper surface of the tooth is almost triangular instead of being long from side to side, as was the original surface. The teeth of the lower jaw now present the appearance shown in figure 5.

At the age of twenty-one years the teeth of the lower

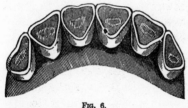

FIG. 6.

jaw become very long from front to rear; this having always been the shape of that part of the tooth which has never until now been made apparent. The teeth at this age are represented in figure 6.

The experience of horsemen has established the following rules for determining the age from the appearance of the teeth (we adopt the classification of Pessina, a German Veterinary Surgeon):

At birth the teeth have not appeared; six or eight days thereafter the two middle nippers of the set of milk teeth are cut; the pair next to them are cut at thirty or forty days; and the corner teeth at six to ten months. These teeth have all the mark, or superficial cavity, when first cut; this however disappears in the teeth of

FIG. 7.

the lower jaw, in the middle nippers, in ten months; in the next pair at one year; in the corner teeth at from fifteen months to two years.

The milk teeth give place to the permanent set as follows: the middle nippers at two and a half to three years, the next pair at three and a half to four years, the corner teeth at four and a half to five years,—these periods may by hastened three or four months by pulling or knocking out the milk teeth.

At five years, the corners are up even with the other teeth, the mark is entirely worn out from the middle nippers, and partly worn from the next pair (fig. 4)

At six years, the mark is almost gone from the second pair, and the *outer edge* of the corner teeth is worn down.

At seven years, the mark is entirely gone from the second pair, the edges of the corner teeth are worn somewhat flat, though there is still a slight cavity in the centre.

At eight years, the teeth of the lower jaw are worn entirely flat, the mark having disappeared from all of them. The form of the surface of the tooth has become oval, and the central enamel is long from side to side, and is near to the front of the tooth.

At nine years, the middle nippers are rounded on the inner side, the oval of the second pair and of the corner teeth becomes broader, the central enamel is nearer to the inner side, and the marks have disappeared from the teeth of the upper jaw (fig. 5).

At ten years, the second pair are rounded on the inner side, and the central enamel is very near to the inner side.

At eleven years, the corner teeth are rounded, and the central enamel becomes very narrow.

At twelve years, the nippers are all rounded, and the central enamel has entirely disappeared from the lower jaw, but it may still be seen in the upper jaw.

At thirteen years, the middle nippers commence to assume a triangular form in the lower jaw, and the central enamel has entirely disappeared from the corner teeth of the upper jaw.

At fourteen years, the middle nippers have become triangular, and the second pair are assuming that form. The central enamel has diminished in the middle nippers of the upper jaw.

At fifteen years, the second pair have become triangular; the central emamel is still visible in the upper jaw.

At sixteen years, all of the teeth in the lower jaw have

become triangular, and the central enamel is entirely removed from the second pair in the upper jaw.

At seventeen years, the sides of the triangle of the middle nippers are all of the same length ; the central enamel has entirely disappeared from the upper teeth.

At eighteen years the sides of the triangle of the middle nippers are longer at the sides of the teeth than in front.

At nineteen years, the middle nippers become flattened from side to side, and long from front to rear.

At twenty years, the second pair assume the same form.

At twenty-one years, all of the teeth of the lower jaw have become flattened from side to side, their greatest diameter being exactly the reverse of what it was in youth.

CHAPTER X.

CONSEQUENCES OF IMPROPER FEEDING—DIFFERENT FOOD FOR DIFFERENT
CONDITIONS—FOOD FOR THE BROOD-MARE—FOR THE FOAL—FOR WORKING
HORSES—GREEN FOOD—CARROTS—CORN—FEEDING HORSES IN TRAINING—
WHILE TRAVELLING—SUMMERING HORSES: THE BEST METHOD—MANAGE-
MENT OF OMNIBUS HORSES IN NEW YORK.

To those who are really acquainted with the horse and accustomed to his use, it is well known that, at the least, one-half
of his availability for work, of his fitness for its performance, of his endurance through a period of years, his health,
his beauty and his value, depends on the quality and
quantity of his food and the manner of his feeding. At
least one-half of the diseases to which he is liable are directly ascribable to bad food, or good food badly administered; to insufficient food or to over-feeding; to want of
judgment in feeding when no food should be given, or in
giving what would be the best at one time, at another
time when it is the worst. Bad stabling, bad grooming
and bad clothing are nearly as bad in their results; but it
may be safely said that the bane of most horses and the
shame of most stables, is bad feeding; and that, too, when
no expense is spared by the owner in providing for the
best and where nothing is wanting but a clear understanding of what ought to be done and what left undone, in the
way of feeding, joined to a system by which the groom,
or whosoever has the duty of attending the animal to perform, shall be compelled or induced implicitly to obey
orders, if he break owners.

The system of feeding horses is diverse and complex;
it cannot be presented once for all, or laid down on a set

6   [121]

formula, for it must constantly vary with the various qualities of horses; the various conditions to which every individual horse is liable; the various kinds of work to
which he is applied, and the various circumstances under
which he may be required to do his work.

Thus, the food of a race-horse or a match-trotter will
and should differ essentially from that of a carriage-horse,
a road-hackney, or a riding-horse; while the food of these
again, as also their stabling and grooming, will and should
differ materially from those of a team-horse, or a slow-
working farm-horse. Again, the food of a gentleman's
show carriage-horses, or roadsters, which are only called
upon to do a few hours light work on four or five days in
the week, and which stand idle in their stalls half the time,
yet are always required to show well in their coats, and execute well as regards wind and speed, will and should
differ materially from that of horses of the same class, in
the hands of another owner who drives or rides his animals over twenty, thirty or forty miles every day, with
now and then, only, a day of rest, and who expects to have
them looking well, working well, in good heart and in
good condition all the time.

Lastly, the food of all horses must vary and differ from
time to time, according to their age, the seasons of the
year, their exact state of health at the time, and the nature
of the work they are doing or will shortly be called upon
to do; and, still more than all, must vary and differ, as
they may be standing in their own comfortable stables, or
travelling on the road in the performance of a journey,
under unusual hardship and fatigue.

In the first place, however, to begin from the beginning,
the system of a horse's feeding, as well as of his grooming
and stabling commences,—and if it be intended that he
shall be a valuable and superior animal, must needs com-

mence, before he is born. If his dam, while pregnant of him, be overworked, be under-fed, be neglected, and kept cold or filthy, or allowed to pick up her own subsistance as she may on open fields or commons, the foal must be a a starveling; and, ten to one, will never attain its full size, or the full possession of its powers. If to neglect before its birth be added neglect of the dam and young creature, both, during its minority ; if they be exposed to cold, to rain, snow, heat, in a word, to the weather and its changes, generally ; if they receive no food,—the dam, but what she can gather from the pasture, and the foal, but the thin and unprofitable milk which the dam can produce from such sustenance,—if they have no comfortable, airy shed to protect them from the scorching suns of summer, no warm stable to shield them from the nipping cold of autumnal nights, the foal will be, from the first to the last, but a wretched, stunted, starveling creature ; and will never repay the breeder the expense or pains of rearing him.

According to the nature, quality and blood of the foal, so should the mare, before and after parturition, and the foal, from the time of its birth, be nurtured, housed and fed. It is not of course to be expected that a cart-mare, in foal to a cart-stallion, a Norman, Canadian, or Cleveland, or Clydesdale, the produce of which expects only to be a cart-horse of improved degree, or, at the best, a heavy carriage-horse, should receive the pains, and have the expense lavished on her which would be expended on a thorough-bred mare, having the blood of twenty generations in her veins, and stinted to a horse inheritor of all the glories of the turf, to the days of its first and noblest champions. Still, it is a truth, that if it be worth the while to breed a beast at all, it is worth the while to breed a good beast,—nay ! but the very best beast, if one can, of the race or family to which he belongs; and this cannot be done unless both the dam, before parturition, and the dam and foal together, after the birth of the latter, be so supplied with food, warmth, and shelter, as to allow the little animal an ample fund whence to draw his bone, his muscles, the development of his size and his blood, and, in a word, sufficient nutriment for the production of all those qualities which one would desire him to possess when he shall have attained his maturity.

Mares and foals should, then, always be supplied, in their summer pastures, with a good, cool, airy shed, for shelter against the sun, or rain; in their winter quarters, with a close, warm, but thoroughly clean and ventilated stable. They should have abundance of good, rich, succulent food of the best quality; especially the dam, before the birth of the foal, and during the time while she is suckling it. It is not necessary, but it is *desirable*, that she should have oats or corn: where it is a thorough-bred mare in foal to a thorough-bred, and expected to produce a racer, she should be cared for almost as if she herself were in work, and should have, at least, her two feeds daily, before parturition; and, after the birth and in the early days of nursing, two good mashes of steamed oats and bran, given moderately warm, in addition to her pasturage. As the foal gains age, she should have her oats regularly, and the young thing should be encouraged to eat of oats, likewise, as early as possible. He will soon take to it, and a quart or two per diem, increased to a full peck during the first year, and to two pecks, added to his pasturage in summer, and his hay, chopped straw, or feed in winter, in his second year, will amply repay the owner in the quality of bone and muscle which the animal will form, and in the increased size, beauty and stamina, which will be his characteristics when he is growing toward maturity. It is not too much to say, that a foal, treated thus, will be, at two years old, the equal of any three year old, allowed to take his chance, without any food but that furnished by his dam from her ordinary commons, or picked up by himself, in his summer pasture or winter straw yard.

Scarcely inferior should be the pains taken with a good half-bred mare, or Canadian, or Norman, in foal to a thorough-bred, and expected to produce an offspring of superior character, as a trotter, a carriage-horse, or a roadster; and we should clearly and decidedly recommend the giving of oats, in small quantities, to both the parent and the young of this second description.

Where ordinary horses are concerned it must be a question, in the main, of dollars and cents; for it is clear that, if a man be breeding from such parents, and under such circumstances that he only expects to realize a hundred dollars, more or less, for his colt or filly, at three years old, there will not be much margin for superfluous expenditures, in the way of early feed or nurture. Still, it is certain that every dollar laid out on the pregnant mare, and on the nursing mare and her foal, will return tenfold to the breeder, in the real goodness of the animal.

We do not believe that it is ever worth the while to breed inferior or second-rate animals of any kind; but that, whatever the kind be, it is the most profitable to breed the best of that kind, and so to keep and care for it, that the creature, when bred, shall attain its perfect standard and full development, and be, in itself, the best attainable specimen and standard of its kind.

This cannot be done, whether the animal is to be an Eclipse, a Flora Temple, a clever roadster, a noble express teamster, a showy carriage-horse, an officer's charger, or a first-rate farm animal, unless it be well-fed and well-cared for while it is growing.

Now, to come to working-horses, we would say, in the first place, that as a general rule, especially for fast-working horses, a great deal too much hay and too little grain, comparatively, and, indeed, too much of both is ordinarily given.   For a gentleman's carriage-horses, or roadsters, at ordinary work, in their own stables, eight pounds, and from that up to ten, of the very best, richest and most succulent hay is amply sufficient, with twelve quarts of good heavy oats, as a daily allowance.

They should be fed with a lock of hay and half a pail of water, the first thing in the morning, on opening the stable; and when the stables have been aired, cleaned and littered, should have, after being thoroughly groomed, their other half-pail of water, and—if they be not going out—four quarts of oats; and when they have eaten these they may have about four or five pounds of hay in their racks, and be left dark and quiet. If they be going out early, they should have six quarts of oats at their morning feed, and no hay.

If they be standing in the stable, and not to be put to work until afternoon, they should be again watered, and have four quarts more at noon; and when they return at night, should be cleaned, watered, fed with oats, and have the remainder of their hay in their racks at night.   This will be found amply sufficient to keep horses in good working condition, when no extraordinary labor—that is to say, not to exceed from ten to twenty miles per diem—is expected of them, and neither extraordinary turns of speed nor feats of endurance.   Half a bushel of nicely-washed carrots, given, a few at a time, every week, will be found to improve the coat, to be particularly beneficial to the stomach and wind, and to be very grateful to the animal; and, in weather and in places where they can be easily provided, a few handfuls of green meat, clover, fine mead-

ow grass, or maize,—long stalks and leaves, sown broadcast and cut young, will cool the blood, give a kindly alterative to the system, keep the bowels moderately open,
and please the appetite of the animal. They should not,
however, be given too freely, when the horse is at hard
work, as they will, perhaps, produce laxity and scouring.
It is a good plan to give a good mash of stewed bran and
oats once a week. Saturday evening—if Sunday be, as it
often is, and always, except in cases of emergency, should
be, a day of rest—is often and appropriately set apart for
this purpose. After an unusually hard day's work, such
a mash is always both useful and grateful to the beast; and
where there is much fatigue and exhaustion, a quart of ale
may be added to the mash with advantage. Nitre and
drugs of all kinds should be studiously avoided, and never
used except when prescribed as medicine. New corn should
never be used as horse feed. It is emphatically dangerous; is heating, apt to swell and produce obstruction of the
bowels, and to cause colic and even acute inflammation.
Old corn may be given, but sparingly and cautiously, and
never in a greater ratio than two quarts where you would
give three of oats. Horses should never be fed within an
hour before being put to work, and then should be worked
slowly until the bowels are fully evacuated; nor within
two hours, if it can be avoided, should they have to perform sharp work. More horses have their winds broken
by being worked quick and hard, with their bellies distended with hay, grain and water, than from all other
causes combined; and more are foundered from being
over-fed while hot, exhausted, and in a state of *quasi* collapse; and are exposed to colic and acute inflammation
of the bowels, from being freely watered and subjected to
drafts of cold air, showers of rain, or being injudiciously
bathed or washed. after sharp work, when their stomachs

are empty, and themselves craving a good dressing and a
warm mash, than one would readily imagine.

The faster and severer the work which a horse is expected to perform, the sounder, more nutritious and more
abundant should be his food. His oats should be increased
and his hay diminished. For a fast trotter, in constant
work, and expected to perform considerable distances in
good time, six pounds of hay will be amply sufficient—
since dry hay, indisputably, is injurious to the wind; but
the oats may be increased to fourteen, or sixteen quarts,
or, in fact, to as much as the animal will eat. The same
may be said of a hunter, of a gentleman's roadster (when
the master is in the habit of calling on him to do long
distances regularly, at a good rate of speed) and, in short,
of all horses, which it is more or less necessary to force,
to keep in an unnatural state, for the performance of unnatural feats. The training of racers and trotters is so
distinctly a science, apart and of itself, and is one limited
to so small a class of persons, comparatively speaking, and
consequently possessed of so little general interest, that it
will not be worth the while to speak of it in detail at present. It consists, of course, in getting the horse for a
short time, into the highest possible state of condition;
hardness of flesh, excitement of spirits, bloom of coat,
speed of foot and depth of wind, which is effected by combining the most nutritious and stimulating system of feeding with such constant and severe exercise, and such medical
treatment as, while exciting and raising every power of
the animal to the utmost, prevents surfeit, prevents fever,
and, for the time, preserves an equilibrium, which, however, at best, is only temporary, and cannot possibly be
prolonged *ad infinitum*. A horse could no more be kept
always in full training than he could always be ridden at
full gallop. It is an abnormal condition; and, while it

develops the utmost powers of the creature, requires the greatest skill and the most constant attention on the part of the person who undertakes to produce it.

Even with horses in full training, or in that half training which is necessarily aimed at by those who keep pleasure horses for fast, continual and long protracted work, the occasional exhibition of carrots and green meat, in small quantities, is of great advantage. It prevents the animals from becoming hide-bound, it keeps their blood cool, and it affords an agreeable change to their over-stimulated appetites, often partially fevered from excess of grain feeding. Mashes are also highly valuable; and it is always desirable to give them, after hard work, and when too hard work is not likely to ensue on the following day. Moistening the hay and oats is not a bad practice, and is especially beneficial to the wind. A small quantity of salt may be occasionally given to advantage in the oats; horses are fond of it, and will often take their feed greedily if a little is intermixed with it, when they would otherwise refuse it altogether. Nitre should never be given in the food, though bad grooms are extremely fond of using it, as a *nostrum* for the production of fine coats. It is a severe diuretic, and injuriously drains the stamina and strength of any horse to which it is supplied as an article of food or a condiment, although it is valuable as a medicine.

It rests only to say, that water, although it should never be given to a horse in large quantities shortly before being put to work; or at all, on his coming off work, while hot; still less, while jaded or exhausted,—should be ordinarily furnished to him often, and in abundance. Not so much in large draughts at a time, which improperly distend the stomach, as in small quantities, at frequently-recurring intervals. Many persons advocate the plan of keeping water constantly within reach of the horse, on the ground that he

6*

actually drinks less, on the whole, when he has it ever before him; and that from never becoming intensely thirsty, he is never tempted to drink to excess; and the argument is certainly good. The difficulty lies in this, that the horse is particularly delicate about what he drinks, and cannot endure tepid, stale, or impure water; and that, if water be supplied constantly, in the stable, with ninety-nine grooms out of a hundred, it will be allowed to stand in the vessel, week in and week out, occasionally filled up, but never drawn off or thoroughly cleansed until it is full of impurities of all kinds impregnated with ammonia from the atmosphere, and alike unfit and unwholesome for the animal to drink.

When metallic mangers can be contrived, having a supply pipe feeding them with constantly running, aërated water, and an escape pipe, which, while they shall be constantly full, shall never allow them to overflow, no plan can be adopted equal to this—as the water, beside supplying the animals with their beverage, will have an admirable effect in purifying, and cooling the heated atmosphere of the stables; but, otherwise, it will be hardly practicable, or desirable, to keep water constantly before horses in their stalls or boxes.

When horses are working on the road, they should be watered, cleaned and fed, very early, at least two hours before it is intended to start them; they should have merely a lock of hay, to play with, while being dressed, and should be then fed with full six quarts of oats. If they be, at all, delicate feeders, it will often succeed to offer them two quarts at a time, and, when that is finished, to refill the mangers. Sometimes, by partially harnessing a horse, particularly if he be a cunning old stager, he will be inclined to go to work as hard at his feed as he can, for fear of losing what is set before him. For the first six or eight miles the horse should be driven gently, until he has unloaded his bowels, when his pace may be increased, until he be within a few miles' distance of his mid-day halting and feeding-place, when he should be pulled up, so as to allow him to come in cool. Horses should be watered often, when at work, say once in every eight or ten miles; but from a few swallows to the extent of half a bucket, at the most, is sufficient. This will not hurt them, even if they be hot, provided they be not exhausted, and provided they be kept standing but a little while, and be instantly put to their work, again, at a moderate pace It is an excellant plan to accustom them to drink water, with a few handfuls of Indian meal, and a little salt stirred into it, as this not only prevents the possibility of a chill, but affords, in some degree, the support of a solid meal. Some horses will drink ale or porter, freely; all horses may be taught to do so, by sweetening it with brown sugar. It is a very useful and desirable quality, in a horse. It is astonishing how much an exhausted animal is sometimes reïnvigorated, on a hot day, by a draught of ale, and if he will—as we have seen many do— eat a rye loaf cut in pieces and steeped in ale or porter, it will do him more good than six quarts of oats.

The mid-day halt of a horse should be long enough to allow of his being thoroughly rested and cleaned, before being fed; he should have, as before, a lock of hay to play with, while cleaning; be watered sparingly, and then be fed with four quarts, and have the rest of his water shortly before starting.

In travelling a journey, it is desirable to start as early as possible in the morning, and to accomplish the most of the days' journey before halting to bait. In summer one would start at four o'clock, travel till ten or eleven, halt and bait until five. and drive on until nine or ten; at this rate one will do his fifty miles for a few days, or his forty, day in and day out, for a month—as the writer has done more than once, without trouble or distress to his team.

On getting to the journey's end, at night, if very much exhausted, the horses should be plentifully supplied, as quickly as they can have it, with tepid gruel, if they will drink it,—the thicker the better; they should be walked about until cool, be thoroughly cleaned, having a bit of hay to amuse themselves with, nicely clothed, and their legs bandaged. Then they should have half a pail of water, and six quarts of oats; and, after giving them the second half pail, their racks should be furnished with six or eight pounds of good hay, and they should be left for the night. Give them good beds, and they will be as fresh as birds, and ready for any work they may be required to perform, to-morrow. Far otherwise, if you feed them lightly, at night and in the morning, and stop them twice, or more during their working hours, to fill their bellies with a mass of hay and oats, and then work them, with their stomachs distended, and their bowels stuffed with crude or undigested food, from which they have derived no real nutriment.

With regard to mere farm-horses, it is, usually, the habit to feed them entirely on hay, or cut straw, with now and then a mash, giving them little, or no oats, or corn. It is certain, however, that this is a mistake. That the value of the work which the horse can do, and of the horse himself, arising from his improved condition and increased .endurance, will be materially raised, while the actual cost of his keep will not be very materially increased by the diminution of the quantity of the cheaper and less nutritious food given to him, and the addition of a smaller or larger portion of the more nutritive grain, which furnished stamina and strength, in a degree greatly in excess of its own increased value, may be assumed as facts.

Slow working horses do not, of course, require so much nutriment of a high quality, as those which are called on to do quick work and perform long distances; but, as a rule, all animals, which have to do hard work, and much of it, must necessarily be so kept as to have hard flesh; and they cannot be so kept, unless they are fed on hard grain.

There is, perhaps, under the head of feeding, one more point, which should be considered. It is that of summering horses, which have been kept up at hard work, in hot stables and on highly stimulating food, for a year or more; and whose feet and legs have become stale, and their whole systems more or less fevered, so that it is desirable to alter their mode of life, for a time; to give them more air, cooler lodgings, and a more natural and less exciting diet. It was, formerly, usual to prepare such horses for grass, by three regular doses of medicine, and then to turn them out, upon some grass land, to fare as they might best, until the summer time should be over, when they are to be taken up again, physiced, as before, and got gradually into condition, by feeding and exercise—a process which could not, with the very best grooms, be accomplished under three or four months, perhaps not in double the time.

The objections to this plan are, first, the length of time. which is required before the horse, which has by this system been thrown wholly out of condition, can be recuperated. Secondly, the great probability of his coming up lame from galloping, gambolling and skylarking with his co-mates, on the pastures, which under our American sunshine are usually burned as hard and nearly as brown as a turnpike road in July. Thirdly, the poorness and innutricious quality of the arid dried up grass at this period.

Fourthly, the want of shade and shelter on most horse pastures. Fifthly, the plague of flies and mosquitoes, which are almost sufficient to torture a thin-skinned animal out of his life; and sixthly and lastly, the result of the whole is, nine times out of ten, that the animal comes up poorer than he was when he went out, sun-bleached, thin, and dry in his coat; his hair staring: his ribs bare; in all respects a failure, unimproved if not actually deteriorated by his summer's run at grass.

For this, it has been lately attempted, we may say now established, with perfect success, to keep the horse partially up, in a large, loose box, if possible, adjoining and opening to a soft, moist, well-sheltered paddock; to take off his shoes, stuff his feet with a cooling paste of tar, tallow, clay, and cow-dung; to reduce his system, by administering two or three mild doses of medicine, not to exceed four drachms each of Barbadoes aloes, the animal having been well prepared for them by assiduous mashing; and then to feed him regularly and plentifully with rich, moist, succulent, green meat, cut for him fresh every day, not forgetting a dessert of carrots, and a standing dish of at least six quarts of oats *per diem*, administered at two feeds. If the horse have the advantage of a good paddock, wherein he can run, he will not so much need other exercise; but, at all events, he will be better for being walked out, or trotted gently, daily, on soft ground. If there be no paddock or natural exercising ground, the walking exercise will be absolutely necessary, and it may be extended advantageously to four hours a day, in two instalments of two hours each, during one of which he should be walked only, and in the other trotted to a little livelier and faster motion.

The advantage of this method is manifold. The animal is not so wholly depleted and reduced; he is not exposed to hot runs, wet nights, or extraordinary changes of temperature; he is not tormented by flies; he has no opportunity of galloping his flesh off his bones, or battering his feet to pieces, on the hard ground. In short, he has all the advantages and none of the drawbacks arising from a run at grass; and, when the time comes when he is again to be brought into condition, it can be done gradually and almost imperceptibly by continually decreasing the supply of green meat, and increasing that of grain, while adding more exercise, putting on more clothing, and keeping the stable warmer, until the animal is brought back into perfect condition.

THE MANAGEMENT OF OMNIBUS HORSES IN NEW YORK CITY.

There is no place in this country where so many horses are kept at regular work, and under circumstances which will admit of systematic feeding and management, or where so good an opportunity for valuable experimenting is afforded, as in the Omnibus and Railroad stables of New York city.

At the request of the Farmers' Club of the American Institute, one of its members made a careful examination of the practice in these stables, the result of which examination is given below.*

There is no farmer who keeps a horse who will not be well repaid for a close study of this paper, in which he will doubtless find reasons for modifying his own practice, and making it to conform more or less to this system, which, as its result shows (these horses being notoriously in good condition, considering the severe labor which they often perform), is the best for horses performing hard work at a moderate pace.

* Transactions of the American Institute for 1855, p. 466.

" STAGE LINES.	No. of Animals.	Miles of daily travel.	Pounds of cut hay daily fed.	Pounds of corn meal daily.	Pounds of salt per month.	Increase of meal for recent severe term of travelling
Red Bird Stage Line, - -	116	17	14	18	1½	3½
Spring St. do - - -	105	21	14	20	4	3⅐
Seventh Av. do - - -	227	22	10	18½	1	2½
Sixth Av. Rail- ⎰ Horses -	117	17	10	14	2	....
road, ⎱ Mules - -	211	17	10	7	2	....
N. Y. Consol'd. Stage Co.	335	21½	8	17	2.9	2⅔
Wash'n Stables, 6 livery horses - - - - -	....	....	12	7½*	....	....

"It is the object of the stage proprietors to get all the work out of their teams possible, without injury to the animals. Where the routes are shorter, the horses consequently make more trips, so that the different amounts and proportions of food consumed are not so apparent when the comparison is made between the different lines, as when it is made also with the railroad and livery horses. The stage horses consume most, and the livery horses least.

"The stage horses are fed on cut hay and corn meal wet, and mixed in the proportion of about one lb. of hay to two lbs. of meal, a ratio adopted rather for mechanical than physiological reasons, as this is all the meal that can be made to adhere to the hay. The animals eat this mixture from a deep manger. The New York Consolidated Stage Company use a very small quantity of salt. They think it causes horses to urinate too freely. They find horses do not eat so much when worked too hard. The large horses eat more than the small ones. Prefer a horse of 1,000 to 1,100 pounds weight. If too small, they get poor, and cannot draw a stage; if too large, they ruin their feet, and their shoulders grow stiff and shrink. The principal

* And 6 quarts oats at noon.

objection to large horses is not so much the increased amount of food required, as the fact that they are soon used up by wear. They would prefer for feed a mixture of half corn and half oats, if it were not more expensive. Horses do not keep fat so well on oats alone, if at hard labor, as on corn meal, or a mixture of the two.

"Straw is best for bedding. If salt hay is used, horses eat it, as not more than a bag of 200 pounds of salt is used in three months. Glauber salt is allowed occasionally as a laxative in the spring of the year, and the animals eat it voraciously. If corn is too new, it is mixed with an equal weight of rye bran, which prevents scouring. Jersey yellow corn is best, and horses like it best. The hay is all cut, mixed with meal, and fed moist. No difference is made between day and night work. The travel is contin. uous, except in warm weather, when it is sometimes divided, and an interval of rest allowed. In cold weather the horses are watered four times a day in the stable, and not at all on the road. In warm weather, four times a day in the stables, and are allowed a sip on the middle of the route.

"The amount that the company exact from each horse is all that he can do. In the worst of the traveling they fed 450 bags per week of meal, of 100 pounds each. They now feed 400. The horses are not allowed to drink when warm. If allowed to do so, it founders them. In warm weather a bed of saw-dust is prepared for them to roll in. Number of horses, 335. Speed varies, but is about four miles an hour. Horses eat more in cold weather than in warm, but the difference cannot be exactly determined."

From this Report we deduce the following hints:

1. It is possible for horses to be kept in good condition, on severe work, when fed on cut hay and corn meal, without oats.

2. An admixture of oats in the feed would be advantageous, when economy is not very closely studied: probably it is always better to use them in the country, where horses are expected to last longer than on hard pavements.

3. Ten pounds of hay per day is a sufficient allowance even for working-horses.

4. Rye bran, mixed with the food, will prevent scouring

CHAPTER XI.

HOW TO STABLE AND GROOM A HORSE.

REQUISITES OF A GOOD STABLE—THE ECONOMY OF PROPER ARRANGEMENTS —VENTILATION—GROOMING—ITS NECESSITY FOR ALL DESCRIPTIONS OF HORSES—HOW PERFORMED—CLOTHING—TREATMENT OF THE HORSE WHEN BROUGHT IN FROM WORK.

WE now propose to give a few brief and comprehensive rules as to the mode of stabling and grooming a horse, premising, always, that both these important branches of horse economy are, for the most part, utterly misunderstood and neglected in the United States, and that, where they are so, it is utterly impossible that the animals can be in a state of health, and comfort to themselves, or in a condition to do good service to their owners.

In a climate so uncertain, changeful, and in which the extremes of heat and cold lie so far apart as in this country, the question of stabling is one of paramount importance. The stable, to be of real utility, must be perfectly cool, airy, and pervious to the atmosphere in summer; perfectly close, warm, and free from all drafts of external air, except in so far as shall be needed for ventilation, in winter; perfectly ventilated, so as to be pure, and free from ill odors, ammoniacal vapors and the like, arising from the urine and excrement of the animals at all times; perfectly dry under foot and well drained, since nothing is more injurious to the horse than to stand up to his heels in wet litter, decomposed vegetable matter, his own ordure, and slops of all kinds; and more than one acute and dangerous disease,—of which we shall only here specify the "scratches," as it is commonly termed in America, or "grease," as one of the most baneful, as it is the most disgraceful to the groom and stable-master,—has its origin. Lastly, it should be perfectly well lighted, as well as thoroughly aired, since it is not only cruel to animals, which are of a gay, cheerful and sociable nature, to keep them constantly in the dark, and not only depresses their spirits, and thus injures their animal health, but it is a frequent cause of blindness. To keep an animal continually in almost total darkness, as is the case in many city stables and in most country farming stables, occasionally bringing him out to do his work, with no protection to his eyes, in the full glare and blaze of an American summer or winter, sunlight, must naturally and necessarily tend to produce blindness.

It is not too much to say that, on nine-tenths of the farmsteads of America, excepting always those of a few model farms, and what may be called show agricultural establishments, the property of wealthy amateurs, the stables are a disgrace to common sense and common humanity; and for the most part are unfit to be used as pig-styes, much less for the dwelling of so noble, so intelligent, so cleanly an animal, and one so acutely sensitive to all impurities of air, food or water, as the horse.

In the first place, a stable should never be under ground, wholly or in part; in the second, it should be, invariably, underdrained, with a sufficient fall to the drains, and with a grating, or perforated slate or flag-stone in the middle of each stall, to which the floor, of whatever substance it is composed, should descend on all sides, with a grade not to exceed an inch to the yard. The expense of this work may seem, to an unthrifty and thoughtless farmer, useless and supererogatory; but, supposing him to work three or more horses of the first cost value of $100 to $150 each, and supposing that these horses last him twice as long, are not half so often ailing, and do him twice as much good work while they do last,—as it is undoubtedly the case that they will do, in wholesome and well-constructed stables,—he will easily find, at the end of fifteen or twenty years, that by the first outlay of a couple of hundred dollars at the outside, in making his stable dry, airy, warm and light, he will have economized many hundreds, if not many thousands. And this will easily appear from a very slight calculation of the losses which will arise from the deterioration of his farm stock, their falling lame, requiring farrier's advice, doing but half work half the time, and finally having to be rejected as useless, sold at half price and replaced at full price, after three or four years, by others which will unavoidably follow the same course; whereas if properly lodged and cared for, the first animals, being sound and hearty at the commencement, might have done good slow farm-work for ten, twelve, or even fifteen years, as well as not; and if mares, might have brought him half-a-dozen good serviceable colts, or fillies, which would owe much of their value to the state of their dam's health, arising from her food and stabling, without materially detracting from her service on the farm. The material of the stable floor should not be the natural soil, for that speedily becomes saturated with moisture, and degenerates into a slough. It should not, we think, be of wood, for wood absorbs the urine, becomes impregnated with ammonia, and is heating to the feet. Very hard beaten clay may answer, but a pavement of small cobble-stones, neatly laid, with such a fall as is mentioned, in clay and sand, or, what is better, of hard bricks laid in cement, and set edgewise, is the best stable floor with which we are acquainted.

The stable should never be less than eight or nine, but had better be ten or twelve feet high from the floor to the rafters. The door should be so placed that when open, the air shall not blow full on the horses; and it is well to have it sawn in two halves, horizontally, in order to allow the upper half to stand open in summer, for the admission of fresh air.

The windows which should be large as in a modern dwelling-house, and as numerous in proportion to the size of the room, should be opposite to one another, so as to allow a free draught of air in summer, but they should never open at the bottom nearer to the ground than at a full distance of six feet, so that the air may not blow on the horses, but circulate above their backs. The stalls should not be less than five, but had better be six feet wide, and nine feet deep; and the stable should not be less than fifteen, or better, seventeen feet, from the head of the stall to the back wall. If hay rooms or feed rooms be placed above the stables, the roof should be of solid, permanent plank, well joined and under-ceiled, and with good trap-doors to the apertures by which the hay is thrown into the cribs. Otherwise the ammoniacal vapors will certainly arise, taint the food, and render it unfit for eating.

Lastly, the stables must be ventilated by a complete and permanent system, which, by the way, is neither difficult nor expensive. This can be done in two ways,—either a single shaft, of a square of two feet on each side, may be carried up through the loft to the roof, made of well-jointed boards, and there fitted with a ventilator of the same size; or, a central shaft equal in space to the square of two feet, for every horse in the stable, may be carried up in the same manner, and fitted with a grand central ventilator, of large dimensions, through which all the heated air will rise, while by the use either of Janes & Beebe's patent valves, or of some other suitable arrangement, no cold air can possibly descend. To this must be added a plan for the regular admission of cold air, at proper places, for the supply of the horses with a suitable quantity of fresh oxygenated air for the purposes of respiration. This is easily done and at very small cost, while the stable is in process of erection. The best plan is to run either a tin tube, or a wooden box pipe, of the capacity of one square foot, through the whole length of the head wall at the height of the horses' nostrils, say four feet from the ground, open to the exterior air at both ends, but protected from the entrance of vermin by a guard of coarse, open wire gauze. From this pipe, there should be bored diagonally upward, through the boarding of the stall, six auger holes, each of one square inch space, into each stall. This will afford to each horse an ample supply of pure, fresh air, which, as it becomes heated and impure, will arise, pass off by the ventilator, and be succeeded by a constant stream of reïnvigorating, vital atmosphere, preserving both the temperature and the odor of the stables even, agreeable and healthful, and adding more of life and health to each animal that one could imagine possible, without an examination of the subject. The whole of this system of ventilation may be added to a new stable, or introduced into an old one remodelled, at a very small price. In fact, the paving, heightening, draining and adapting proper windows, doors and ventilators to an old stable, if so situated as to be capable of improvement, or the introducing all these as additions, into a new one, the site of which can be selected with a view to them, will not. with reasonable economy, by any possibility exceed a couple of hundred dollars for a stable capable of containing from four to six horses; and undeniably, the owner of horses who will try it will find that, at the end of twenty years of horse-keeping, he will be an actual gainer of twenty times two hundred dollars. We will here add, that for country stables there is no better than a good, framed building, rather loosely weather-boarded externally, lined at the distance of nine inches, or, better, one foot, with well grooved and tongued inch boards, or inch and a quarter planks,—having the intermediate space filled with tan bark. This will preserve an equal temperature through the whole year, and the stable will always be cool in summer and warm in winter. If external sliding shutters be appended to the windows, contrived to open and shut by means of a cord and pulley, and if fly-nets of coarse gauze be added in summer, to exclude the winged pests, which are such tor- ments to horse-flesh, the expense will not be one of many dollars, and will add hundreds of dollars worth to the com- fort of the horses. We will only add that the new construc- tion of concrete moulded walls is excellently well adapted for country stables, and will, more easily than any other form, admit the introduction of air pipes, as described above.

And now, the question of stabling disposed of, we pass to that of grooming and clothing, which is the next in im- portance, and scarcely secondary to those of food and sta- bling, as regards the health and comfort of the horse, and, what is the same thing, the true interest of his owner.

GROOMING. " Of this," says Mr. Youatt, " much need not be said to the agriculturist; since custom, and appar- ently without ill effect, has allotted so little of the comb and brush to the farmer's horse. The animal that is worked all day and turned out at night, requires little more to be done to him than to have the dirt brushed off his limbs. Regular grooming, by rendering his skin more sensible to the alteration of temperature and the inclemency of the weather, would be prejudicial. The horse that is altogether turned out needs no grooming. The dandruff or scurf which accumulates at the roots of the hair, is a provision of nature to defend him from the wind and the cold.

This, however, which may be true, and correct as of the horse which is turned out every night, during the greater part of the year, and which feeds only on grass, with some slight addition of oats, and mashes, certainly is not applicable to the farm-horses of the United States; which are, for the most part, if not altogether, stabled for the greater part of the year, or in winter, at least; fed on artificial food; kept warm, to a certain extent; and which, of course, must be cleaned daily, especially after severe work, or exposure to wet, if they are to be kept in health and working condition.

"It is to the stabled horse," Youatt continues, "highly fed, and little or irregularly worked, that grooming is of the highest consequence. Good rubbing with the brush, or the currycomb opens the pores of the skin, circulates the blood to the extremities of the body, produces free and healthy perspiration, and stands in the room of exercise. No horse will carry a fine coat, without either unnatural heat, or dressing. They both effect the same purpose, but the first does it at the expense of health, and strength; while the second, at the same time that it produces a glow on the skin, and a determination of the blood to it, rouses all the energies of the frame. It would be well for the proprietor of the horse if he were to insist, and to see that his orders are really obeyed, that the fine coat in which he, and his groom so much delight, is produced by honest rubbing, and not by a heated stable and thick clothing, and, most of all, not by stimulating, or injurious spices. The horse should be regularly dressed every day, in addition to the grooming that is necessary after work."

It is true, in a measure, that the necessity of regular dressing, wisping, currying, brushing and, hard rubbing is far greater in the case of highly pampered horses, fed in the most stimulating manner, principally on grain, kept in hot stables, always a little above their work, and ready at

7

all times to jump out of their skins from the exuberance of their animal spirit; yet it is necessary to all housed and stabled horses; and the farmer, no less than the owner of fast trotters, will find his advantage in having his horse curried and washed, before feeding in the morning, in the increased play of his spirit, and in the gayety and fitness of the animal for his work; and if, when he brings him in at night, reeking with sweat, drenched with rain or snow, his thighs and belly plastered with thick mud, and his legs covered, as cart-horses' legs mostly are, with thick hair, saturated with cold water and clogged with particles of mud and sand, he neglects to have him thoroughly cleaned, and made dry and comfortable for the night, he not only commits an act of gross cruelty, but wholly disregards his own interest. Unless a horse be cleaned and groomed when in such a condition, he cannot be kept in health; and if he be fed freely when in such a state,— although the cart-horse is less liable to such ailments from his hardier habits and less impressive constitution,—the chances are that soon he will be attacked by inflammation of the bowels, or lungs, or with spasmodic colic—the race-horse, fast trotter, or highly bred and highly fed roadster would be so attacked, to a certainty—and the failure to dry and cleanse the legs of such a horse, especially if there be a draft of cold wind blowing upon the heels from a crevice under the stable door, as is generally the case in common farm stables, will be almost certainly succeeded by that troublesome, dangerous and foul disease, known as "grease," or more commonly in America as "the scratches."

It may be well to say here, that the best average heat for a gentleman's stable should be from 60, to not to exceed 65 degrees; that the air should be perfectly dry; for if there be any moisture about the stables, it will hang about the horses in the shape of a mist, and the animals, when they are brought into the open air, although their skins will be as fine as can be imagined, will shiver as if they had just made their exit from a warm bath.

In stables such as this, a single good blanket, breast-plate and roller, will be a sufficient clothing, though a holland sheet, under the woollen rug, is very serviceable in keeping the skin smooth and the coat unruffled. A hood and cover should be added when the horse is taken out for slow exercise. It is common, in America, in winter, in unusually cold weather, where horses are expected to be driven fast, and to have to stand still, alternately, at shop doors or in visiting, to see them clothed, under their harness, in hoods and blankets. This plan can, evidently, do no good; the animal, while working fast, is as much more heated by the covering, as he is afterward more protected by it when standing still; add to which, if the clothing be, as probably it will, saturated with perspiration while the animals are in motion, it will be frozen, or rendered entirely cold and clammy, so soon as the motion ceases; and will in that state affect the animals injuriously instead of beneficially; just as it would affect a man, to wrap him up, when sweating profusely, in a heavy wet overcoat. If anything of this sort be required, the only rational way is to have the rugs or blankets at hand, dry and warm, in the boot of the carriage, and to throw them over the backs of the animals, and buckle them across their chests, so soon as they are pulled up, removing them and restoring them to a dry place before again getting under way. Such is the rationale of out-door clothing. There is, however, no objection to the use of a water-proof covering over the loins of a horse, when he is taken out to be used through the whole of a cold, rainy or sleety day, particularly if it be at an even, slow pace, as is the case with carmen's horses, in New York, which are often so equipped. Another excellent plan adopted by these men, in summer, is the affixing an arched bow to the shafts of the cart, rising eighteen inches over the withers of the animal, from which an awning of duck is extended to a cross-yard, supported by an upright, at the front of the truck, affording a complete protection against the scorching sun, to the animal, and promoting a draft of air over his whole body, from the current caused by his mere motion through the atmosphere; which must be in the highest degree refreshing and delightful to the creature, during his day-long toil, in the dog days.

But to return to the article of grooming. "When the weather will permit the horse," continues Mr. Youatt, "to be taken out, he should never be groomed in the stable, unless he be an animal of peculiar value, or placed for a time under peculiar circumstances. Without dwelling on the want of cleanliness, when the scurf and dust that are washed from the horse lodge in his manger, and mingle with his food,—experience teaches, that if the cold is not too great, the animal is braced and invigorated to a degree that cannot be attained in the stable, by being dressed in the open air. There is no necessity, however, for half the punishment which many a groom inflicts upon the horse in the act of dressing, and particularly on one whose skin is thin and sensitive. The currycomb should be, at all times, lightly applied. With many horses, its use may be almost dispensed with; and even the brush need not be so hard, or the points of the bristles so irregular as they often are. A soft brush, with a little more weight of the hand, will be equally effectual, and a great deal more pleasant to the horse. A hair-cloth, while it will seldom irritate or tease, will be almost sufficient with horses which have a thin skin, and which have not been neglected   After all, it is no slight task to dress a horse, as it ought to be done. It occupies no little time, and demands considerable patience, as well as dexterity. It will be readily ascertained whether a horse has been well dressed, by rubbing him with one of the fingers. A greasy stain will detect the idleness of the groom. When, however, the horse is changing his coats, both the currycomb and the brush should be used as lightly as possible."

In ordinary cleaning, in the morning, the head should be first dressed. The hair should be lifted, and deranged lightly, not stretched, or torn, with the currycomb, and then rubbed well, in all directions, both against and across the grain of the hair, as well as with it, until it is entirely clear from dust and dandruff. The ears should be gently pulled and stripped with the hand, from the roots to the points; and the whole head should then be washed smoothly and evenly, as the hair ought to lie. The neck, back, shoulders, loins, croup, and quarters, follow; the same plan being used, except that, in dressing these parts, while the comb is used lightly and dexterously with one hand, the brush is employed in removing the scurf with the other. The flexures of the skin, at the insertion of the limbs, are parts which require especial care, as the dust is most apt to collect in these places. This done, the horse must be thoroughly wisped, all over, with bunches of dry straw, till his coat is quite clean and glossy, when it may be gone over, for the last time, with a fine, soft brush, or a light duster. His clothes may be then put on, and the legs cleaned in the same manner, and finished off by a careful hand rubbing. Flannel bandages, steeped in cold water, well wrung out, and applied loosely to the legs, and again covered by a tighter drawn linen bandage, are often of great advantage, after severe work, in keeping down and checking inflammation, as well as in fortifying and strengthening the sinews, when in a sound state, and in remedying and alleviating any slight slip, or casual strain. The mode of dressing, when the horse is brought in, wet, weary, hot, dirty and exhausted, is nearly identical. The ears should be first stripped and pulled, and the head made comfortable. The dry dirt should be scraped from the legs and belly. The legs should be plunged into tepid water, and have all the dirt washed carefully away; they should be then carefully dry-rubbed with wisps of clean straw, and tightly swathed in flannel bandages, steeped in water as warm as the hand will bear. The whole neck and body should then—or, if there be sufficient force of hands in the stable—at the same time while the legs are being arranged, be thoroughly rubbed, till perfectly clean, dry, and in a glow of vigorous animal heat, with straw wisps. After this they should be lightly curried, brushed, and arranged; and then, nor until then, the clothes may be put on, the animal fed, his stall well bedded and littered down, and himself left to his repose, which, however hard his day's work may have been, will, if these precautions be taken, be both soft and light.

This, in brief, is the whole theory of grooming. It requires care, dexterity, exactness, and honest application of work. It cannot be procured without some expense; or relied on, without the active and intelligent supervision of the master; but without it no stables can be in order,— no horses healthy, happy, or in condition for doing the work for the performance of which they are kept.

As of feeding and stabling, it may be said of grooming, without fear of contradiction, that, for every dollar expended, the horse-owner will receive in the results the recompense of, at least, a hundred; and that without attending to this essential branch of stable economy, he can never expect to be satisfied with, much less proud of, the performances of his horses, and the state of his stables.

CHAPTER XII.

HOW TO BREAK AND USE A HORSE.

WHAT IS REQUIRED IN A WELL-BROKEN HORSE—HIS EDUCATION SHOULD COMMENCE WHEN A COLT—BITTING—PUTTING HIM IN HARNESS—HOW TO USE A HORSE—TRAVELLING—WORKING—PLEASURE HORSES—PUNISHMENTS.

IT is not too much to say, that not one horse in a hundred, if one in a thousand, in the United States, is ever properly broken; or one in fifty, when offered for sale as a finished horse, entered in the merest rudiments of his education. Horses in America,—we cannot say wherefore, but, perhaps, from the general absence of a very high degree of blood, from the general absence of extremely high and stimulating feeding and grooming, which not only act directly on the individual horse, but exert an influence, increasing generation after generation, over the progeny of horses long kept up in an unnatural condition,—are very rarely actively, and almost never savagely, vicious. Nothing more than this, as a general thing, is required. If a horse will carry his rider without kicking him over his head, or draw him in his wagon or buggy without kicking it to shivers; if he will go off at a walk, increase his speed to the top of his gait, and stop again when pulled upon, without running away; if he will hold back going down hill, and if he will not balk going up hill; and more particularly, if he will stand at a door without tying, he is held to be fully broken, and is willingly received, credited, and paid for as such.

It is needless, however, to say to a real horseman, that such a horse is as far as possible from being broken at all, especially from being well broken. To be really well broken,

a horse must be so disciplined as to have apparently no
will but his-rider's. He must have been so educated as to
carry his body, his head, all his limbs, in the easiest, the
most graceful and the most accurate position. His neck
must be like a steel bow, yielding to the pressure of the
hand, but returning with the head to its natural position
the moment that the pressure ceases. His mouth must be
like velvet to the touch ; and if the animal at times pull
or resist the pressure of the bit and the command of the
rider's finger, it must be from exuberance of animal
spirits and force of animal courage, not from hardness of
mouth, as it is usually called, or in truth, from rigidity
and intractability of the muscles of the jaw and neck—as
has been demonstrated by M. Baucher, the great French
equestrian teacher.

He must change his leg, alter his paces, moderate his
paces, all at the will of his rider or driver, and must, in
fact, be little or nothing more than a living and spirited
automaton in his hands.

The next question that arises is, how shall this be done ?
Clearly, we answer, not by allowing the colt or filly to go
wild and run riot, until it shall have attained its full
strength, its full energies, and the full sway of its natural
temper unconstrained, without making an effort to train,
or teach, or even tame it, until it be two and a half or three
years old, and then to take it up, saddle it and bridle it by
force, and, putting it into the hands of some fearless, hard-
hearted, mutton-fisted, rough-riding fellow, scarce less a
brute, in all points of humanity, than that which he professes to teach, expect it to be turned out, by dint of whip
and spurs, a gentle animal, rendered gentle by brute violence, and a well-instructed animal.

The education of a horse should commence when he is
a colt. He should be handled frequently by different per-

sons, and should be made accustomed to whatever is likely to attract his attention when he is put in harness. The more he is accustomed to straps the less likely will he be to become frightened by accidental breaking of the harness, by the falling of a trace about his heels, or by having the reins thrown on his back by a careless driver.

Young horses, while mere foals nursing by their mothers' sides, should be accustomed to be fearless; should be accustomed to feed from the hand, to suffer themselves to be handled, to have their feet lifted, and tapped with the hands or a hammer on the soles, to be led to and fro by the forelock, to endure the pressure of the hand on the back, to rejoice in being constantly flattered, caressed and spoken to; nay, even to understand words of gentle reproach. They should be very early equipped with a headstall, having a ring appended to which a halter can be attached, and by these means they can be easily taught to follow at any pace the person leading them, walking, running or stopping as he may desire. Punishment at this period should never be resorted to, but rewards should be continually offered. Bits of bread, or carrots, should be carried in the pocket, and given to the little creature, with a caress, when it has done what is required of it.

Soon after this a pad may be strapped on the back for a few hours daily; and, after a time, stirrup-leathers, and then stirrups appended to it, and suffered to flap about, by which means all fear of such things will be removed long enough before it will become necessary to saddle him for any real purpose. When he is about a year old the colt's bits should be occasionally put in his mouth, and he should be reined up gently to his surcingle, and allowed to play with them or mouth them: and, after this, he may stand for an hour or two between the pillars, with reins attached

7*

from the colt's bit to rings placed at a proper height in the standards. But here it is necessary to observe, above almost any other thing in the world, that it is fatal to the formation of the animal's mouth to place the rings too high, or to bear up the head above its ordinary and natural elevation. This is a thing often done, with a view to giving a lofty carriage to the colt's head, and to produce a proud bearing. It does nothing of the kind. It causes the horse, weary with having its head forced into an unnatural position, to bear, to weigh, to hang upon the bits,—to become accustomed to their pressure, and to find pleasure instead of pain from it, so that, at the last, it acquires a mouth perfectly unimpressive, and muscles set and rigid.

Shortly after this the colt should be longed, or worked in a circle, with a long cord attached to the breaking bits, in a smooth grass field; by which means he is taught his paces, taught to regulate them, taught to moderate, to increase or diminish his speed, to change his leg, to come toward the operator, or to stop dead short at a signal, either of the voice or of the crack of the whip. All this it requires only time, patience and good temper to effect; and, when effected, half the business is done. The rest must be accomplished when the animal is backed.

Experience, practice, patience, added to individual aptitude, natural tact, and acquired skill and habit, are the only things by which a man may become a horse-breaker.

No attempt should be made to put the colt to work before he is three and a half to four years old, and it would be far better to exact no work, beyond what is necessary for gentle exercise, before he is six years old; this, although not at first remunerative, is eminently so in the end, for the two years' loss in early life will generally add six to eight years to a horse's working time.

If the colt has been treated as previously directed, there

will be little difficulty in breaking him to harness work. It will be only necessary to put him in by the side of an old and steady horse, and light wagon without a load, and to handle him gently, until he is made to understand what is required of him.

If he is a wild colt, whose whole life has been spent at pasture, or in the straw-yard, it becomes a more serious matter. He should be kept in the stable for a few days, visited and handled frequently, and gradually made acquainted with the harness, wearing it for a few hours at a time in his stall. He should next be taken into a large stable, or shed, or into a small yard, and made to advance, or turn to the right or to the left, as he is spoken to or guided by the reins. The trainer should use only the most gentle means, and should in no case allow himself to show the least impatience. Whatever he desires to have done should always be within the power of the horse to comprehend, and then be strictly enforced, but always with persevering calmness. If it be necessary to whip the colt, it should be done thoroughly, and under such circumstances as will preclude the possibility of his resisting with any effect: for every compliance with our wishes he should be rewarded with caresses.

If it is not convenient to put him by the side of a well-broken horse, as before directed, he may be brought out and have the wagon shown to him, being allowed to examine it with his nose until he has become familiar with every part of it, and until he can be led or backed toward it from any direction without fear. He should then be put into the shafts and securely attached, so that no straps can strike against him; he should then be made to advance, and the wagon pushed gently from behind, that he may not at first feel its weight. When he has in this way become accustomed to its presence, the pushing from behind may be gradually lessened. It is a very good plan to set the wagon on ground which is slightly descending, so that it will nearly run from its own weight; but the hill should not be steep enough to cause the wagon to run on to him.

In this way any colt, not absolutely vicious—and very few, if any, are so until they have been badly treated—may be brought, by imperceptible degrees, to be a good harness horse, without in any way ruffling his temper, or giving him any disagreeable recollections which shall interfere with his future usefulness. This is properly *training* a horse, and it differs widely from the old method of *breaking*, which was usually a struggle between the man and horse, to see whose will or neck should first be broken; and which was sure, in nine cases out of ten, to produce a bad and lasting effect on the horse's disposition. The time to be occupied in the exercise of training will be long or short, in proportion to the skill of the trainer and the nature of the animal, but it can never be so long that it will not be a hundred times repaid in the docility and usefulness of the horse.

Every part of the harness and wagon should be so strong and well made that there can be no possibility of breaking. When it is possible to do so, it is always best to put the young colt in double harness, by the side of a strong, steady, well-trained horse, until he is perfectly quiet, and will bear the whip and the rein well. Greater docility, better subjection to the hand, and generally better style and action will be attainable, if the colt be thoroughly trained to the saddle before being put in harness; usually, however, in this country, it is very difficult to find a proper person to train a colt in this way. The same course of bitting should be resorted to as will be described for the preliminary training of the saddle horse.

HOW TO USE A HORSE.

It is not, after all, every one who owns a horse that knows how to use him, whether for his own pleasure or the horse's, which is, in other words, the owner's best advantage. Nor is it very easy to lay down rules how a horse should be used, considering the many different purposes for which horses are kept, the different natures and constitutions of the animals, and the different circumstances of their owners.

Horses may, in general, be divided into two classes,—those kept for work, and those kept for pleasure. In the former class may be included farm-horses, stage, coach and omnibus horses, team-horses, employed in the transportation of goods, and moving heavy and bulky masses, carmen's horses,—and lastly, the road horses of all professional men, who, like lawyers, doctors of medicine, and the like, are compelled to drive or ride many hours *per diem*, regularly, in the performance of their business.

In the latter class may be included race-horses, match-trotters, private gentlemen's saddle-horses, carriage-horses, or roadsters, and many other animals belonging to business men, which being employed during half the time or more in actual service, are used during spare hours on the road for purposes of amusement.

With regard to the first class of these horses, the exigencies of the business to which they are applied are, for the most part, such as to supersede and override all rules. In some cases the natural hours of the day and night have to be reversed, and the animals are called upon to do their work by night, and to rest and feed by day. Under these circumstances it may be laid down as an immutable law, that at whatever hour the horses are to be worked, they must have full time, beforehand, to digest their food and water; they must be carefully cleaned, and made comfortable; they must have sufficient intervals for halting and baiting, on the road, must be cleaned and well fed during the intervals of work, and must have ample time for undisturbed repose. The distance which horses in perfect condition can go upon the road, varies greatly with the powers of the animal, the degree of pains bestowed on him, the skill of his driver, and the amount of his load, as well as the state of the roads. But it may be taken as a rule, that strong, able horses, of moderate speed, can travel forty miles a day, with a moderate load, without distress, for many days in succession. It may be observed, that it is the better way to start at an easy pace when on a journey, to increase it slightly in the middle of the day, and again to relax it before coming in at night, in order to allow the animals to enter their stables cool, in good order, and ready, after a short rest, and cleaning, to feed with an appetite.

It may also be observed, in this point of view, that it is a mistake to fancy that horses are benefited by being driven or ridden very slowly when they have a long distance to perform. If a horse have to get over forty miles in a day, the roads being good, the temperature of the day pleasant, and the load not excessive, he will do it with more ease and less inconvenience to himself, going at the rate of seven or eight miles the hour, and doing the whole distance in five or six hours,—with a single stoppage, in the middle of the day, to feed and rest,—than if he be kept pottering along at the rate of four or five miles, and be kept out of his stable, hungry and thirsty, and leg-weary to-boot, for a longer time.

Farm-horses, whose work is necessarily slow and continuous, lasting ordinarily from sunrise to sunset, with the exception of a mid-day halt for baiting, are under different circumstances. Their work being always slow, and rarely, if ever, severe, at the moment, or toilsome, except from its long duration, they need not be subject to the same condition as fast-working horses, of being fed long before they are put to work and allowed to evacuate their bowels thoroughly before being harnessed. They may, therefore, be fed and watered at the last moment, and put to slow work immediately, and will rarely take harm from travelling on full stomachs. In the same manner, when they are loosed at noon-day, being rarely overheated, after a slight rest and a slighter rubbing down—which, by the way, they rarely receive—they may take their mid-day feed without delay, and without fear of evil consequences. In the like manner may be treated carmen's horses, and team-horses, the labor of which is heavy and continuous rather than rapid. All horses, however, whatever the work to which they are applied, should have ample time to rest at night, and should be thoroughly rubbed down, dried, clothed and made comfortable, before feeding them and closing the stables for the night,—and the more so, the more trying the day's work.

With regard to pleasure-horses, which are usually in the stables, more or less, twenty hours out of every twenty-four, which are only taken out for the gratification of the owner at such times as it suits his humor or necessity, they should never be taken out or driven fast on full stomachs; which can always be avoided by letting the groom know, in case that they will be required at an unusual hour or for unusual work—when he can adapt his feeding hours to the circumstances of the case.

When harnessed and ready for a start, the driver should mount his seat quietly, gather his reins, and get his horses under way, slowly and gradually, by speaking or chirruping to them; never starting them with a jerk, or striking them with a whip,—allowing them to increase their pace by degrees to the speed required, instead of forcing it on a sudden.

It is far better for horses, to drive them steadily at a regular pace, even if it be ten or twelve miles an hour, than to send them along by fits and starts—now spinning them over the road at sixteen or eighteen miles, now plodding along at six or seven; and of two pairs of horses, driven the same distance, after the two different methods, that which is driven evenly will, at the end of the day, be comparatively fresh and comfortable, while the other will be jaded and worn out.

In regard to punishment, the less that is administered the better. A sluggish or lazy horse must, it is true, be kept up to his collar and made to do his share of the work, or the free-goer will be worn out before the day is half done; and for this the whip must be occasionally used. Even good and free-going horses will occasionally be seized with fits of indolence, at moments, induced perhaps by the weather, and it may be necessary to stimulate them in such cases; again, at times when roads are bad, when time presses, and certain distances must be accomplished within certain times, recourse must be had to punishment; as it must occasionally, also, in cases where the animals are vicious or refractory, and where the master must show himself the master. Still, as a general rule, punishment should be the last resort. It should never be attempted with a tired, a jaded, or an exhausted horse; for to apply it in such cases is utter barbarity; little or no immediate advantage is gained to the driver, while it may probably result in the loss of an excellent animal. It is common to see horses punished for stumbling, punished for starting; and whenever a new horse, which one may chance to be trying, starts off into a gallop after committing either of these offences, one may be sure that he is an habitual starter or stumbler, and that he has frequently undergone chastisement for them, and undergone it in vain. It is altogether an error to punish for either starting or stumbling; the one is the effect of fear, which cannot be cured by the whip, the other, in most cases, of malformation or of tenderness in the foot, which certainly cannot be treated successfully by chastisement, which, in fact, aggravates and confirms instead of alleviating or curing.

In speaking of driving at an equal pace, we would not, of course, be understood to mean that horses should be driven at the same gait and speed over all roads, and over grounds of all natures. Far from it. A good driver will, while going, always, at the rate of ten miles—we will say—an hour, never, perhaps, have his horses going at exactly the same rate for any two consecutive twenty minutes. Over a dead level, the hardest of all things except a long continuous ascent of miles, he will spare his horses. Over a rolling road, he will hold them hard in hand as he crosses the top and descends the first steep pitch of a descent; will swing them down the remainder at a pace which will jump them across the intervening flat and carry them half way up the succeeding hill; and will catch them in hand again and hold them hard over the top, as we have shown before.

Horses in work should be watered about once, with not to exceed two quarts, after every ten miles, or every hour, if one be travelling fast; and if travelling far, they should be well fed once in the middle of their journey. This point, however, has been discussed already under the head of feeding.

In closing, we would say, always remember, in using a horse, that it cannot be done with too much coolness, too much gentleness, too much discretion, or too much kindness.

There is no better beast in the world than a horse, nor any one which, though often most cruelly misused by man, so well deserves, and so amply, by his services, repays the best usage.

CHAPTER XIII.

HOW TO PHYSIC A HORSE—SIMPLE REMEDIES FOR SIMPLE AILMENTS.

CAUSES OF AILMENTS—MEDICINES TO BE GIVEN ONLY BY THE ORDER OF THE MASTER—DEPLETION AND PURGING—SPASMODIC COLIC—INFLAMMATION OF THE BOWELS—INFLAMMATION OF THE LUNGS—HOW TO BLEED—BALLS AND PURGATIVES—COSTIVENESS—COUGHS—BRONCHITIS—DISTEMPER—WORMS—DISEASES OF THE FEET—SCRATCHES—THRUSH—BROKEN KNEES.

IT is not too much to say that more than one-half the ailments of horses arise, in the first instance, from bad management,—or, to speak more correctly, from absence of all management,—from an improper system of feeding, from ill-constructed, unventilated, filthy stabling, from injudicious driving, and neglect of cleaning. When disease has arisen, it is immediately aggravated and, perhaps, rendered ultimately fatal, either by want of medical aid, or, what is far more frequent as well as far more prejudicial, ignorant, improper, and often violent treatment, either on a wrong diagnosis of the affection, or on a still more wrong system of relieving it. Over-medicining and vulgarly quacking slightly ailing horses is the bane of half the private stables in cities, and of nearly all the farm stables in the country; and one or the other, or both combined, cause the ruin of half the horses which "go to the bad" every year.

There is no quack on earth equal to an ignorant, opinionated groom; and every one, now-a-days, holds himself a groom, who is trusted with the care of a horse, even if he do not know how to clean him properly, or to feed him so as not to interfere with his working hours. Every one of these wretched fellows, who has no more idea of a horse's structure or of his constitution than he has of the model of a ship or the economy of an empire, is sure to have a thousand infallible remedies for every possible disease, the names of which he does not know, nor their causes, origin or operation; and which, if he did know their names, he is entirely incapable of distinguishing, one from the other. These remedies he applies at haphazard, wholly in the dark as to their effect on the system in general, or on the particular disease, and, of course, nine times out of ten he applies them wrongfully, and aggravates fifty-fold the injury he affects to be able to relieve.

These are the fellows who are constantly administering purgative balls, diuretic balls, cordial balls, on their own hook, without advice, orders, or possible reason—and such balls, too! some of them scarcely less fatal than a cannon ball—who are continually drugging their horses with nitre in their food, under an idea that it is cooling to the system and that it makes the coat sleek and silky; never suspecting that it is a violent diuretic; that its operation on the kidneys is irritating and exhausting in the extreme, and that the only way in which it cools the animal's system is that it reduces his strength and acts as a serious drain on his constitution. These, lastly, are the fellows who are constantly applying *hot oils*, fiery irritants, and stimulants, to wounds, strains, bruises, or contusions, which in themselves produce violent inflammation, and to which, requiring as they do the exhibition of mild and soothing remedies, cold lotions, or warm fomentations, the application of these stimulating volatile essences is much what it would be to administer brandy and cayenne to a man with a brain fever.

It should, therefore, be a positive rule in every stable, whether for pleasure or farm purposes, that not a drachm of medicine is ever to be administered without the express orders of the master. Even if a horse-keeper be so fortunate as to possess a really intelligent, superior servant, who has served his apprenticeship in a good stable, and has learned a good deal about horses, he should still insist on being invariably consulted before medicine is administered. He should acquaint himself with the man's reasons for wishing to administer medicine at all; his idea of the ailment which he supposes to exist; of the symptoms from which he diagnoses it, and of the nature and action of the drug which it is proposed to exhibit. If he see that the symptoms do exist, and learn that the nature of the medicine is such as would be expected to counteract such an ailment—which a very small share of common sense will enable him to discover—he will do well to sanction the proceeding. But if there be the least doubt about the symptoms, and still more, unless the man have a clear conception *why* he should give this dose for that disease, and what is its effect on the constitution, he should put an absolute veto on all proceedings until the advice of a regular practitioner can be obtained. Even these—unless they chance to be men of superior ability, and, what is very rare in America, even in the large cities, and almost unknown in the country, men of real education also—will be very likely to overdo the matter. In the first place, when called in, they judge it necessary to order something in order to show that they know what is the matter and what is wanting. In the second place, they almost always have recourse to violent, drastic, aloetic purges, and to extreme measures generally, when, half the time, no medicine at all, or at most a simple alterative, or a diaphoretic, or an enema, is all that is required.

Of course, any sensible man, if his horse be dangerously and acutely affected, whether he do or do not himself know precisely what is the disease, will call in the best medical aid his neighborhood will afford as soon as possible. But, in the mean time, palliations may be always used, innocent in themselves, if not useful ; and, in many acute and sudden diseases, if immediate relief be not applied, the malady will have gained such headway that when advice arrives it will be too late to check it; whereas, if some simple but active treatment be adopted on the spot, much time will be saved, in the least important view of the matter, and, in the worst, possibly life itself. Again : in the case of accidents, wounds and sudden casualties, it is often imperatively necessary to act upon the spot ; and it is always highly desirable to do so, insomuch as, if nothing else, it by so much expedites the cure. Once again : there are many ailments of so trifling a character and so simple of treatment that it would be entirely superfluous for a horse-keeper to call in the aid of a veterinary surgeon on each occurrence of one of these, even if he were close at hand, since they are such that every stable should be capable of managing its own cases within itself.

It is to these three classes of cases that we intend to confine ourselves in the remarks which we propose to offer for the use of our readers, whether urban, suburban or rural, who keep horses and desire to promote, what fortunately go hand-in-hand together, the utility and the well-being of that noble animal. And first, we would have our readers divest themselves of the idea that there is anything portentously secret, wonderful, or out of the course of nature in the ailments of horses, or that it requires either extraordinary sagacity or intense study to treat their commoner and more usual maladies so as to give them immediate relief, and to enable them to resume their labors for our own benefit in a short period. The truth is the very reverse of this. The more ordinary diseases and affections of the horse are very similar to those with which we are affected ourselves; their treatment is always analogous, often almost exactly identical; the processes by which relief is to be obtained are the same, and the medicines do not materially differ from those suitable to the human race. It is not too much to say that any intelligent man, gifted with good reasoning powers and not deficient in observation, who knows how to keep his own bodily health in a good state, and to deal with his own ordinary ailments, can, within twelve months, qualify himself to treat a horse in all the cases that are likely to befall him, under ordinary circumstances, as well as any body else, and fifty times better than the stable-keepers, who will sneer at his efforts until they perceive that they are successful, and then will suddenly discover that the means he took are precisely those which themselves recommended. The things of great importance which he has to learn, in order to guard against danger, are, how much depletion the system of a horse can endure without danger, and what extent of purgation his bowels can resist undamaged. And to these questions it may be answered, generally, that the horse can bear much more depletion and less purgation than is generally imagined, especially of the drastic drugs usually exhibited. We are very decided opponents of purgatives in general, and have been gratified by observing that the recent cause of veterinary practice, both in France and England, is tending to the entire abandonment of the old system; according to which every horse, whether anything ailed him or not, was put through two annual courses of purgation, each of three doses, in the Spring and Fall, beside having to bolt a diuretic ball fortnightly, or oftener, according to the whim of the groom, when his kidneys no more required stimulation than his hocks did blistering.

A horse of ordinary size contains, on an average, from twenty to twenty-four quarts of blood, and the loss to him of four quarts is not so much as a pound, or pint, to a human being. In cases of acute inflammation, a horse may be bled eight or ten quarts at a time, or until he lies down, with advantage; and if the symptoms do not abate, may be bled again at intervals of an hour or two, to an extent which a person, ignorant how rapidly blood is made, would suppose must drain the animal of his life. Purgatives, in our opinion, on the other hand, should be very cautiously administered; *never* when there is any inflammation of the lungs or bowels; very rarely when there is any *internal* inflammation; and when given, should never, or hardly ever, in our judgment, exceed five drachms of new Barbadoes aloes. Injections, diet, and mashes are vastly superior, for general practice, to acute purgatives, horses being extremely liable to super-purgation, and many valuable animals being lost in consequence of it yearly.

The first branch of this subject on which we propose to treat, is the early application of remedies to horses, suddenly seized with violent and acute diseases, anticipatory to the calling in of regular medical assistance. It is highly necessary that this should be done as soon as the horse is known to be seized, and the nature of his seizure is fully ascertained, since, in several of the diseases to which the horse is most liable, the increase of the malady is so rapid that, if early steps be not taken to relieve the sufferer, the evil becomes so firmly seated that the remedy, if long delayed, comes too late, and an animal is lost which by timely assistance might have easily been preserved. These ailments, especially, are of common occurrence with the horse, of highly dangerous character, and so rapid in their development and increase that, if steps be not taken for their relief almost immediately after their commencement, all treatment will be useless;—these are spasmodic colic, inflammation of the bowels, and inflammation of the lungs.

The two former of these have, in their early symptoms, a close resemblance one with the other; and as the treatment of the two should be very different, it is necessary to be exceedingly careful, and to be well acquainted with the diagnosis of the two ailments before attempting to treat the patient, as a mistake might well be fatal, while a delay is almost surely so.

"The attack of colic," says Mr. Youatt, "is usually very sudden. There is often not the slighest warning. The horse begins to shift his posture, look round at his flanks, paw violently, strike his belly with his feet, lie down, roll, and that frequently on his back. In a few minutes the pain seems to cease, the horse shakes himself and begins to feed; but on a sudden the spasm returns more violently, every indication of pain is increased, he heaves at the flanks, breaks out in a profuse perspiration, and throws himself more violently about. In the space of an hour or two either the spasms begin to relax and the remissions are longer in duration, or the torture is augmented at every paroxysm, the intervals of ease are fewer and less marked, and inflammation and death supervene."

As all the more violent symptoms of this disease and of acute inflammation of the external coats of the intestines, such as looking round at the flanks, pawing, kicking at the belly, rolling violently, and, in a word, all the manifestations of excessive pain are nearly identical, and, as the causes which lead to the two diseases are also nearly the same, so that one might be liable to suspect the occurrence of either, from a knowledge of the antecedents to which the horse has been exposed, it was well done in Youatt to present briefly in a tabular form the distinctions between the symptoms of the two, which, if carefully observed, cannot be misunderstood, and will prevent the possibility of confusion, which might lead to the most fatal consequences. We proceed to present his table, accompanied by his remark that the treatment recommended for the former (colic) would often be fatal in the latter:

COLIC.	INFLAMMATION OF THE BOWELS.
Sudden in its attack, and without any warning.	Gradual in its approach, with previous indications of fever.
Pulse rarely much quickened in the early period of the disease, and during the intervals of ease, but evidently fuller.	Pulse very much quickened, but small, and often scarcely to be felt.
Legs and ears of natural temperature.	Legs and ears cold.
Relief obtained from rubbing the belly.	Belly exceedingly painful, and tender to the touch.
Relief obtained from motion.	Pain evidently increased by motion.
Intervals of rest and ease.	Constant pain.
Strength scarcely affected.	Great and evident weakness.

Of these differences the most strongly and decidedly marked are the different affections of the pulse, the different conditions of the extremities, the remissions of the pain in the one, and the constant increase of it in the other, and the extreme weakness which rapidly comes on in inflammation, and does not show in colic.

It will be well, here, to state that the pulse of the horse is most conveniently felt at the lower jaw; a little behind the spot where the submaxillary artery and vein and the parotid duct come from under the jaw: in other words, close to the junction of the head and neck. The thumb should be placed on the cheek externally, with the nail upward, and the tips of the fingers passing under and

8

within the jaw-bone, will readily feel the artery, and, by compressing it against the bone, will ascertain not only the number of pulsations, but the manner in which the blood passes, and the quantity. By feeling the heart, through the side, as is the ordinary practice of horsemen, nothing can be ascertained beyond the number of pulsations.

We will here add that, in temperate climates, about thirty-six in a minute is the ordinary beat of the pulse in a common or farmer's horse, which will be increased to forty, or even forty-two, in thorough-breds. It varies but little in horses of different sizes, but is slightly increased in hot weather, and very materially so in hot climates. The pulse of the thorough-bred horse is said to range ten higher in New Orleans than in New York; and we can readily believe this to be the case, as we have observed the same thing to occur when the horse is kept in a very hot stable. Sudden alarm often quickens the pulse by ten beats; wherefore particular care should be had to go up to the patient as gently, and to handle him as tenderly and caressingly, as possible, in order to avoid producing this excitement, which will lead to a false diagnosis.

COLIC is usually produced by sudden cold, often the result of drinking cold water when heated; sometimes by exposure to cold wind, in a draft, when heated; sometimes by overfeeding on green meat, or new corn. The causes of inflammation in the bowels are somewhat similar, though not identical. Horses used to high feeding and warm stabling, which, after sharp exercise and being for some hours without food, are exposed to cold wind, or are allowed to drink freely of cold water, or are drenched with rain, or have their legs and belly washed with cold water, are almost sure to be attacked with inflammation of the bowels. An overfed or overfat horse, which is subjected to severe and long-continued exertion, if his lungs be weak, will be attacked, probably the same night, by inflammation of the lungs; if the lungs be sound, the attack will be on his bowels on the following day.

The diagnosis being made, and the disease being fully established to be spasmodic colic, and not inflammation, the treatment should be as follows: Give at once, in a drench, by a horn or bottle, three ounces of spirits of turpentine and an ounce of laudanum in a pint of warm ale, the effect of which will often be instantaneous. If these ingredients cannot be quickly obtained, a drench of hot ale, with ginger, a wine-glass full of gin and a teaspoonful of black pepper, with, if possible, the laudanum added, will succeed as a substitute. If the paroxysm returns, or if relief of a decided kind do not take place within half an hour, from four to six quarts of blood may be taken, with advantage, in order to prevent inflammation. The dose of turpentine should be repeated, and clysters of warm water, with an ounce of finely powdered Barbadoes aloes dissolved in them, should be injected, at intervals, until the counter-irritation puts a stop to the spasms. For the injections, a common wooden pipe with an ox bladder will answer, although the patent syringe is far better. The pipe should be greased and introduced gently and tenderly, great care being had not to alarm or startle the animal. The operation and effect of the medicines will be promoted by gentle friction of the belly, with a brush or hot flannel cloth, and by walking the horse, or trotting him very gently about; but all violence, or violent motions, must be avoided, as tending to produce inflammation. These remedies, which can be procured with ease in any village, almost in any house, will almost to a certainty remove the disease. When relief is obtained, the horse's clothes should be changed, which will be found to be saturated with sweat;

he should be slightly cleaned; warmly and dryly littered down, if possible, in a loose box, and should be fed, for two or three days, on warm bran mashes, and suffered to drink warm water only. It is evident that the above treatment, which is stimulating, would be probably fatal, as it would aggravate all the worst features, in a case of inflammation, which must be treated, as nearly as possible, on the opposite plan—that is, antiphlogistically.

INFLAMMATION OF THE BOWELS.—The first step, in decided cases where the extremities are cold and the pulse very quick and very feeble—observe, here, that fifty-five is very quick, indicating considerable fever, and seventy-five perilously quick—is to take eight or ten quarts of blood as soon as the malady appears,—for there is no other malady that so quickly runs its course. If this do not relieve the pain, and render the pulse more moderate, and fuller, and rounder, four or five quarts more may be taken, without any regard to the weakness of the animal. That weakness is a part of the disease, and, when the inflammation is subdued by the loss of blood, the weakness will disappear. We have said that most of the acute diseases of the horse and the man are closely similar, and their treatment analogous. In acute inflammation of the bowels there is an exception. The human practitioner properly uses strong purgatives, in cases of acute inflammation of the bowels. The irritablility of the horse's bowels will not allow their exhibition. The most that can be done is, to throw up copious injections—they can hardly be too copious—of thin gruel, in which half a pound of Epsom salts, or half an ounce of Barbadoes aloes, has been dissolved. The horse should be encouraged to drink freely of warm, thin gruel, and he should have a draught, every six hours, of warm water, with from one to two drachms,—never more,— of aloes dissolved in it   Above all, the whole belly should be blistered as quickly as possible after the nature of the disease is fully ascertained, with tincture of cantharides well rubbed in. The legs should be well bandaged, to restore the circulation; and the horse should be warmly clothed, but the stable kept cool. No hay or oats must be allowed during the attack, but merely bran mashes and green meat; of the latter, especially, as much as he will eat. As the horse recovers a little oats may be given, a handful or two at a time, twice or thrice a day, but not more; and they should be increased sparingly and gradually. Clysters of gruel should be continued for two or three days, and hand-rubbing and bandaging to restore the circulation. There is another kind of inflammation of the bowels, which attacks the inner or mucous membrane, and is produced by super-purgation and the exhibition of improper medicine in improper quantities. Its characteristics are incessant purging, laborious breathing, pulse quick and small, but less so than in the other form of disease; and, above all, the mouth is hot, and the legs and ears warm. In this disease, no food must be allowed, least of all laxative food, such as mashes or green meat; but draughts and clysters of gruel, thin starch and arrow-root may be given frequently. If the pain and purging do not pass away within twelve hours, astringents must be given. The best form is powdered chalk 1 oz., catechu ¼ oz., opium 2 scruples, in gruel, repeated every six hours till the purging begins to subside, when the doses should be gradually decreased and discontinued. Bleeding is not generally necessary, unless the inflammation and fever are excessive. The horse should be kept warm, and his legs rubbed and bandaged as directed in the former type of the disease.

INFLAMMATION OF THE LUNGS.—This disease, which in a state of nature is almost unknown to the horse, is one to which in his domesticated state he is most liable, and which is most fatal to him. It requires immediate and most active treatment. It is sometimes sudden in its attack, but is generally preceded by fever. The pulse is not always much quickened, in the first instance, but is indistinct and depressed. The extremities are painfully cold; the lining membrane of the nostrils becomes intensely red; the breathing is quick, hurried, and seems to be interrupted by pain, or mechanical obstruction. The horse stands stiffly, with his legs far apart, so as to distend his chest to the utmost, and is singularly unwilling to move, or to lie down, persisting in standing up, day after day and night after night: and if at last compelled by fatigue to lie down, rises again after a moment's repose. The pulse soon becomes irregular, indistinct, and at last almost imperceptible. The legs and ears assume a clay-like, clammy coldness,—the coldness of death. The lining of the nostril turns purple; the teeth are violently ground; the horse persists in standing, until he can stand no longer, when he staggers, drops and soon dies.

For this disease, the only remedy that can be depended upon is the lancet. The horse must be bled, not according to quantity, not only till the pulse begins to rise, but until it begins to flutter or stop, and the animal begins to faint. The operator should watch this effect, with his finger on the pulse, while the bleeding is in process. At the end of six hours, if the horse still persist in standing and the laborious breathing still continue, the bleeding should be repeated to the same extent. This will generally succeed in conquering the strength of the disease. If a third bleeding be necessary, as is sometimes the case, it must not be carried beyond four or five quarts, lest not only the disease, but the recuperative power be subdued. After this, if the symptoms return, successive bleedings to the extent of two or three quarts should be used, to prevent the reëstablishment of the disease. The instrument for bleeding should be a broad-shouldered thumb lancet, and the stream of blood should be full and strong. Some of the blood, from each bleeding, should be set aside in a glass tumbler, and suffered to grow cold, in order to note the thickness of the buff-colored, adhesive coat which will appear on the top of it, and which indicates the degree of inflammation at the time the blood was drawn. We have seen it occupy above one half the depth of the tumbler. As the condition of the blood improves, and the symptoms of the animal decrease, the bleeding may be gradually discontinued.

The whole of the horse's chest and sides, up as far as to the elbows, should now be thoroughly blistered, the hair having been previously closely shaved, with an ointment of one part of Spanish flies, four of lard, and one of rosin, well rubbed in. In making the ointment, the rosin and lard should be melted together, and the flies then added.

A horse with inflammation of the lungs must never be actively purged; the bowels and lungs act so strongly in sympathy, that inflammation of the former would surely supervene, and prove fatal. The horse must be back-raked, and clystered with warm gruel containing eight ounces of Epsom salts. Castor oil must never be given; it is a most dangerous medicine to the horse. Doses of nitre, digitalis and tartar emetic, in the proportion of three ounces of the first, one of the second and one and a half of the third may be given, morning and evening, until the animal begins to amend, when the dose may be reduced to one-half. The horse must be warmly clothed, but kept in a cool box. As he recovers, his skin should be gently rubbed with a brush, if it do not irritate him; but his legs *must* be constantly and thoroughly hand-rubbed and bandaged. He should not be coaxed to eat, but may have a little hay to amuse him, cold mashes and green meat, but on no account a particle of oats. Eight-and-forty hours generally decides the question of death or life. But in case of recovery, it is necessary long to watch for a relapse, which is of frequent, one might say of general, occurrence. It is to be met at once by the same energetic treatment. And now, one word to the owner of a horse which has had one bad attack of inflammation, either of the lungs or of the bowels. Get rid of him as soon as possible! It is ten to one that he will have another, and another, and, as in the former instance, end by becoming broken-winded,—in the latter by being useless, from a nearly chronic state of the disease.

The second class of ailments, which every horse-keeper ought to be prepared to treat himself, without assistance, are those natural and constantly occurring cases which are almost habitually present in large stables or farming establishments, and in aid of which to call in a veterinary surgeon on every occasion would be both an absurd expense and a useless waste of time. Such are, for instance, costiveness, common cough, bronchitis, or catarrhal disease, strangles or colt-distemper, worms, difficulty in staling, and some others, which any man who keeps a horse ought to be able to treat successfully himself, without any advice, and with ordinary medicines, easily procurable from any druggist. Condition, in its proper sense, is more dependent on proper and systematic feeding, exercising, clothing and lodging, than on medicine ; and if a horse be of good, sound constitution, and be judiciously fed, regularly worked, warmly yet not too warmly clothed and stabled, in a building properly ventilated and aërated; and, above all, if he be kept scrupulously and religiously clean, there will for him be but little need of medicine of any kind. From ill-constructed stables arise half the worst diseases, those for instance of the lungs, from want of ventilation ; many of those of the eyes, from the excess of ammoniacal vapors and unnatural darkness; many of those of the feet, as cracked heels, thrushes, grease—which in America is known as scratches—from filth and neglect; and most of those of the bowels, and the bowels and lungs combined, from bad food, or good food badly administered. Still diseases will and do arise from other causes, in the best stables, and among the best-attended horses. And again, they do arise, and when arising must be dealt with medically, owing to the causes above enumerated.

It may be well in this place to describe briefly the most approved modes of bleeding and administering medicine. The former operation is performed in the jugular vein; the hair is smoothed, along the course of the vein, with the moistened finger; then, if the fleam be used—which, in our opinion, ought to be discarded—with the third and little fingers of the left hand, which holds the fleam, pressure is made upon the vein sufficient to bring it into full view; the fleam is to be placed on the vein, in the direct line of its course, precisely over the centre of it, not exactly touching it, but as near to it as possible without doing so. A smart blow is then given to the back of the fleam with an instrument called the blood-stick, which gives it force sufficient to pierce the skin and open the vessel. A much neater way, however, is to use a broad-bladed lancet. The vein is secured and pressed sufficiently to bring it into full view and cause it to swell, with the divided fingers of the left hand, when the point of the lancet is sent in, without an effort, so as to cut slightly upward and to open a clean and sufficient aperture. By this method the danger of cutting the neck foul without touching the vein, owing to the horse starting at the moment the blow is given upon the fleam, and the yet worse danger of dividing both sides of the vein, are both avoided. When enough blood has been

8*

taken, the edges of the wound should be brought smoothly together, and secured by a sharp pin, around which a little tow or a few hairs of the horse should be twisted. The blood, while it is flowing, should be made, by a gentle pressure on the vein below the aperture, to spring out in a clear, full jet, and to fall into the centre of the vessel used to receive it. If it be allowed to trickle down the sides of the pail, it will not undergo the changes by which the extent of inflammation may be judged. The operator should accurately know the size of the vessel he uses, so as to calculate the flow of blood.

In giving medicine, if balls be used, they should never weigh above an ounce and a half, or be above an inch in diameter, and three in length. The horse should be lashed in the stall, the tongue should be drawn gently out with the left hand on the off side of the mouth, and fixed there, not by continuing to pull at it, but by pressing the fingers against the side of the lower jaw. The ball is then taken between the tips of the fingers of the right hand, the arm being bared and passed rapidly up the mouth, as near the palate as possible, until it reaches the root of the tongue, when it is delivered with a slight jerk, the hand is withdrawn, and the tongue being released the ball is forced down into the oesophagus. Its passage should be watched down the left side of the throat, and if it do not pass immediately, a slight tap under the chin will easily cause the horse to swallow it. The only safe purgative for a horse is Barbadoes aloes, or the flour of the Croton bean, for some peculiar purposes; but its drastic nature renders it undesirable as a general aperient. When aloes are used, care should be taken to have them new, as they speedily lose their power, and they should be freshly mixed. Very mild doses only should be used; four or five drachms are amply sufficient, if the horse have been prepared, as he should be, by being fed for two days at least, entirely on mashes, which will cause a small dose to have a beneficial effect, equal to double the quantity administered to a horse not duly prepared for it. The immense doses of eight, nine, ten and even twelve drachms, which were formerly in vogue, and which are still favored by grooms, ostlers and carters, are utterly exploded; and it is well known that eight or nine good fluid evacuations are all that can be desired, and far safer than twice the number.

Four and a half drachms of Barbadoes aloes, with olive or linseed oil and molasses sufficient to form a mass in the proportion of eight of the aloes to one of the oil and three of the molasses, is the best general ball, though often four drachms given after a sufficiency of mashes or green food will accomplish all that is needed or desirable. Castor oil is a most dangerous and uncertain medicine. Linseed oil is not much better. Olive oil is safe, but weak. Epsom salts is inefficient, except in enormous doses, and is then dangerous. It is, however, excellent, given in clysters of weak gruel; which, by the way, except where very searching and thorough purging is required, as in cases of mange or grease, is by far the safest, most agreeable and mildest way of purging the horse, and evacuating his bowels. Where, however, his intestines are over-loaded with fat, where he shows signs of surfeit, or where it is necessary to prepare him to undergo some great change of system, as from a long run at grass to a hot stable, or *vice versa*, a mild course of two or three doses of physic, with a clear interval of a week between the setting of one dose and the giving of another, is necessary, and cannot be properly dispensed with.

COSTIVENESS.—Ordinary cases can generally be conquered without medicine, by diet, such as hop or bran mashes, green meat and carrots; but where it is obstinate, the rectum should be cleared of dry fæces by passing the naked arm, well greased, up the anus; and the bowels should be then thoroughly evacuated by clysters of thin gruel, with half an ounce of Barbadoes aloes, or half a pound of Epsom salts dissolved in it. If the patent syringe be used, the injection will reach the colon and cæcum and dispose them also to evacuate their contents.

COMMON COUGH is generally subdued without much difficulty, though it often becomes of most serious consequence if neglected. It is accompanied by a heightened pulse; a slight discharge from the nose and eyes, a rough coat, and a diminished appetite, being its symptoms. The horse should be kept warm, fed on mashes, and should have a dose or two of medicine. If the cough be very obstinate, bleeding may be necessary.

BRONCHITIS is cough, with catarrh extending to the entrance of the lungs superadded. It is characterized by a quick, hard breathing, and a peculiar wheezing, followed and relieved by coughing up mucus. It must be treated by bleeding, though by no means so copious as in cases of inflammation of the lungs. Repeated bleedings of four or five quarts, at intervals, until relief is obtained, are preferable to the abstraction of large quantities at once. The chest should be blistered, and digitalis, nitre and tartar emetic exhibited, as with inflammation of the lungs; bronchitis, if neglected, is apt to degenerate into thick wind.

STRANGLES, or colt-distemper, is a disease which shows itself in all young horses, and from which, when they have once passed through its ordeal, they have no more to fear. It is preceded by some derangement of circulation, quickening of the pulse, some fever, cough, and sore throat. The parts around the throat swell, the maxillary glands are swollen and tender, and sometimes the parotids also. The animal refuses to drink, and often declines his food. There is a flow of saliva from the mouth and a semi-purulent discharge from the nose. The jaws, throat and glands of the neck should be poulticed with steaming mashes, the skin stimulated by means of a liquid blister, and the head steamed, in order to promote suppuration. As soon as fluctuation can be perceived, the swelling should be lanced, and a rowel introduced, to keep the abscess open and the discharge flowing for a few days. The animal should have walking exercise, and be treated with green food, until the symptoms abate, when he will require liberal and generous food to recruit his strength.

WORMS are sometimes troublesome to a horse, but in a far less degree than is generally supposed. Botts have long since, been proved to be perfectly harmless while they are within the stomach,—all the stories of their eating through its coats being pure *myths*, although they are very often troublesome after they have passed out of the œsophagus and rectum and begin to adhere to the orifice of the anus. Common purgatives will often bring away vast numbers of the long, white worm, *teres lumbricus*, which occasionally, when existing in great numbers, consume too large a proportion of the animal's food, and produce a tight skin, a tucked-up belly, and a rough coat. Calomel should never be given, as it too frequently is, for the removal of these worms, which will readily yield to balls of two drachms of tartar emetic, one scruple of ginger, with molasses and linseed oil *quantum suff.*, given alternate mornings half an hour before feeding time. The smaller worm, *ascaris*, which often causes serious irritation about the fundament, is best removed by injecting a quart of linseed oil, or an ounce of aloes dissolved in warm water, which is a most effectual remedy.

DISEASES OF THE BLADDER are many, serious, and often mistreated They require, however, so much skill and so accurate a diagnosis, that none but a regular practitioner should pretend to treat them. Simple difficulty of staling can generally be relieved by cleansing the sheath with the hand, and giving gentle doses of nitre. These are most of the simpler diseases, which may be simply and successfully treated at home, and with which every horse-keeper ought to be at least superficially and generally acquainted. We shall touch upon the subject of accidents, strains, simple lameness, contusions, and the like, which can often be perfectly cured by cold lotions, or simple, warm fomentations, without any further or more difficult process,—though ignorant persons make much of them, as if their cure proved marvelous skill, and required magnificent appliances.

Before proceeding to the consideration of simple accidents and their treatment, we shall devote a few words to an affection of the feet, or, to speak more correctly, heels, which although not exactly an accident, is not a natural disease, but arises from filth, neglect, cold, wet, and the omission to clean and dry the feet and legs of the horse, after work and exposure to weather. It has been rightly called the disgrace, as it is the bane, of inferior stables, both in the city and the country, but more commonly in the latter, where, to pay any attention to the legs and feet of a farmhorse, is an almost unheard-of act of chivalric Quixotism. This is the ailment known in England as "the grease," in the United States, generally, as "the scratches." It is perfectly easy to be prevented, and easy to be cured if taken in the first instance; but if neglected and allowed to become virulent, is nearly incurable.

GREASE.—The first appearance of "grease," which is caused by the feet and heels being left wet after work in muddy soil, and exposed to a draft of cold air, is a dry and scurfy state of the skin, with redness, heat and itching. If neglected, the hair drops off, the heels swell, the skin assumes a glazed appearance, is covered with pustules, cracks open, and emits a thin, glairy discharge, which soon becomes very offensive. In the last, worst, and incurable stage, the leg, half-way to the hock, is covered with thick, horny scabs, divided into lozenge-shaped lumps by deep cracks, whence issues an extremely offensive matter. In this stage, the disease is called "grapy heels," and is scarcely curable. In the first stage, all that is necessary is frequent washing with tepid water and Castile soap, and the application of a flannel bandage, evenly applied over the whole limb, moistened with warm water and allowed to dry on the part. An ointment of one drachm of sugar of lead in an ounce of lard, will supple, soften and relieve the parts. The cracks may be washed with a solution of four ounces of alum in a pint of water, which will in most cases suffice. A dose of medicine is now desirable, for which the horse should be well prepared by the administration of bran-mashes, as before advised, for a couple of days; after which, a ball of four or five drachms of Barbadoes aloes will suffice. An injection will not answer in this case, as the object is, not to empty the bowels, but to cool the system. The horse should be fed on mashes, carrots, and green meat; oats, Indian corn, and high food of all kinds, are to be avoided as too heating.

When the disease has reached the second stage, the physicing must be persevered in for three doses, with the regular intervals; carrot poultices must be applied to the heels. This is best done by drawing an old stocking, minus the foot, over the horse's hoof, confining it around the fetlock joint with a loose bandage, and filling it from above with carrots, boiled and mashed into a soft pulp. This mass should be applied tolerably hot, and repeated daily for three days. When removed, the heels should be anointed with an ointment of one part of rosin, three parts of lard, melted together, and one part of calamine powder, added when the first mixture is cooling. The cracks should be persistently washed with the alum lotion, and the bandage applied whenever the poultices are not on the part. The benefit of carrot poultices for all affections where there is fever, swelling and a pustular condition of the skin, cannot be over-rated. Stocked legs and capped hocks we have seen completely cured by them; and, on one occasion, at least, we have known incipient farcy to give way before their emollient and healing influence. Where "the grease" has degenerated into "the grapes," the aid of a veterinary surgeon must be invoked; but he will rarely succeed, as the ailment is now all but incurable. It is, however, only the height of neglect which ever allows the ailment to degenerate into this filthy and malignant stage of disease.

THRUSH.—Among the more common of the simple ailments of the foot is that known as "thrush." This is a discharge of offensive matter from the cleft of the frog, produced by inflammation of the lower surface of the sensible frog. In the fore feet, it is often the consequence of contraction of the hoofs. It constitutes a legal unsoundness, and is generally, although not always, accompanied by lameness. Any moderately astringent application is of advantage, but it must not be of too caustic a nature. Common ægyptiacum, or honey boiled with vinegar and verdigris, is a good liniment; but the best of all applications is a paste, composed of two ounces of blue and one of white vitriol, powdered as finely as possible, and rubbed down with one pound of tar and two of lard; a pledget of tow covered with this should be introduced into the cleft of the frog, as far as is possible, without undue force, every night, and removed before the horse goes to work in the morning. The feet should be kept moist by being stuffed nightly with equal parts of tar, cow-dung and soft clay.

A very common and dangerous accident to the foot arises from pricking the hoof, by awkward driving of the nails in shoeing, either through the horny crust of the foot into the sensible flesh, or so near to it as to give acute pain and produce violent lameness. When a horse falls lame immediately after shoeing, the foot should be carefully examined, in order to see if this be not the cause. If it be so, the seat of the injury will often be detected by a sensible heat and inflammation of the injured part; if not, on tapping the hoof externally all round with a hammer, the animal will flinch when the hammer is struck opposite to or above the puncture. The shoe must then be withdrawn, the nail which has done the mischief must be removed, the puncture must be opened out and enlarged by paring away the horn quite down to the quick, when a pledget of tow, dipped in Friar's balsam, should be inserted into the puncture. The feet must be kept cool and moist, by stuffing them, as described above, and the cure, beyond this, must be left to time and rest to accomplish.

BROKEN KNEES.—In cases of knees broken by a fall, the wound should be carefully washed with tepid water; all extraneous matter, as earth, sand, or gravel, must be carefully removed; any ragged edges of skin should be clipped off with a pair of sharp scissors; a pad of linen, dipped in Friar's balsam, should be applied, and kept in its place by a moderately tight bandage. The wound should be washed daily with tepid water; if there be much swelling or inflammation, it may be well fomented, but not poulticed, as it is an object to prevent, not to encourage, suppuration. But all hot oils, astringents, or stimulating applications of any kind, which grooms are almost sure to recommend, and to apply contrary to orders if not watched, must be avoided as one would avoid poison.

The treatment for over-reach, tread, or wounds produced by injuring one foot by the caulks of the other, are to be treated precisely in the same manner as broken knees.

For all strains, wrenches, or contusions, where the skin is not broken, hot fomentations of vinegar and water, applied by means of flannel bandages, and constantly repeated, are the best possible treatment. Where there is much swelling and acute inflammation, linseed, turnip, or carrot poultices may be applied with advantage; and the parts should be kept tightly bandaged, when not under other treatment. When the swelling and inflammation have passed, but weakness and lameness continue, the part should be wrapped nightly with a close, but not tight, Harpocrates bandage of cotton cloth, saturated in cold water, and above that tightly swathed in a double flannel bandage. This treatment, if resolutely persevered in, will, nine times out of ten, remove the injury. If it do not so, the veterinary surgeon must be called in, and blistering, or other stronger means, resorted to. But these measures should not be tried until the disease is becoming chronic, and until all inflammation is at end.

It is believed, that if applied carefully and with considerate judgment, the above-described simple remedies will be found all-sufficient for the simple ailments and simple accidents mentioned; and they can all be applied from materials to be found in every house, and by any one with ordinary sense and common judgment. For all more serious accidents and complicated disorders, good medical treatment is actually necessary; and, in such cases, it is even greater folly to attempt home treatment, than it is not to attempt it in such cases as we have referred to.

CHAPTER XIV.

FARRIERY, ETC.

BY farriery we generally understand the performance of those common operations which do not require the aid of a Veterinary Surgeon, but may be practiced, with pretty good success, by men of practical experience, who have little or no scientific knowledge of the anatomy and physiology of the horse. It is true that very many, if not all of these, would be performed much better by a skilled Veterinary Surgeon, but they are of such a character that his services are not absolutely essential. These operations are chiefly such as affect only the external parts and organs of the animal; and they may be safely entrusted to any person, who has had a fair amount of experience in the management of sick horse-flesh. It is to be premised, however, that very few of those smiths on whose signs there appears, "*Horse Shoer and Farrier*," are better than quacks into whose hands it would not be safe to place the control of the simplest case.

As a general rule, every horse owner should, if possible, appeal only to skilled veterinary surgeons, for any surgical operation, no matter how trifling, of which his horse may stand in need. Where he has to depend on the services of an uneducated country farrier, he should take pains to inform himself, as far as lies in his power, of all the conditions on which the difficulty in question, and the mode of curing it, depends; this will enable him at least to prevent much injury which an ignorant quack might occasion, if allowed to have entirely his own way.

CASTRATION.

This operation is, of course, a very delicate one, and should never be attempted, on a living subject, except by a person of experience and skill.

The following directions are given by Mr. Youatt:

"The period at which this operation may be best performed depends much on the breed and form of the colt, and the purpose for which he is destined. For the common agricultural horse, the age of four or five months will be the most proper time, or, at least, before he is weaned. Few horses are lost when cut at that age. Care, however, should be taken, that the weather is not too hot nor the flies too numerous.

"If the horse is designed either for the carriage or for heavy draught, the farmer should not think of castrating him until he is at least a twelvemonth old; and, even then, the colt should be carefully examined. If he is thin and spare about the neck and shoulders, and low in the withers, he will materially improve by remaining uncut another six months; but if his fore-quarters are fairly developed at the age of a twelvemonth, the operation should not be delayed, lest he become heavy and gross before, and perhaps has begun too decidedly to have a will of his own. No specific age, then, can be fixed; but the castration should be performed rather late in the spring or early in the autumn, when the air is temperate, and particularly when the weather is dry.

"No preparation is necessary for the sucking colt, but it may be prudent to bleed and to physic one of more advanced age. In the majority of cases, no after treatment will be necessary, except that the animal should be sheltered from intense heat, and more particularly from wet."

Moderate exercise taken in grazing will be preferable to perfect inaction. The old method of pinning the scrotum (testicle bag) on either side, and cutting off the testicles,—preventing bleeding by a temporary compression of the vessels while they are seared with a hot iron,—must be abandoned; and there is no necessity for this extra pain when the spermatic cord, (the blood vessels, and the nerve) is compressed between two pieces of wood, as tightly as in a vice, and there left till the following day, or until the testicle drops off.

Another method of castration is by torsion. An incision is made into the scrotum, and the *vas deferens* is exposed and divided. The artery is then seized with a pair of forceps contrived for the purpose, and twisted six or seven times around. It retracts without untwisting the coils, and the bleeding ceases; the testicle is removed, and there is no sloughing, or danger. The most painful part of the operation, that with the firing iron or the clamp, is avoided, and the wound readily heals.

Mr. Spooner, the editor of Youatt's works, recommends the use of chloroform, and says that he has performed the operation in seven minutes, without any pain to the animal.

DOCKING AND NICKING.

These barbarous methods of depriving the horse of his natural form and appearance, in order to make him conform to the fashion of the time, is, fortunately, very fast going into disuse. If the tail of the horse were given to him for no good purpose, and if it were not a design of nature that he should have the power of moving it forcibly to his sides, there might be some excuse for cutting it off, within a few inches of his body, or for separating the muscles at its sides to lessen this power; but, that this is not the case, must be acknowledged by all who have seen how a horse, whose tail has been abridged by "Docking," or weakened by nicking, is annoyed by flies.

If a horse have a trick of throwing dirt on his rider's clothing, this may be prevented by cutting off the *hair* of the tail, below the end of the bones, as is the custom with hunters in England, where the hair is cut squarely off about eight or ten inches above the hocks.

No apology is offered for not giving in this work a description of these two operations; they are so barbarous and so senseless, that they are going very rapidly out of fashion, and it is to be hoped that they will ere long, have become obsolete, as has the cropping of the ears, formerly so common in England.

A more humane way of setting up the horse's tail, to give him a more stylish appearance, is by simply weighting it for a few hours each day, in the stall, until it attains the desired elevation. This is done by having two pulleys at the top of the stall, one at each side, through which are passed two ropes, which come together and are fastened to the tail, the ropes having at their other ends weights (bags of sand or of shot are very good for the purpose), which must be light at first, and may be increased from day to day. The weighting should be continued until the tail has taken a permanent position as desired. It is true that this method requires a somewhat longer time than that of cutting the muscles, but while it is being done the horse is never off his work, and he suffers infinitely less pain.

The method of nicking or pricking, as usually performed in this country, is not quite so cruel nor so hazardous as the cutting of the muscles; it is thus described by **Mr.** Allen:*

The tail has four cords, two upper and two lower. The upper ones raise the tail, the lower ones depress it, and these last alone are to be cut. Take a sharp penknife with a long slender blade; insert the blade between the bone and under cord, two inches from the body; place the thumb of the hand holding the knife against the under part of the tail, and opposite the blade. Then press the blade toward the thumb against the cord, and cut the cord off, but do not let the knife cut through the skin. The cord is firm, and it will easily be known when it is cut off. The thumb will tell when to desist, that the skin may not be cut. Sever the cord twice on each side in the same manner. Let the cuts be two inches apart. The cord is nearly destitute of sensation; yet when the tail is pricked in the old manner, the wound to the skin and flesh is severe, and much fever is induced, and it takes a long time to heal. But with this method the horse's tail will not bleed, nor will it be sore, under ordinary circumstances, more than three days; and he will be pulleyed and his tail made in one half of the time required by the old method.

BLEEDING.

Bleeding, like physic and many other artificial measures for assisting nature, is very much over-estimated—as a means of bringing horses into condition; and its evil effects on horses in health are not sufficiently appreciated. It is a well known fact, that those men who are in the habit of being bled every few months, because of a supposed over-supply of blood, invariably become so much inclined to congestion, that the bleeding has, after a time, to be more

* Stewart's Stable Book.

frequently repeated, and it can be dispensed with only at the risk of serious temporary illness; many who have been bled with unnecessary frequency present the appearance of an apoplectic condition. These results are supposed to arise from an unnaturally vigorous action of the blood— forming power, acquired in the attempt of nature to make up for the loss of bleeding. The same result is observed in the case of horses, and it is believed that they arise from the same cause.

Blood-letting is, in the hands of a "cautious physician," a most valuable agent for reducing inflammation or congestion, but in the hands of the ordinary horseman, or farrier, it is subject to great abuse and is the occasion of many evils. Of course, in a case of blind staggers, or of great inflammation from a wound or other cause, it is well that the person having charge of the horse should be able to apply this means of relief; but for ordinary depletion of the system, for bringing horses into condition, etc., it is absurd to resort to bleeding. The end desired may be more safely attained by administering a proper diet.

The operation of bleeding is thus described by Youatt:

This operation is performed with a fleam or a lancet. The first is the common instrument, and the safest, except in skilful hands. The lancet, however, has a more surgical appearance, and will be adopted by the veterinary practitioner. A bloodstick—a piece of hard wood loaded at one end with lead—is used to strike the fleam into the vein. This is sometimes done with too great violence, and the opposite side of the coat of the vein is wounded. Bad cases of inflammation have resulted from this. If the fist is doubled, and the fleam is sharp and is struck with sufficient force with the lower part of the hand, the bloodstick may be dispensed with.

For general bleeding the jugular vein is selected. The

horse is blindfolded on the side on which he is to be bled, or his head turned well away. The hair is smoothed along the course of the vein with the moistened finger; then, with the third and little fingers of the left hand, which holds the fleam, pressure is made on the vein sufficient to bring it fairly into view, but not to swell it too much,— for then, presenting a rounded surface, it would be apt to roll or slip under the blow. The point to be selected is about two inches below the union of the two portions of the jugular at the angle of the jaw. The fleam is to be placed in a direct line with the course of the vein, and over the precise centre of the vein, as close to it as possible, but its point not absolutely touching the vein. A sharp rap with the bloodstick or the hand on that part of the back of the fleam immediately over the blade, will cut through the vein, and the blood will flow. A fleam with a large blade should always be preferred, for the operation will be materially shortened, and this will be a matter of some consequence with a fidgety or restive horse. A quantity of blood drawn speedily will also have far more effect on the system than double the weight slowly taken, while the wound will heal just as readily as if made by a smaller instrument. There is no occasion to press hard against the neck with the pail, or can; a slight pressure will cause the blood to flow sufficiently fast.

When sufficient blood has been taken, the edges of the wound should be brought closely and exactly together, and kept together by a small sharp pin being passed through them. Round this a little tow, or a few hairs from the mane of the horse, should be wrapped, so as to cover the whole of the incision; and the head of the horse should be tied up for several hours, to prevent his rubbing the part against the manger. In bringing the edges of the wound together, and introducing the pin, care should be taken

9

not to draw the skin too much from the neck,—otherwise blood will insinuate itself between it and the muscles beneath, and cause an unsightly and sometimes troublesome swelling.

The blood should be received into a vessel, the dimensions of which are exactly known, so that the operator may be able to calculate at every period of the bleeding the quantity that is subtracted. Twenty-four hours after the operation, the edges of the wound will have united, and the pin should be withdrawn. When the bleeding is to be repeated, if more than three or four hours have elapsed, a fresh incision will be better than opening the old wound.

For general bleeding the jugular vein is selected as the largest superficial one, and most easily got at. In every affection of the head, and in cases of fever or extended in flammatory action, it is decidedly the best place for bleeding. In local inflammation, blood may be taken from any of the superficial veins. In supposed affection of the shoulder, or of the fore leg, or foot, the *plate* vein, which comes from the inside of the arm, and runs upwards directly in front of it towards the jugular, may be opened. In affections of the hind extremity, blood is sometimes extracted from the *saphœna*, or thigh-vein, which runs across the inside of the thigh. In foot cases it may be taken from the coronet, or, much more safely, from the toe; not by cutting out a piece of the sole at the toe of the frog, which sometimes causes a wound difficult to heal, and followed by festering, and even by canker; but cutting down with a fine drawing-knife, called a searcher, at the union between the crust and the sole at the very toe until the blood flows, and, if necessary, encouraging its discharge by dipping the foot in warm water. The bleeding may be stopped with he greatest ease, by placing a bit of tow in the little groove hat has been cut, and tacking the shoe over it.

TREATMENT OF STRAINS AND WOUNDS.

STRAINS.—Strain is a wrenching or torsion of the mus-cles, tendons or ligaments, and is generally followed by pain and lameness.

"Muscular strains consist of an absolute tearing of the fibrous tissue composing the muscles; or else of such an approach to a disruption as to have an equally prejudicial effect in producing lameness. In some cases the whole of a small bundle of fibres is torn across; but this is not the usual degree in which strains occur, and the most common amount of mischief is only a slight separation of a few of the very small fibres of which the bundle is composed; and this state is then generally spread over a considerable surface, producing considerable soreness from inflamma-tion. Tendinous and ligamentous strains are very similar in their nature, and consist either in an absolute tearing apart of these fibres, or such an approach to this as to cause great inflammation, and consequent incapacity for using them. Sometimes what is supposed to be a strain of the tendon is really an inflammation in its sheath, which causes great swelling and pain, and the limb is thereby rendered quite useless for the time being."*

Of *Shoulder Strain,* Youatt says:

The muscles of the shoulder-blade are occasionally injured by some severe shock. This is effected oftener by a slip or side fall, than by fair, although violent exertion. It is of considerable importance to be able to distinguish this shoulder-lameness from injuries of other parts of the fore extremity. There is not much tenderness, or heat, or swelling. If, on standing before the horse, and looking at the size of the two shoulders, or rather their points, one should appear evidently larger than the other, this must

* Stonehenge.

not be considered as indicative of sprain of the muscles of the shoulder. It probably arises from bruise of the point of the shoulder, which a slight examination will determine.

In sprain of the shoulder the horse evidently suffers extreme pain while moving, and, the muscle underneath being inflamed and tender, he will extend it as little as possible. *He will drag his toe along the ground.* It is in the lifting of the foot that the shoulder is principally moved. If the foot is lifted high, let the horse be ever so lame, the shoulder is little, if at all affected.

In shoulder-lameness, the toe alone rests on the ground. The circumstance which most of all characterizes this affection is, that when the foot is lifted and then brought considerably forward the horse will express very great pain, which he will not do if the lameness is in the foot or the leg.

In sprain of the internal muscles of the shoulder, few local measures can be adopted. The horse should be bled from the vein on the inside of the arm (the plate vein), because the blood is then abstracted more immediately from the inflamed part. A dose of physic should be given, and fomentations applied, principally on the inside of the arm, close to the chest, and the horse should be kept as quiet as possible. The injury is too deeply seated for external stimulants to have very great effect, yet a blister will properly be resorted to, if the lameness is not speedily removed.

Its best treatment consists of rest, cooling diet, blistering, or the use of the seton or rowel.

" *Setons* are pieces of tape or cord, passed by means of an instrument resembling a large needle, either through abscesses or the base of ulcers, with deep sinuses, or between the skin and the muscular or other substances beneath. They are retained there by the ends being tied together, or by a knot in each end. The tape is moved in the wound twice or thrice in the day; occasionally wetted with spirits of turpentine, or some acrid liquid, in order to increase the inflammation which it produces, or the discharge which is intended to be established.

To form a *rowel*, the skin is raised between the finger and thumb, and with a lancet, or with scissors contrived for the purpose, a slit is cut an inch in length. The finger, or the handle of the improved roweling scissors, is introduced, and the skin is forcibly separated from the muscular or cellular substances beneath, until there is a circular cavity two or three inches wide; into this a piece of tow is inserted sufficient to fill it, and previously smeared with blistering ointment. This causes considerable inflammation and discharge. If a little of the tow be left sticking out of the incision, the discharge will conveniently dribble down it. The tow should be changed every day, with or without the ointment, according to the action of the rowel or the urgency of the case." *

If either of these be applied to the front of the shoulder, it will produce such a counter irritation as will reduce the inflammation in the locality of the strain, and aid in its cure. They take the place of the blistering mentioned by Mr. Youatt.

Other Strains.—The following directions of Dr. Dadd, concerning strain of the back, and those given under the head of *shoulder strain*, will serve as a guide to the treatment of all strains, supposing the mode of procedure to be changed as is required by the locality of the affected part:

The diagnostic symptoms of this form of strain are,— pressure over the lumbar region elicits symptoms of pain; the part feels hot; and the horse, when compelled to describe a circle, shows, by the careful manner in which he turns, that it gives him great pain.

* Library of Useful Knowledge.

Treatment—Rest; applications of cold water; light diet; and cream of tartar water as a drink.　One ounce of cream of tartar to a bucket of water daily.　It was customary, but a few years ago, to apply charges, and plasters, to the back, for the cure of strain and lameness.　But the day of plasters in human, as well as veterinary practice, has gone by; they are now only used by those who have never taken the trouble to understand the exhalatory function of the skin,—which salutary function plasters obstruct; the wet sheet next the skin, and a blanket over it, will be more likely to do good than a plaster.　Should the horse show more than ordinary symptoms of pain, a fomentation of hops should be resorted to; if, after a day or so, the pain is still manifest, the trouble is something more than mere strain, and the owner had better consult a medical man.

GALLS OF THE SKIN.

A horse newly put to work, and working in a new harness, or under a new saddle, which touches parts not inured to the pressure, are very likely to have the skin of the back, and shoulders abraded.

Unless there is an absolute necessity for the animal to be used, he should, in all cases, be allowed a few days rest, that the wound may heal and become somewhat hard; and even then, until the hair has fairly grown out, the greatest care must be used to see that the chafing of the harness is entirely obviated, as when the skin is in the least sore it is peculiarly susceptible to irritation.　When a gall is fresh and bleeding, nothing will so soon dry it and cause it to cicatrise, as a little dry table salt sprinkled upon it.

After the wound is in a measure healed, if it be absolutely necessary to use the horse, a careful examination of the harness or saddle should be made, and padding should be taken out, or parts of the leather removed, to prevent any part of it from touching the wound. To prevent friction, when caused by the saddle or collar, there is nothing so useful as a piece of raw sheep-skin, worn with the *flesh* side next to the horse. In riding long journeys, it is the safest plan to have such a protection always under the saddle.

If the chafing is caused by loose straps striking and rubbing against the skin, they should be covered with sheep-skin having its *woolly* side turned towards the horse.

Saddle galls are unlikely to occur if the saddle fits the back, and is left on the horse for at least one hour (and it had better remain on two or three hours) after he is put into the stable. If convenient, he should be saddled half an hour before going out, as it is much better that the saddle should become warm, or slightly softened by the insensible perspiration of the back, before the rider's weight is put upon it.

The following is a good lotion for galls of the skin:

> Sal ammoniac, 1 ounce.
> Vinegar, 4 ounces.
> Spirits of wine, 2 ounces.
> Tincture of arnica, 2 drachms.
> Water, half a pint. Mix.

If no other remedy is used, a mixture of burned leather, gunpowder and lard should be occasionally rubbed on the gall to prevent the growth of white hair.

SIT FASTS, and their treatment, are thus described by Stonehenge:

Sit Fast is merely a name for an obstinate and callous galled-sore, which has repeatedly been rubbed by the saddle, and has become leathery, and disinclined to heal. If time can be allowed, there is nothing like a small quantity of blistering ointment rubbed on; or the application of a small piece of fused potass; or even the nitrate of silver in substance, or blue-stone; all of which will produce a new action in the part, and if followed by rest from the saddle, will generally effect a cure.

FLESH WOUNDS.

The following, on the treatment of ordinary flesh wounds, is from Dadd's Modern Horse Doctor:

INCISED WOUNDS are those inflicted by sharp instruments. On the human body they often heal without any subsequent inflammation beyond what nature sets up in the restorative process; but the difficulty in the horse is, that we cannot always keep theparts in contact, and therefore it is not so easy to unite them. . . . .
If the wound is seen immediately after infliction, and there seems to be the least probability of healing by first intention, we place a twitch on the horse's nose, and examine the part. If there be found neither dirt nor foreign body of any kind, the blood had better not be washed off; for this is the best healing material in the world. The edges are then to be brought together by interrupted sutures, taking care not to include the hair between the edges of the wound, for that would effectually prevent union. Nothing more is needed but to secure the animal so that he cannot get at it. If he is to be kept in the stable, without exercise, for any length of time, he had better be put on half diet.

CONTUSED WOUNDS.—These are generally occasioned by hooks, or some blunt body connected with the harness or vehicle. They generally leave a gaping wound with bruised edges. We have only to remember that nature possesses the power of repairing injuries of this kind—of filling up the parts and covering them with new skin; all we have to do is, to attend to the general health of the animal, and keep the wound in a healthy condition. Our usual application is the compound tincture of myrrh. If the part assume an unhealthy aspect, a charcoal poultice will rectify that. If such cannot be applied, owing to the situation of the wound, dress it with pyroligneous acid.

LACERATED WOUNDS.—Lacerated wounds are gene-rally in the form of a rent rather than cut, inflicted (as we have seen cases) by the caulking of a shoe tearing off the integuments and subcellular tissue, leaving a sort of tri-angular flap. In these cures we generally employ sutures, and treat them the same as incised wounds.

PUNCTURED WOUNDS are those inflicted by a pointed body, as a nail in the foot, the point of a fork, or a splin-ter of wood. These are the most dangerous kinds of wounds, for they are frequently the cause of fistula and locked-jaw.

We make it an invariable rule, in the treatment of punctured wounds, to first examine by probe, or otherwise, and remove any foreign body that may be present, and then poultice with flaxseed, into which we stir a small quantity of fir balsam. In puncture of the foot by nail, instead of plastering it with tar, and forcing a tent into the orifice, and then covering the sole with leather, as most blacksmiths are wont to do, we have the shoe taken off, the foot washed clean, and a moderately warm poult'ce applied, and renewed daily, until the suppurative stage commences. That once established, we consider our patient safe; for many men, as well as animals, have lost their lives from the absorption of pus formed in the wound after the external breach had healed. When a bone is injured by the point of a nail, or fork, the cure is rather tedious; the primary means, however, are the same. The poultices may be followed by astringent injections, as alum water, &c.

9*

In case of injury to the bone, we use pyroligneous acid, to be thrown into the wound by means of a small syringe: If extensive disease of the bone sets in, the services of a veterinary surgeon will be required. A very profuse or unhealthy discharge from a punctured wound must be met by constitutional remedies. Sulphur and sassafras, to the amount of half an ounce each, every other day, to the amount of three or four doses, will arrest the morbid phe- nomenon. The local remedy in all cases of this kind is, diluted acetic or pyroligneous acid.

CRACKED HEELS.—Horses that are so neglected that they have a tendency to inflammation of the legs, and feet, are often troubled with what is known as *cracked heels*, which is a very troublesome affection, and causes a great loss of useful service, in the case of animals otherwise well cared for.

Cracked heels may be cured on the same general principles as are employed in the case of scratches or grease, which is thus described by Percival :

The etiology of grease throws considerable light upon its veritable nature. Horses which are at pasture or in straw yards—in situations, in fact, where heat and cold are not naturally, and cannot be artificially, made suddenly operative upon the heels—rarely have grease. Those that have grease in stables are mostly coach and cart-horses, with thick, fleshy heels and white legs; which are subject to get their heels wet, and do not commonly have such pains bestowed upon them, to dry the legs, as hackneys, hunters, and racers have. Indeed, among the latter, grease is a very uncommon disease. Such horses also stand in stables hot and filthy from dung and urine, the very ex- halations from the litter of which proves an additional excitement.

Grease formerly made great ravages in the English cavalry and ordnance service; whereas, at the present day the disease is scarcely known. This change for the better is ascribed to three causes;—to proper ventilation of the stables; the greater attention paid to grooming; and to the presence of a veterinary surgeon, who checks, at the onset, such a casual occurrence.

The best remedy for this disease is probably the following, which has been recommended by Professor Morton, of the Royal Veterinary College:

> Pyroligneous acid,)
> Linseed oil, } . of each equal parts.
> Turpentine,)

Mix; let the heels first be washed with lukewarm water and Castile soap; after wiping them dry, apply the mixture. Repeat night and morning.

In order to keep down morbid granulations—denominated by some "*proud flesh*"—the parts may be sprinkled daily with one of the following articles:

> Powdered bloodroot.
> "   burnt alum,
> "   bayberry bark.

Put on a good coating of one of the above articles; cover the sore with dry lint; and apply a bandage over all. It should be borne in mind that bandages should always be dispensed with, if possible; for they invariably irritate and inflame whatever parts they are applied to. This is owing to the high state of sensibility in the skin of the horse.*

CLIPPING AND SINGEING.

It has for a long time been the custom to clip the coats of many well kept horses in the fall of the year, that they may present a less shaggy appearance during the winter months than if their hair were allowed to grow to its natu-

* From Dadd's Modern Horse Doctor.

ral length. For this practice there has been recently substituted that of singeing with burning gas, by means of an
apparatus made for the purpose, which may be obtained
at most saddlers' in cities where gas is consumed.

This is an operation which requires to be performed by
a person who thoroughly understands it, and it is unnecessary to give any directions for it in this work.

There have been opposed to this practice many objections, most of which were groundless, in the case of horses
which are highly prized and proportionately well cared
for. It would, of course, be unwise to apply it to horses
receiving only ordinary care, such as working-horses; but
for all that are kept for pleasure driving, or for fast work,
there can be no doubt that it is judicious, inasmuch as it
gives them a much better appearance, prevents their breaking out in cold sweats in the stable, or carrying wet coats
after perspiring freely. Indeed, it is at least questionable,
whether in the case of all horses that are not required from
the nature of their work to stand, unblanketed, in the cold,
it would not cause a great saving of their natural heat and
strength by keeping their coats generally in a dryer condition.
To prove that there is less danger of taking cold in consequence of this treatment than would be supposed, the following extract is made from an English work on "Stable
Practice" (by Cecil):

I was returning home one evening, in the month of
November, and, passing through a gentleman's park under
some trees, the branches of which I could not discern, in
consequence of the excessive darkness, I was thereby pulled
off my hack, a mare which had been clipped only the day
previous. This disaster gave her her liberty; and, although
I obtained the aid of the keeper, and other assistance, I
could not succeed in finding the mare. She therefore remained in the park, without shelter, all night. Moreover,

it was bitterly cold, foggy, and frosty. When daylight appeared, the mare was discovered; and I fully expected, especially as I had ridden her fast up to the time we parted company, that she would be laid up with a violent cold. That, however, was not the case. On her return home she had a bran mash, with two ounces of spirit of nitric ether, and, on the following day, gave no evidence of the slightest indisposition. Had she not been clipped I am inclined to think the result would not have been so fortunate; because, from the pace I had ridden her, with the perspiration in the coat, she would have been wet all night, whereas she quickly became dry; hence the coldness of the atmosphere had not such an injurious effect as might have been expected."

TRIMMING THE HAIR OF THE LEGS AND HEELS.

On the subject of trimming the hair of the legs and heels, we find the following sensible remarks in Stewart's Stable Book:

The hair of the fetlock, the hollow of the pastern, and the posterior aspect of the legs, is longer on heavy draught-horses than on those of finer bone. It is intended to keep the legs warm, and perhaps, in some degree, to defend them from external violence. It becomes much shorter and less abundant after the horse is stabled, kept warm, well fed, and well groomed. The simple act of washing the legs, or rubbing them, tends to make the hair short and thin, and to keep it so. Nevertheless, it is a very common practice, especially in coaching-stables, to clip this hair away almost close to the root.

The heels* are trimmed in three different ways: the most common and the easiest is, to clip away all the long

* The word *heel* is applied to the back and hollow of the pastern. In this place, all that is said of the heels is applicable to the legs.

hair, near or close to the roots;—another way is, to switch
the heels,—that is, to shorten the hair without leaving any
mark of the scissors; the groom seizes the hair and cuts
off a certain portion in the same manner that he shortens
a switch tail;—the third mode is, to pull the long hairs out
by the roots. Switching and pulling, which is little practised, are generally confined to the foot-lock; some neat
operators combine these different modes so well, that the
hair is rendered thin and short without presenting any
very visible marks of the alteration. By means of an iron
comb with small teeth and a pair of good scissors, the hair
may be shortened without setting it on end or leaving scis-
sor marks, but every groom can not do this.

When the horse is carefully tended after his work is
over, his legs quickly and completely dried, the less hair
he has about them the better. The moisture which that
little takes up can be easily removed: both the skin and
the hair can be made perfectly dry before evaporation
begins, or proceeds so far as to deprive the legs of their
heat. It is the cold produced by evaporation that does all
the mischief.

Whenever the legs *must* be dried by manual labor, they
should have little hair about them. But in coaching and
posting-studs, and among cart-horses, the men can not, or
will not, bestow this care upon the legs; they have not
time, and they would not do it if they had time. A team
of four horses, perhaps, comes in at once, the legs all wet,
and, it may be, the whole skin drenched in rain. Before
eight of the legs can be rubbed dry, the other eight have
become almost dry of themselves, and are nearly as cold
as they can be. These horses should never have the heels
trimmed: they cannot have too much hair about them.
They do indeed soak up a great deal of water, and remain
wet for a much longer time than those that are nearly

naked; but still they never become so soon nor so intensely cold.

DRESSING THE MANE, TAIL, AND EARS.

THE MANE.—When it is desired to make the mane lie on the opposite side from that toward which it naturally grows, it should be combed and wetted several times a day. This will suffice if it is not very short and bushy; in such case, some of the hair may be pulled out from the under part, on the side toward which it is desired to make it grow; this will generally cause it to fall easily. If this does not suffice, the mane should be plaited in eight or ten braids, the end of each being loaded with a bit of lead. When the mane becomes too long, or too thick, a few of the hairs should be pulled out, but it is necessary that this should be done with care and judgment.

THE TAIL.—If the tail of a horse is tolerably good, it may be kept in proper order by being combed daily with a strong comb. If the hair is inclined to be too wiry, and to stand on end, it may sometimes be made to lie well by being moistened, and either tied together at the ends or bound around with a straw rope. If the tail become unhealthy (which may be known by a dry scurf in the hair, accompanied by itching), it should never be combed, but should be dressed by frequent wiping down with wet straw. It is not the custom in this country to square the end of the tail, and the only directions, therefore, which it is necessary to give, are what refers to the pointing of the switch tail. To do this properly requires some skill. The tail must be taken in the left hand, a small portion at a time, and the knife, which is held in the right hand, with its edge resting directly across the hair, should be moved up and down over the hair in such a way as to rasp it off, leaving the ends irregular in their lengths.

THE EAR.—Custom to the contrary, notwithstanding, the hair on the inner side of the ear of the horse should never be cut away. It is necessary to protect that delicate organ from dust, rain, and cold. The only treatment which should be allowed, is to close the edges of the ear together, and to clip off the hair that projects beyond them.

ADMINISTERING MEDICINE TO THE HORSE.

On this subject Stonehenge gives the following directions:

The most common form in which medicine is given to the horse is by means of the ball,—an oblong mass of rather soft consistence, yet tough enough to retain its shape, and wrapped up in thin paper for that purpose. The usual weight of the ball is from half an ounce to an ounce, but they may be given of a larger size, if they are made longer but not wider. Every groom should know how to give a ball, which is managed either with or without a balling-iron, an instrument which is seldom wanted, and which sometimes occasions considerable mischief to the roof of the horse's mouth. Occasionally a horse cannot be managed by any other means; but, generally speaking, they are only an excuse for bad management. In giving a ball in the ordinary way, the horse's tongue is drawn out of his mouth on the off or right side, and held there firmly with the left hand grasping it as near the root as possible, but to a certain extent yielding to the movement of the horse's head, so as not absolutely to tear it out. While the tongue is thus held, the ball is placed between the fingers and thumb of the right hand, extended in a wedge-like or conical form, so as to pass as far down the swallow as possible; and the hand in this form, with the arm bared to the shoulder, is carried over the root of the tongue till it feels the impediment caused by the contraction of the swallow when the fingers leave the ball there, and the hand is withdrawn quickly yet smoothly, while at the same moment the tongue is released, and the head is held up till the ball is seen to pass down the gullet on the left side of the neck, after which the head may be released. When the balling-iron is used, the oval ring of which it is composed is passed into the mouth, so as to keep it open, being first well guarded with tow or cloths wrapped round it; the handle is then held in the left hand, together with the halter, so as to steady the head, and yet to keep the horse from biting; and while thus held the hand can freely be carried over the tongue, and the ball be deposited in the pharynx. When a horse is very determined, it is sometimes necessary to keep the iron in the mouth by means of the check-pieces of an ordinary bridle buckled to the sides of the oval ring; but this expedient is seldom required if the halter is firmly grasped with the handle of the iron. In the usual way the horse to be *balled* is turned round in his stall, which prevents his backing away from the groom; and if the latter is not tall enough, he may stand upon a *sound* stable-bucket, turned upside down. Balls should be recently made, as they soon spoil by keeping; not only losing their strength, but also becoming so hard as to be almost insoluble in the stomach, and frequently passing through the bowels nearly as they went into the mouth. When hard they are also liable to stick in the horse's gullet. If ammonia, or any other strong stimulant, is given in this way, the horse should not have his stomach quite empty, but should have a little gruel or water just before; for if this is put off till afterwards, the nauseous taste of the ball almost always prevents his drinking. When arsenic forms an ingredient of the ball, it should be given soon after a feed of corn; or a quart or two of gruel should be given instead, just before the ball.

The administration of a drench is a much more troublesome affair than the giving of a ball; and in almost all
cases more or less of the dose is wasted. Sometimes, however, a liquid medicine is to be preferred, as in colic or
gripes, when the urgent nature of the symptoms demands
a rapidly-acting remedy, which a ball, from its requiring
time to dissolve, is not; and, besides this, a ball cannot
contain any of the sprituous cordials. The best instrument
for giving a drench is the horn of the ox, cut obliquely, so
as to form a spout. Bottles are sometimes used in an emergency, but their fragile nature always renders them dangerous. In giving a drench, the tongue is held in the same
way as for the delivery of a ball, but the head must be
more elevated; the drench is then carefully poured into
the throat, after which the tongue is let go, but the head
still kept up till it is all swallowed. Allowance should
always be made for some waste in giving a drench.

The mode of managing all horses while 'in physic,' is that
which I shall here describe. In all cases, if possible, the
horse should be prepared by bran mashes, given for two
or three nights, so as to make the bowels rather loose than
otherwise, and thus allow the dose to act without undue
forcing of the impacted *fœces* backwards. If physic is
given without this softening process, the stomach and bowels pour out a large secretion of fluid, which is forced back
upon the rectum, and met by a solid obstacle which it
takes a long time to overcome, and during that interval the
irritating purge is acting upon the lining membrane, and
often produces excessive inflammation of it. Purging
physic should generally be given in the middle of the
day, after which the horse should remain in the stable, and
have chilled water as often as he will drink it, with bran
mashes. By the next morning he will be ready to be
walked out for an hour, which will set the bowels to act

if they have not already begun. It is usual to tie up the tail with a tape or string, so as to keep it clean. The horse should be warmly clothed, and if the physic does not act with an hour's walk, he may be gently trotted for a short distance, and then taken home; and, if still obstinate, he may be exercised again in the afternoon. As soon as the physic operates pretty freely the horse is to be taken into his stable, *and not stirred out again, under any pretence whatever,* for forty-eight hours after it has "set," or, in common language, stopped acting. When the purging has ceased, the mashes may be continued for twenty-four hours, with a little corn added to them, and a quantity of hay. The water, during the whole time, should be in small quantities, and chilled; and the clothing should be rather warmer than usual, taking great care to avoid draughts of cold air. Every horse requires at least three days' rest for a dose of physic, in order to avoid risk of mischief.

The mode of giving a clyster is now rendered simple enough, because a pump and tube are expressly made for the purpose; and the groom has only to pass the greased end of the tube carefully into the rectum, for about eight or nine inches, and then pump the liquid up until a sufficient quantity is given. From a gallon to six quarts is the average quantity, but in colic a much larger amount is required.

Lotions are applied by means of calico bandages, if used to the legs; or by a piece of calico tied over the part, if to any other surface.

Fomentations are very serviceable to the horse in all recent external inflammations, and it is astonishing what may be done by a careful groom, with warm water alone, and a good-sized sponge. Sometimes by means of an elastic tube and stop cock warm water is conducted in a continuous stream over an inflamed part, as in severe wounds, &c., in which this plan is found wonderfully successful in allaying the irritation, which is so likely to occur in the nervous system of the horse. A vessel of warm water is placed above the level of the horse's back, and a small India-rubber tube leads from it to a sponge fixed above the part, from which the water runs to the ground as fast as it is over-filled. It is a plan very easily carried out by any person of ordinary ingenuity.

DISEASES OF THE FEET.

THRUSH is inflammation of the lower surface of the sensible frog, which while so inflamed secretes *pus*, instead of horn; this offensive matter being exuded from the cleft of the frog renders it sensitive to pain. The direct cause of thrush is doubtless too much secretion, especially of a foul kind; but this result will never occur unless the horse is, or has been, so shod, as to prevent a natural expansion of the foot; and even where thrush has appeared it may sometimes be cured by the adoption of the "one-sided nailing."

CORNS in the feet of horses are injuries to the sole, usually occurring in the angle between the crust and bar on the inner side of the fore foot. They are caused by the pressure of the shoe, or of gravel which is lodged under the shoe. They are easily prevented, and when they occur they are a disgrace to the smith who shoes the animal, or to the groom who neglects to clean out the gravel which accumulates between the shoe and the foot.

They may be cured, if recent, or greatly relieved, if of long standing, by a proper adaptation of the shoe. The sole should be (in the sound foot, as well as in that which has corns,) cut away from the angle in question until it is lower than both the crust and the bar, and these should be so prepared as to afford an elevated support for the shoe.

which, if properly made, will rest always upon them and will be in no danger of pressing upon the sole at the "corn place." If the case is a bad one, and if the frog is sufficiently sound to withstand the pressure, a bar-shoe may be used, which is chambered over the affected point, and so formed as to rest upon the frog. This treatment, however, should not be constant, as the frog would not long bear the pressure, and as the heel being relieved from pressure might become softened, and thus induce permanent lameness. There are few cases in which a bar-shoe, thus formed, can be used for more than two successive shoeings.

If a horse, whose feet are already sound, be shod according to the directions given in the chapter on that subject, there need be no fear of his having corns, if proper care be taken to prevent an accumulation of gravel under the shoe.

CUTTING, or INTERFERING, is the striking of the fetlock joint with the opposite foot, or its shoe. It arises sometimes from a defective formation of the legs, but generally from improper shoeing. On this subject Youatt says:

Many expedients used to be tried to remove this; the inside heel has been raised and lowered, and the outside raised and lowered; and sometimes one operation has succeeded, and sometimes the contrary; and there was no point so involved in obscurity, or so destitute of principles to guide the practitioner. The most successful remedy, and that which in the great majority of cases supersedes all others, is Mr. Turner's shoe, of equal thickness from heel to toe, and having but one nail on the inside of the shoe, and that near the toe; care being taken that the shoe shall not extend beyond the edge of the crust, and that the crust shall be rasped a little at the quarters.

When the leg is at all swollen from the cutting, it should be protected by a boot, which should in all cases remain on until the cure is complete, as if the swelling remained it might throw the parts so far into the line of the other foot, when in motion, as to cause the cutting to continue in spite of every attempt to prevent it.

SPEEDY CUT is a cut of the knee, by the striking of the shoe of the opposite foot, when the horse is cantering, or throwing his feet very high in the trot. The only remedy, when the shoeing has been properly performed, and the cutting still continues, is to use the boot on the wounded knee; but, in such a case of constitutional defect, the boot can never be dispensed with, as an unlucky step might at any time cause the horse to fall from the pain occasioned by the blow.

NAIL PRICKING, from careless shoeing, is very common, especially in country districts, where the smith is very often guided only by the horse flinching, in deciding whether a nail has gone too deep. Injury from these causes is not always perceptible at the time of shoeing, but it will be certain to appear in a few days. When an injury arising from this cause is detected, the shoe should be removed and the foot examined, that the extent of the injury may be learned. Stonehenge gives the following directions for the treatment of such cases:

On removing the shoe it is found that there is great tenderness at some particular part of the foot, and sometimes a slight bulging; but this is seldom evident so soon. It is the better plan to place the foot in a cold bran poultice, without a shoe on, and wait for a day or two, when, if the foot continues very hot, the smith must pare down the horn over the suspected place, and let out the matter, if there is any; or, if necessary, bleed at the toe, which is likely to relieve the inflammation, and prevent suppuration, if it has not already occurred. If matter has formed, and is let out a little, friar's balsam is pushed into the abscess on a piece of lint, and the shoe tacked on; but the lint must be so left as to be capable of being pulled out on the next day, so as to leave a clear opening for the matter to escape. In a few days the shoe must be taken off again, and any ragged pieces of horn removed, as well as the opening enlarged, if necessary. Sometimes a prick occurs from a nail picked up on the road, and then the accident must be treated exactly as if it occurred in shoeing.

QUITTOR is a disease very nearly allied to, and frequently growing out of, neglected cases of nail-pricking. Concerning this disease, Dr. Dadd writes as follows: *

Quittor is a fistulous opening running between the sensible and insensible *laminæ* of the foot; the opening, or *sinus*, runs in various directions downward; at other times, the lateral cartilages are in connection with it, and become diseased. It generally makes its appearance on the inside of the foot, near the matrix of the hoof. In such case, its origin is from bruise or wound. It arises also from pricks in shoeing, gravel, neglected corns, &c. Should a nail enter the sensitive laminæ of the foot, and cause suppuration, and the lower outlet become plugged up, the matter moves upward, burrowing through the tissues, until it gains exit above the hoof.

Treatment.—We first examine the sinus by means of a small-sized, flexible bougie, such as are used on young persons. Being *flexible*, we are enabled to trace the cavity, whatever direction it may take. Having discovered that, we make up our mind as to the treatment. Should it descend towards the sole, it is caused either by prick, corn, or gravel, which can be ascertained on careful examination. In order to make such, we remove the shoe, pare the foot, and perhaps poultice it, with the double object of softening the hoof and removing obstructions to the lower outlet, if any there be. Whether the cause be evident or not, we

* Dadd's Modern Horse Doctor.

waste no time in injecting the sinus, (which is practised by many,) but make a small opening in the sole, as near the base of the sinus as possible, and invite a discharge from it by means of a poultice placed only in contact with the sole. A free discharge once secured from the lower outlet, we have no fears of a cure. So soon as a discharge sets up, inject from below strong tincture of bloodroot, two or three times, and then sprinkle some bloodroot in the cavity; there is no need of any bandage; let the matter have free vent. The upper orifice will now close; it is only necessary to moisten this region with compound tincture of aloes, or some other traumatic.

During this treatment the horse must be kept on light, soft food, and his bowels must be kept in a somewhat relaxed condition.

OVER-REACHING consists in the striking of the heel of the fore foot with the toe of the hind shoe. It seldom occurs except in saddle-horses which are too slow in moving their fore feet, and this faulty action may be remedied by training the horse to a light "gathered" movement, as directed in the chapter on Baucher's method of training. When a wound has been inflicted by over-reaching, the best treatment is to dry up the discharge as soon as possible, which may best be done by the use of tincture of arnica, of full strength, or, in the absence of this, of gunpowder. If the discharge is allowed to continue, it is very apt to degenerate into *Quittor*, and to cause much trouble.

The cut of the heel in over-reaching is caused not by the clip of the hind shoe, but by the back part of the web at the toe of the shoe, which, being made square at first, is soon worked to a sharp edge. If, when the shoe is made, that part of the web be filed to a round edge, there will be little danger of a severe cut.

CLICKING, OR FORGING, which is a limited over-reach,

and which is often noticed in trotting horses, whether under the saddle or in harness, is a striking of the shoe of the fore foot with the toe of the shoe of the hind foot. The parts of the fore shoe which are thus struck may be known from being worn brighter than the rest of the shoe, and if these parts are filed away the diffiulty will generally cease.

STOPPING THE FEET, which belongs to "Grooming" rather than to "Farrieing," consists of filling the space between the shoe and the hoof, and all within the inner circumference of the shoe, with some material which will gradually impart moisture to the foot. It should always be resorted to whenever there is the least tendency to dryness or fever· in the feet, and there is an advantage in stopping the feet of all horses as often as every other night. The stopping should be very carefully removed before the horse goes out.

The best material for stopping are:

1—Pure cow-dung,—recently dropped.

2—Wet clay.

3—Cow-dung and clay, mixed.

4—Wet oakum.

5—Linseed meal.

6—A mixture of tar, tallow, clay and cow-dung.

A change from one of these to another will be found beneficial, though, in the country, cow-dung is usually the most convenient, and it is quite as good as any cf the others.

10

CHAPTER XV.

HOW TO SHOE A HORSE.

ALTHOUGH it is an almost universal custom to entrust the shoeing of horses to the Knight of the Hammer and Tongs who happens to be nearest to one's stable, and to pay but little regard to the manner in which the work is done, there are very few who are not ready to admit that the operation is frequently performed in an unskilful manner, and that their horses would be more serviceable, and would perform their work with much greater comfort to themselves, if their owners knew exactly how and when the shoeing should be done; and would insist on its being done at the right time, and in the right manner.

There is hardly any other class of mechanics who combine so much ignorance of the principles on which their art is founded, with so much conceit of their knowledge, as do ordinary horse-shoers; and it should be one of the first duties of the horse owner to inform himself of the construction and nature of the horse's foot, the reasons why shoeing is necessary at all, what parts of the foot it protects, what is the best form of shoe to effect the purpose, how it may be best fastened to the foot, and how often it should be removed.

To illustrate these fundamental points, cuts are here introduced, showing the construction of the horse's foot.

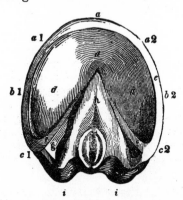

FIG. 8.

Shows the ground surface of the hoof prepared for receiving a shoe; and marks very distinctly the difference between the curvature of the outer and inner quarters.

a The toe—rasped away to receive the turned-up shoe. *a 1.* The *inner* toe. *a 2.* The *outer* toe. *b 1.* The *inner* quarter. *b 2.* The *outer* quarter. *c 1.* The *inner* heel. *c 2.* The *outer* heel. *d d d.* The sole. *e e.* The crust or wall of the hoof. *f f.* The bars. *g g.* The commissures. *h k l.* The frog.
{ *h.* The part immediately under the navicular joint.
{ *k.* The oval cleft of the frog.
{ *l.* The elevated boundary of the cleft.
i i. The bulbs of the heels.

As the various parts of the horse's foot cannot be better lescribed for the purposes of this work than they have been by Mr. Miles (from whose manual the above cuts are transferred), extracts are here made from his description:

The hoof is divided into horny crust or wall, sole, and frog.

The horny crust is secreted by the numerous blood-vessels of that soft protruding band which encircles the upper edge of the hoof, immediately beneath the termination of the hair; and is divided into toe, quarters, heels, and bars   Its texture is insensible, but elastic throughout its whole extent; and, yielding to the weight of the horse, allows the horny sole to descend, whereby much inconvenient concussion of the internal parts of the foot is avoided. But if a large portion of the circumference of the foot be fettered by iron and nails, it is obvious that that portion, at least, cannot expand as before; and the beautiful and efficient apparatus for effecting this necessary elasticity, being no longer allowed to act by reason of these restraints, becomes altered in structure: and the continued operation of the same causes, in the end, circumscribes the elasticity to those parts alone where no nails have been driven,— giving rise to a train of consequences destructive to the

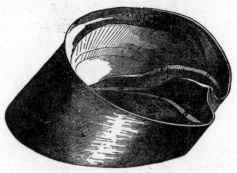

FIG. 9.

a. Is a broad flat mass of horn, projecting upwards into the middle of the elastic cushion, and is called the "frog stay."

b b. Are two horny projections rising into the cavity of the hoof formed by the commissures.

c c. Are portions of the same projections, and are situated just under the two ends of the navicular bone, and mark the point on either side where diminution in the natural elasticity of the fatty frog would be felt with the greatest severity by the navicular joint : for under the most favorable circumstances, the quantity of cushion between these points and the navicular joint cannot be very large ; and hence the importance of our doing all we can to preserve its elasticity as long as possible.

soundness of the foot, and fatal to the usefulness of the horse.*

The toe of the fore foot is the thickest and strongest portion of the hoof, and is in consequence less expansive than any other part, and therefore better calculated to resist the effect of the nails and shoe. The thickness of the horn gradually diminishes towards the quarters and

* The horse's foot, and how to keep it sound, with illustrations, by Wm Miles, Esq

heels, particularly on the inner side of the foot, whereby
the power of yielding and expanding to the weight of the
horse is proportionably increased, clearly indicating that
those parts cannot be nailed to an unyielding bar of iron,
without a most mischievous interference with the natural
functions of the foot. In the hind foot, the greatest thickness of horn will be found at the quarters and heels, and
not, as in the fore foot, at the toe. This difference in the
thickness of horn is beautifully adapted to the inequality of
the weight which each has to sustain, the force with which

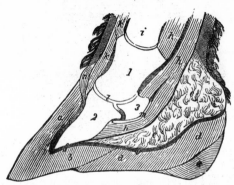

Fig. 10.—A section of the Foot.

1. The coronet bone. 2. The coffin bone. 3. The navicular bone.
a. The wall. b. The sole. c. The cleft of the frog. d d. The frog. e e. The fatty
   frog, or elastic cushion. f. The sensitive sole. g. The sensitive frog. h h h. Tendons of the muscles which bend the foot. i. Part of the pastern bone.
   k k. Tendons of the muscles which extend the foot. l. The coffin joint. m. The
   navicular joint. n. The coronary substance. o. The sensible laminæ, or
   covering of the coffin bone.

it is applied, and the portions of the hoof upon which it
falls. The toe of the fore foot encounters the combined
force and weight of the fore hand and body, and consequently in a state of nature is exposed to considerable
wear and tear, and calls for greater strength and substance
of horn than is needed by any portion of the hind foot,
where the duty of supporting the hinder parts alone is

distributed over the quarters and heels of both sides of the foot.

The *bars* are continuations of the wall, reflected at the heels towards the centre of the foot, where they meet in a point, leaving a triangular space between them for the frog.

The whole inner surface of the horny crust, from the centre of the toe to the point where the bars meet, is everywhere lined with innumerable narrow, thin and projecting horny plates, which extend in a slanting direction from the upper edge of the wall to the line of junction between it and the sole, and possess great elasticity. These projecting plates are the means of greatly extending the surface of attachment of the hoof to the coffin bone, which is likewise covered by a similar arrangement of projecting plates, but of a highly vascular and sensitive character; and these, dovetailing with the horny projections above-named, constitute a union combining strength and elasticity in a wonderful degree.

The horny sole covers the whole inferior surface of the foot, excepting the frog. In a well-formed foot it presents an arched appearance and possesses considerable elasticity, by virtue of which it ascends and descends, as the weight above is either suddenly removed from it, or forcibly applied to it. This descending property of the sole calls for our especial consideration in directing the form of the shoe: for, if the shoe be so formed that the horny sole rests upon it, it cannot descend lower; and the sensible sole above, becoming squeezed between the edges of the coffin bone and the horn, produces inflammation, and perhaps abscess. The effect of this squeezing of the sensible sole is most commonly witnessed at the angle of the inner heel, where the descending heel of the coffin bone, forcibly pressing the vascular sole upon the horny sole, ruptures a small blood-vessel, and produces what is called a corn, but which is, in fact, a bruise.

The horny frog occupies the greater part of the triangular space between the bars, and extends from the hindermost part of the foot to the centre of the sole, just over the point where the bars meet; but is united to them only at their upper edge: the sides remain unattached and separate, and form the channels called the "Commissures."

If we carefully observe the form and size of the frog in the foot of a colt of from four to five years old, at its first shoeing, and then note the changes which it undergoes as the shoeings are repeated, we shall soon be convinced that a visible departure from a state of health and nature is taking place. At first it will be found large and full, with considerable elasticity; the cleft oval in form, open, and expanding, with a continuous, well-defined, and somewhat elevated boundary; the bulbs at the heels fully developed, plump and rounded; and the whole mass occupying about one-sixth of the circumference of the foot. By degrees the fulness and elasticity will be observed to have diminished; the bulbs at the heels will shrink, and lose their plumpness; the cleft will become narrower, its oval form disappear, the back part of its boundary give way, and it will dwindle into a narrow crack, extended back between the wasted, or perhaps obliterated bulbs, presenting only the miserable remains of a frog, such as may be seen in the feet of most horses long accustomed to be shod.

The bones proper to the foot are three in number,—viz., the coffin bone, the navicular bone, and part of the coronet bone: they are contained within the hoof, and combine to form the coffin joint; but the smallest of them, the navicular bone, is of far more importance as connected with our subject of shoeing, than either of the others; for upon the healthy condition of this bone, and the joint formed between it and the tendon, which passes under it to the coffin bone, and is called the navicular joint, mainly depends the usefulness of the horse to man.

This small bone, which in a horse sixteen hands high measures only two and a quarter inches in its longer diameter, three-fourths of an inch at the widest part of its shorter diameter, and half an inch in thickness in the centre, its thickest part, has the upper and under surfaces and part of one of the sides overlaid with a thin coating of gristle, and covered by a delicate secreting membrane, very liable upon the slightest injury to become inflamed; it is so placed in the foot as to be continually exposed to danger; being situated across the hoof, behind the coffin bone, and immediately under the coronet bone; whereby it is compelled to receive nearly the whole weight of the horse each time that the opposite foot is raised from the ground.

The coffin bone consists of a body and wings; and is fitted into the hoof, which it closely resembles in form. Its texture is particularly light and spongy, arising from the quantity of canals or tubes that traverse its substance in every direction, affording to numerous blood-vessels and nerves a safe passage to the sensitive and vascular parts surrounding it; while the unyielding nature of the bone effectually protects them from compression or injury, under every variety of movement of the horse.

In an unshod foot, the front and sides of the coffin bone are deeply furrowed and roughened, to secure the firmer attachment of the vascular membranous structure, by which the bone is clothed; but in the bone of a foot that has been frequently shod, this appearance is greatly changed, the furrows and roughness giving place to a comparatively smooth surface. This change I imagine to be produced by the shoe limiting, if not destroying, the expansive power of that part of the horn to which it is nailed; whereby a change of structure in the membrane itself, as well as absorption of the attaching portions of the bone, is induced; for it is an invariable law of the animal economy not to continue to unemployed structures the same measure of efficient reparation that is extended to parts constantly engaged in performing their allotted tasks. The shoe restricts or prevents expansion; while nature, as the secret influence is called, immediately sets to work to simplify the apparatus for producing the expansion, which art has thus rendered impracticable, and substitutes for it a new structure, less finely organized, but admirably suited to the altered condition of the parts.

The wings extend from the body of the bone directly backwards, and support the "lateral cartilages" of the foot.

The sensitive sole, or, as it is sometimes called, the fleshy sole, is about the eighth of an inch thick, and is almost entirely made up of blood-vessels and nerves; it is one of the most vascular and sensitive parts of the body, and is attached to the lower edge of the sensitive covering of the coffin bone,—to the bars,—and point of the frog,—and also with great firmness to the whole of the arched under-surface of the coffin bone.

The sensitive frog includes not only the part corresponding to the sensitive sole, but also the peculiar spongy elastic substance which intervenes between it and the navicular joint, and fills the space between the cartilages. The proper sensitive frog is thicker, and less finely organized, than the sensitive sole, possessing fewer blood-vessels and nerves.

Before treating of the preparation of the foot for the reception of a shoe, it is desirable to correct the generally received, but erroneous opinion, that the shape of a per-

10*

fect foot is circular, or very nearly so. It is this opinion
that leads the generality of smiths to direct their energies
towards reducing the foot to that shape as soon as possible;
indeed, so impatient are some persons to commence this
work of setting nature right, that they cause their colts'
feet to be "*put in order*,"—as the mischievous interference
is called,—long before the process of "breaking" has rendered the evil of shoeing necessary. There are very few
things so little varied in nature as the form of the *ground*
surface of horses' feet; for whether the hoof be high
heeled and upright,—or low-heeled and flat,—large or
small,—broad or narrow,—the identical form of ground surface is maintained in each, so long as it is entirely left to
nature's guidance. The outer quarter, back to the heel,
is curved considerably and abruptly outwards, while the
inner quarter is carried back in a gradual and easy curve.
The advantage of this form is so obvious, that it is matter
for wonder it should ever be interfered with. The enlarged outer quarter extends the base and increases the
hold of the foot upon the ground; while the straighter
inner quarter lessens the risk of striking the foot against
the opposite leg.

The inclination of the front of the horny crust of the
foot should be at an angle of about 45 degrees. If the
foot is much steeper than this it is very liable to contract,
while, if it is much more slanting, it constitutes what is
called the "oyster shell" foot, in which there is an undue
flatness of the sole, and a tendency to pumiced feet.

Bearing in mind, now, the nature of the various parts of
the foot of the horse, we will consider the manner in
which the practical operations of shoeing should be conducted, and the reasons for adopting some improvements
on the general custom of our smiths.

Before removing the old shoe, care should be taken to

raise all the clinches of the nails to prevent injury to the crust, and to avoid giving pain to the horse; even after clinches are raised, if the shoe cannot be easily drawn off, those nails which seem to hold most firmly should be punched, or drawn out, that the shoe may be removed without injury to the hoof, and without weakening the nail hold for the new shoeing.

The shoe being removed, the *edge* of the crust should be well rasped to remove so much of the horn as would have been worn away by contact with the ground, had it been un-shod. In no case should the rasp be used on the surface of the hoof, except to make the necessary depressions for the clinches, after the new shoe has been put on, and to shape the hoof *below* the line of the clinches of the nails. The hoof, above this line, will inevitably be injured by such treatment, which is one of the most fertile sources of brit-tleness of the horn, which often results in " sand crack."

The operation of paring out the horse's foot is a matter requiring both skill and judgment, and is, moreover, a work of some labor, when properly performed. It will be found that the operator errs much oftener by removing *too little* than *too much;* at least it is so with the parts which ought to be removed, which are almost as hard and unyielding as a flint, and, in their most favorable state, re-quire considerable exertion to cut through.

It would be impossible to frame any rule applicable to paring out of all horses' feet, or, indeed, of the feet of the same horse at all times: for instance, it is manifestly un-wise to pare the sole as thin in a hot, dry season, when the roads are broken up, and strewed with loose stones, as in a moderately wet one, when they are well bound and even; for, in the former case, the sole is in perpetual danger of being bruised by violent contact with the loose stones, and consequently needs a thicker layer of horn for its protection; while the latter case offers the most favorable surface that most of our horses ever have to travel upon, and should be taken advantage of for a thorough paring out of the sole, in order that the internal parts of the foot may derive the full benefit arising from an elastic and descending sole; a state of things very essential to the due performance of their separate functions. Again: in horses with upright feet and high heels, horn grows very abundantly, especially towards the toe; and such are always benefited by having the toe shortened, the heels lowered, and the sole well pared out; while in horses with flat feet and low heels horn grows sparingly; and the toe of such feet, being always weak, will admit of very little shortening. Such heels being already too low, should scarcely be touched with the rasp; and the sole presents such a small quantity of dead horn, that the knife should be used with great discretion.

The corners formed by the junction of the crust and bars should be well pared out, particularly on the inside; for this is the common seat of corn, and any accumulation of horn in this situation must increase the risk of bruising the sensible sole between the inner point or heel of the coffin bone and the horny sole. I very much doubt either the utility or wisdom of leaving the bars projecting beyond the surface of the sole; it cannot possibly increase the power of resisting contraction, and this projecting rim is left exposed to the danger of being broken and bruised by contact with stones and other hard substances; and it is further attended with the disadvantage of making the cleaning out of these corners a work of considerable ingenuity with so unwieldy an instrument as a common drawing-knife. I prefer paring them down to a level with the sole, or very nearly so; avoiding, however, every approach to what is called "opening out the heels." a most reprehensible practice, which means cutting away the sides of the bars, so as to show an apparent increase of width between the heels, which may for the time deceive the eye; but it is a mere illusion, purchased at the expense of impaired power of resistance in the bars, and ultimate contraction of the feet. It is self-evident, that the removing any portion from the sides of the bars must diminish their substance, and render them weaker, and consequently less able to resist contraction.

Youatt says, on the same subject:

The act of paring is a work of much more labor than the proprietor of the horse often imagines. The smith, except he is overlooked, will frequently give himself as little trouble about it as he can; and that portion of horn which, in the unshod foot, would be worn away by contact with the ground, is suffered to accumulate month after month, until the elasticity of the sole is destroyed, and it can no longer descend, and its other functions are impeded, and foundation is laid for corn, and contraction, and navicular disease, and inflammation. That portion of horn should be left on the foot, which will defend the internal parts from being bruised, and yet suffer the external sole to descend. How is this to be ascertained? The strong pressure of the thumb of the smith will be the best guide. The buttress, that most destructive of all instruments, being, except on very particular occasions, banished from every respectable forge, the smith sets to work with his drawing-knife and removes the growth of horn, until the sole will yield, although in the slightest possible degree, to the strong pressure of his thumb. The proper thickness of horn will then remain.

The quantity of horn to be removed, in order to leave the proper degree of thickness, will vary with different feet. From the strong foot, a great deal must be taken.

From the concave foot the horn may be removed, until the sole will yield to a moderate pressure. From the flat foot, little need be pared; while the pumiced foot should be deprived of nothing but the ragged parts.

The crust should be reduced to a perfect level all round, but left a little higher than the sole, or the sole will be bruised by its pressure on the edge of the seating.

The heels will require considerable attention. From the stress which is thrown on the inner heel, and from the weakness of the quarter there, the horn usually wears away considerably faster than it would on the outer one; and if an equal portion of horn were pared from it, it would be left lower than the outer heel. The smith should therefore accommodate his paring to the comparative wear of the heels, and be exceedingly careful to leave them precisely level.

Miles, after forcibly recommending that the frog (except in very rare cases, of horses with unusually fast-growing frogs), should never be cut or pared; and giving instances which have come under his own observation, and which have demonstrated the truth of his theory, says:

The first stroke of the knife removes this thin horny covering altogether, and lays bare an under surface, totally unfitted, from its moist, soft texture, for exposure either to the hard ground or the action of the air; and in consequence of such unnatural exposure it soon becomes dry and shrinks: then follow cracks,—the edges of which turning outwards form rags; these rags are removed by the smith at the next shoeing, whereby another such surface is exposed, and another foundation laid for other rags; and so on, until at last the protruding, plump, elastic cushion, interposed by nature between the navicular joint and the ground, and so essential to its preservation from injury, is converted by the mischievous interference of art into the dry, shrunk, unyielding apology for a frog, to be seen in the foot of almost every horse that has been regularly shod for a few years. The frog is provided within itself with two very efficient modes of throwing off any superfluous horn it may be troubled with; and it is very unwise in man to interfere with them: the first and most common is the separation from its surface of small branlike scales, which, becoming dry, fall off in a kind of whitish scurf, not unlike the dust that adheres to Turkey figs. The other, which is upon a larger scale, and of rarer occurrence, is sometimes called "casting the frog." A thick layer of frog separates itself in a body, and shells off as deep as a usual paring with a knife; but it is worthy of remark, that there is this very important difference between the two operations: nature never removes the horny covering until she has provided another horny covering beneath, so that although a large portion of the frog may have been removed, there still remains a perfect frog behind, smaller, it is true, but covered with horn, and in every way fitted to sustain exposure; while the knife, on the contrary, removes the horny covering, but is unable to substitute any other in its stead. My advice, therefore, is, to leave the frog to itself; nature will remove the superfluous horn, and the rags can do no harm, and, if unmolested, will soon disappear altogether.

The shoe should have these general features:—1st. It should be, for ordinary work, rather heavy, in order that it may not be bent by contact with hard, uneven roads; 2nd. It should be wide in the web, and of equal thickness and width from the toe to the heel, that it may protect, as much as possible, the sole, without altering the natural position of the foot. 3rd. It should be well drawn in at the heels, that it may rest on the bars, and extend to the outer edge of the crust on the outside, and reach beyond

the bar nearly to the frog, so that there may be no danger
of its pressing on the "corn place" or angles between the
bar and the crust.   4th. It should, in no part, extend beyond the outer edge of the crust, lest it strike against the
opposite leg when the horse is travelling, or be stepped
on by another horse, or be drawn off by a heavy soil.

Such a shoe, and its position on the foot, is shown in
figure 11.

FIG. 11.

Represents the foot with the shoe rendered transparent, showing what parts of the foot
are covered and protected by bringing in the heels of the shoe.

    a a a. The crust, with the shoe closely fitted all round.
    b b. The bars, protected by the shoe.
    c c. The heels, supported by the shoe.
    d. The situation of corns protected from injury.

The shoe should be made as nearly of this form as the
shape of the foot will allow; but one must never lose sight
of the fact that the shoe is made for the foot, and not the
foot for the shoe, and that it is eminently proper to make
the shoe to fit the natural form of the foot, instead, as is
too often the case, of paring, burning, and rasping the foot,
until it fits the shoe, which is made to suit the ideas of the

smith as to what *should* be the form of the horse's foot. No amount of paring can bring the foot of a horse to an unnatural figure, and leave it sound and safe to work with. Miles says:

The truth really is, that the shape of the shoe cannot by possibility influence the shape of the foot; for the foot, being elastic, expands to the weight of the horse in precisely the same degree, whether it be resting upon the most open or the most contracted shoe: it is the *situation of the nails*, and not the shape of the shoe, that determines the form of the foot. If the nails be placed in the outside quarter and toe, leaving the heels and quarters of the inside, which are the most expansive portions, free, no shape that we can give to the shoe can of itself change the form of the foot. I would not however be understood to mean, that the shape of the shoe is therefore of no importance; for I trust I have already proved the contrary. Seeing then that the shape of the foot is in no way changed by the form of the shoe, both wisdom and interest would prompt us to adopt that form which possesses the greatest number of advantages with the fewest disadvantages.

A small clip at the point of the toe is very desirable as preventing displacement of the shoe backwards; it need not be driven up hard; it is merely required as a check or stay. The shoe should be sufficiently long fully to support the angles at the heels, and not, as is too often the case, so short, that a little wear imbeds the edge of it in the horn at these parts. The foot surface of the shoe should always have a good flat even space left all around for the crust to bear upon; for it must be remembered, that the crust sustains the whole weight of the horse, and needs to have a perfectly even bearing everywhere around the shoe. In this space the nail-holes should be punched, and not, as is too often the case, partly in *it*, and partly in the seating. In what is technically called "back-holing the shoe," which means completing the opening of the nail-holes on the foot surface, great care should be taken to give them an outward direction, so as to allow the points of the nails to be brought out low down in the crust. The remainder of the foot surface should be carefully seated out, particularly around the elevated toe, where it might otherwise press inconveniently upon the sole; and I would have the seating carried on fairly to the point where the crust and the bars meet, in order that there may be no pressure in the seat of corns: the chance of pressure in this situation will be further diminished by bevelling off the inner edge of the heels with a rasp.

The ground surface should be perfectly flat, with a ful-lering or groove running round the outer edge, just under the plain surface, whereon the crust bears. The principal use of the fuller is to receive the heads of the nails that secure the shoe, and prevent their bending or breaking off:—it is further useful in increasing the hold of the shoe upon the ground, and with this view I always have it car-ried back to the heels.

In fitting the shoe to the foot, it should never, while red hot, be *burned* into its place, as this would so heat the sen-sitive sole as to produce a serious derangement of its parts, but it may with safety be touched lightly to the foot, that by a slight burning it may indicate those points where the foot needs paring ; indeed, it is necessary to pursue this course in order to make the shoe so exactly fit the foot that there will be no danger of its moving sufficiently to loosen the hold of the nails. It is desirable to have the shoe made with steel in front, this being sloped backward to a line running at right angles with the upper slope of the hoof. Old shoes are always worn to about this form, and new ones should be so made. The steel will prevent their being unduly worn.

Having so fitted the shoe that the foot exactly touches it in every part, the next point is to nail it fast to the hoof; and on this subject we can do no better than to quote Miles' very valuable remarks:

The next circumstance to be considered is one of vital importance to our subject, as upon it depends the amount of disturbance that the natural functions of the foot are destined to sustain from the shoe; viz., the number and situation of the nails which are to secure it to the foot. If they be numerous, and placed back in the quarters and heels, no form of shoe, be it ever so perfect, can save the foot from contraction and navicular disease. If on the contrary they be few, and placed in the outside quarter and toe, leaving the inside quarter and heels quite free to expand, no form of shoe is so bad that it can, from defective form alone, produce contraction of the foot.

Three years ago I commenced a series of experiments upon shoeing, with a view, among other things, of ascertaining how *few* nails are absolutely necessary, under ordinary circumstances, for retaining a shoe securely·in its place. The subjects of my experiments were six horses of my own, and three belonging to friends; the nine among them representing very fairly the different classes of pleasure horses,—not, indeed, including hunters or race-horses, each of which requires a separate and totally different treatment, but carriage-horses, ladies' horses, and roadsters; and they also included the common variations in form and texture of the generality of horses' feet.

When my attention was first directed to the subject of nailing, I was employing seven nails in each fore, and eight in each hind shoe. I then withdrew one nail from each shoe, thus reducing the number to six in the fore and seven in the hind shoes; and finding at the end of a year that the shoes of all the horses had been as firmly retained as formerly, I withdrew another nail from each shoe, leaving only five in the fore shoes and six in the hind. I found, however, that six nails would not retain the hind shoe of a carriage-horse, without allowing it sometimes to shift; so I returned to seven in the hind shoes, and have continued to employ that number ever since: but five have retained all the fore shoes as firmly during the whole of the last year and a half, as six had previously done.

I have invariably directed and superintended the whole operation of shoeing during these experiments; and have always been very careful to mark that the nails were not driven high up in the crust, but brought out as soon as possible; and that they were very lightly driven up before the clinches were turned down, and not, as is generally the case, forced up with all the power that the smith can bring to bear upon them with his hammer.

The clinches should not be rasped away too fine, but turned down broad and firm. The practice of rasping the whole surface of the hoof after the clinches have been turned down, should never be permitted; it destroys the covering provided by nature as a protection against the too rapid evaporation of the moisture of the hoof, and causes the horn to become dry and brittle.

Two of the horses alluded to above, worked for some time with only four nails in their fore shoes.

I have detailed these experiments with a view to expose the groundless nature of the fear that expects to cast a shoe at every step, unless it be held to the foot by eight or nine nails, driven high into the crust. If the presence of a nail in the crust were a matter of no moment, and two or three more than are necessary were *merely useless*, there would be no great reason to interfere with this practice of making "assurance doubly sure;" but it is far otherwise ;—the nails separate the fibres of the horn, and they never by any chance become united again, but continue asunder and unclosed, until by degrees they grow down with the rest of the hoof, and are ultimately, after repeated shoeings, removed by the knife.

If the clinches should happen to rise, they must be replaced without delay; as such rising imparts to the nails a freedom of motion which is sure to enlarge the size of the holes,—and this mischief is often increased by the violent wrenching which the shoe undergoes from side to side in the process of removal by the smith.

Now as these holes cannot possibly grow down and be removed under three shoeings, it will be found that even with seven nails, the crust must always have twenty-one of these separations existing in it at the same time; and as they are often from a variety of causes extended into each other, they necessarily keep it in a brittle, unhealthy state, and materially interfere with the security of the future nail-hold.

During the last six months I have arranged my five nails upon this "system of one-sided nailing," and the result has been most satisfactory ; the shoes have not only been firmly, but *easily* held to the feet, as is evidenced by the clinches not having risen in one single instance,—a clear proof that the struggle between the expansion of the foot and the resistance of the shoe is entirely overcome by this mode of fastening. This very desirable end appears to be attained in the following manner : the outer side of the foot, being the only part nailed to the shoe, carries the whole shoe with it at every expansion; while the inner side, being unattached, expands independently of it, whereby all strain upon the nails is avoided, and the foot is left, with respect to its power of expansion, as nearly as possible in a state of nature.

An unexpected benefit has arisen to one of my horses

from this plan, in the total disappearance of two very trou
blesome corns: they had existed in his feet for ten years,
during seven of which I tried every plan that I had ever
heard of as likely to effect a cure,—both in form of shoe
and local application,—without, however, any decided advantage; but the adoption of this plan of fastening the
shoe to the foot, by removing all restraint and pressure
from the part, has accidentally achieved that which I had
so long sought in vain.

The hind foot certainly does not demand the same measure of attention as the fore foot, inasmuch as its position
and the nature of its office render it less liable to injury, and consequently it is less frequently lame. It is,
however, by no means entirely exempt, nor does it always
escape disease of its navicular joint; for I have myself found
disease in a navicular bone taken from a hind foot. This
being the case, then, we should endeavor to guard against it
by interfering as little as possible with its expansive power;
and that will be best done by keeping the nails on the inside as far removed from the heel as we conveniently can,
to which end I recommend the employment of seven nails
only,—four to be placed in the outer and three in the inner
side of the shoe. The holes in the inner side are to be
punched closer together, and kept more towards the toe
than those on the outside, which need to be more spread
out, as affording greater security of hold to the foot. The
shoe should be carefully fitted to the hoof all round, particularly at the heels, which are too commonly left without
any support whatever; and the mischievous custom of
turning down the outer heel only must be avoided, because
it throws the weight entirely upon the inner quarter, which
is the part the least able to bear it, and causes much uncomfortable strain to the fetlock joint above. Calkins,
even though they may be turned down of perfectly even

lengths on each side, which, however, is very rarely done, are objectionable appendages, and had better be dispensed with, excepting, perhaps, for very heavy draft, where their ends, by entering the ground, may prevent the foot from slipping backwards, and may thus enable the toe to obtain a firmer hold.

The form of shoe here referred to, and the position of the nail holes, are shown in figure 12.

Fig. 12

a a. The heels of an even thickness with the rest of the shoe.
b b. Show the points at which the heels of the hoof terminated.
c c. The seating carried back, so as to clear the angles at the heels, and leave the
    seat of corns free from pressure.
   d. The nail-holes placed in the flat surface which supports the crust, where they
    should always be.
   e. The hindermost nail of the inner side at the inner toe, whereby the whole of
    the quarter and heel are left free to expand.

The directions for properly shoeing horses having now been as fully given as the limits of this work will allow, the attention of the reader is called to certain evils which are produced by bad shoeing.

CONTRACTED FEET,—that is, feet that have shrunken and become narrow at the heels, and of which the frog has become materially reduced in size,—are often caused by in flammation, arising from various causes, but most frequently, without doubt, from improper shoeing. It is the custom of many smiths to " set the shoes well off at the heels," and to carry the seating or bevel of the upper side of the shoes so far back that the heels, instead of resting on a flat surface, as they would on a properly fitted shoe, rest on the slope of the seating, which are, in this respect, simply two inclined planes, so placed that, at each step taken by the horse, his heels must be pressed together until a greater or less contraction is made manifest, too late for us to remedy the evil; for there is no means by which this contraction of the foot can be cured,—though, when it exists only to a slight extent, the internal portions of the foot will sometimes accommodate themselves to its new form. So far as disease is the result of bad shoeing, it can be obviated by so forming the shoe that it will afford a sufficient and perfectly secure and level support for the heels.

For the cause, and treatment of diseases of the feet, including those which result from improper shoeing, the reader is referred to the chapter on Farriery.

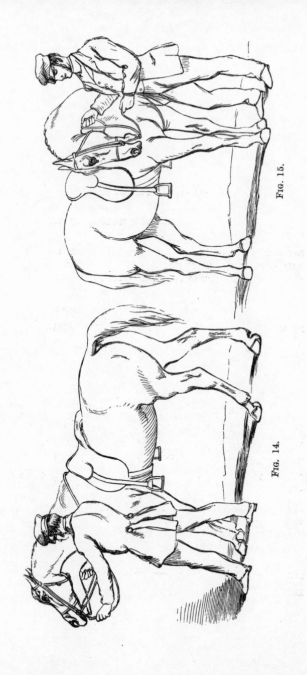

FIG. 15.

FIG. 14.

CHAPTER XVI

WHAT CONSTITUTES A WELL-TRAINED HORSE—TO MAKE HIM COME AT YOUR
CALL—THE PHILOSOPHY OF TRAINING—FLEXIONS OF THE JAW—FLEXIONS
OF THE NECK—FLEXIONS OF THE CROUP—BACKING—THE PACES—LEAPING.

THERE is nothing which so much conduces to the pleasure and safety of a rider, as the proper training of his
horse.   Indeed, no matter how good a rider one may be,
it is impossible for him to ride gracefully, easily or safely
on a horse that has not been properly broken to the work.
It is true that a good rider can, by a sufficient exercise of
prudence, get on passably well with an unbroken horse, or
even a poor rider may, by putting his horse into a fast
gallop, make up in some degree, and for a short time, for
want of training; but it is very certain that both are la-
boring under great disadvantages, and that neither the rider
or his horse is working with ease.

It is too often supposed that all that is necessary to constitute a good saddle-horse is, that he should allow a bit to
remain in his mouth, and should carry his rider without
attempting to throw him, and without viciously trying to
make himself disagreeable.   If he have a dozen different
gaits; if he carry his head low. and his nose out,—these

11   [241]

faults are ascribed to his *nature*, and it is not deemed possible to give him an elegant carriage. If he bear with his full force on the bit, it is considered an advantage, because it gives the rider a firm support, by enabling him to steady himself in his seat by bearing his weight on the bridle.

There have been for ages more or less imperfect directions given for overcoming these difficulties, and for bringing ordinary horses into a tolerably good condition for the saddle; but they were so tedious and so uncertain in their results, that their application was limited to Military schools, and similar institutions, where it was worth while to take a great amount of trouble to train horses for special work.

More recently M. Baucher, a French equestrian of great distinction, has, after giving many years to the subject, advanced on entirely new method for training horses to the saddle, which seems to be founded on natural principles and to be equally applicable to all cases. M. Baucher does not claim that he can make all horses equally good for the saddle, but he does claim, and he seems to prove, that all horses can be made, by his method, as good saddle-horses as they are capable of becoming, with an outlay of very much less time and labor, and with far less pain to the animal, than was necessary under the old system. He also asserts that any horse, not actually deformed, no matter how sad a jade he was when taken in hand, will become, after proper suppling and instruction, a light and graceful saddle beast.

If the horse to be trained be vicious, and will not allow himself to be approached and properly handled, he should of course be subjected to the processes described in the chapter on Rarey's method of *taming* horses; but supposing him to be already tamed, and tolerably docile, he may be proceeded with according to the following directions:—

TO MAKE THE HORSE COME TO THE MAN,

AND TO RENDER HIM QUIET WHILE BEING HANDLED AND MOUNTED.

The rider or trainer should approach the horse, without haste or timidity, holding his whip under his arm. He should speak to him in an ordinary tone of voice, and should pat him caressingly on the face and neck; he will then take the reins of the curb-bit in the left hand, at a distance of six inches from the branches, and in such a manner as to be able to present as much resistance as possible to the efforts which the horse will make to release himself. Take the whip in the right hand, and raise it quietly to the height of the horse's breast, against which it should be struck at intervals of a second, and with a steady and uniform movement. This will, of course, cause the horse to draw back, in order to get away from the whip; as he recedes, follow him steadily, keeping a uniform pull upon the reins, and tapping the breast with the same steady movement of the whip. The horse will soon tire of his unsuccessful attempts to back away from the pain, and will try another movement, making a start forward. At that instant the pressure on the bit should be discontinued, and by caresses the horse should be made to understand that he has done as we desired, by coming toward us, and that in this way he can avoid being whipped. Repeat this exercise, and continue it for half an hour, being careful always to follow the horse as he recedes, and to reward him for compliance, by slacking the hold of the reins, and caressing him. Be sure not to caress him when he has not done well, and not to punish him after he has yielded. This first lesson having been given in the morning, it should be repeated for half an hour in the afternoon. This will be sufficient to cause the most timid or stubborn horse to respond to the least intima-don of the wish of his master, and without being whipped he will come forward at the first touch of the reins; it will be gratifying to the trainer, and useful to the horse to repeat the foregoing operation once or twice before each lesson during the subsequent training. Occasionally during the exercises the hand may be borne down, so as to depress the head, to teach the horse more ready submission to the instructions which are to follow. When a horse will come freely forward at the least gesture, his progress may be slightly checked by the hand, which will cause him to arch his neck, and draw in his chin, approaching to the perpendicular position of the face, which Baucher so strongly recommends.

If the horse be very unruly, it may be necessary, in rare cases, to use the cavesson, (a nose-band of iron, supported by an arrangement similar to the common halter); but such aids should be eschewed as far as possible.

The following exercises are, like the calisthenic exercises of schools, intended to give strength and pliability to the muscles, and grace to the movements. They are not immediately useful, but they render the horse much more serviceable to his rider than he would be in a state of nature, because they enable him to perform smoothly many movements which, naturally, he would perform but awkwardly; and to respond more readily to the indications of the hand or leg.

It is one of the first principles of M. Baucher's system, that all the resistances of the young horse *originate* in a physical cause, and that they have a moral cause only when the horse has been perplexed, and made resentful, by the unskilfulness, ignorance, or brutality of the rider.

It is often remarked that horses which are considered indomitable are those which develop the greatest energy and vigor, as soon as we know how to remedy their phys-

FIG. 16.

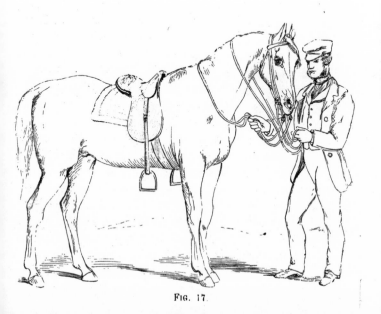

FIG. 17.

ical defects; as with those which, in spite of their bad conformation, are subjected by a bad system of training to a semblance of obedience, we have to thank nothing but the gentleness of their natures. If they consent to submit to the simplest exercise, it is on condition that we do not exact anything more difficult; for they would soon recover their energy to resist any further attempts.

A well constituted horse is one, all of whose powers are regularly harmonized, so as to bring about a perfect equilibrium of the whole.

If we once admit these truths:

That the education of the horse consists in the complete subjection of his forces;

That we can make use of his forces only by annulling all of his involuntary resistances;

And, that these resistances have their source in the contractions resulting from physical defects;—

It is only necessary to seek out those parts in which these contractions operate, to combat them, and to cause them to disappear.

Whatever be the fault of conformation which prevents a just disposition of the forces of the horse, it is always in the neck that the most immediate effect is felt. There is no false movement, no resistance, that is not preceded by a contraction of this part; and as the jaw is intimately connected with the neck, a stiffness of the one is instantly communicated to the other. These two points are the prop on which the horse depends to annul all of the efforts of the rider. We can easily conceive of the immense obstacles which they present, because the neck and the head are the two principal levers by which we control and direct the animal, and it is impossible to obtain any influence over him so long as we do not entirely master these two indispensable means of action. Behind, the parts

where the forces most contract for resistance, are the loins
and the croup (the haunches).

The contractions of these two opposite extremities are, to
each other, causes and effects; that is to say, the stiffness
of the neck induces that of the haunches, and *vice versa.*

FLEXIONS OF THE JAW.—The flexions of the jaw, as
well as the two flexions of the neck, which are to follow,
are performed standing still, the trainer on foot. The
horse will be led on to the ground and the reins passed
over his neck. The trainer will first see that the bit, which
is of the double sort (see fig. 13), is properly placed, and

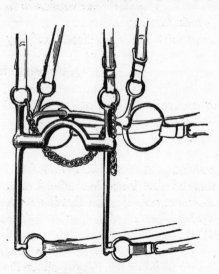

FIG. 13.—The Bit and Bridoon Bridle.

that the chain is so fastened that the finger can be easily
introduced between it and the chin. Then, looking the
animal kindly in the eyes, he will place himself opposite
his neck, and near to his head; the body should be firm
and the legs a little apart, to strengthen the position and to

enable the trainer to contend with advantage against every resistance of the horse.

In order to execute the flexions to the right, the trainer, being on the near side of the horse (see fig. 14), will take the right curb rein in his right hand, at a distance of about six inches from the branch of the bit, and the left rein in the left hand, at a distance of about four inches from the branch. He will then draw the right rein toward him, and at the same time stretch out the left hand, turning the bit in such a way as to force the horse's mouth open. The force employed ought to be proportioned to the resistance of the neck and the jaw, in order not to render unsteady the position of the trainer. If the horse incline to back, to avoid the flexion, he should be prevented from doing so by holding the hands firmly forward. If the previous exercise has been practiced completely and with care, it will be easy, with the aid of the whip, to arrest this retrograde movement, which is a powerful obstacle to all flexions of the jaw and neck.

As soon as the horse yields to the pressure, and allows his head to be drawn around to the right shoulder, draw gently and evenly on the two reins until the line of the face is perpendicular to the ground, and until the animal will sustain his head in this position without bearing on the bit. The champing of the bit by the horse is an evidence that he is completely in hand, and entirely under subjection. Figure 14, shows the position at the commencement of this exercise, and fig. 15, that at the termination. He should now be recompensed by a slackening of the reins, and by being allowed, after a few seconds, to regain his natural position. The flexion of the jaw to the left is executed on the same principles, and by opposite means, and the flexions should be alternated from the right to the left.

DEPRESSION OF THE NECK AND DIRECT FLEXION OF THE JAW.—The trainer will stand as before directed; he will take the reins of the snaffle in the left hand, at about six inches from the rings, and the curb reins in the right hand, close to the bit (see fig. 16). He will then bear down with the left hand, and will draw back with the right,—the force with which either effort is made being nicely adjusted to the resistance of the horse. This figure represents the position at the commencement, and fig. 17 that at the close of this exercise.

As soon as the horse's head shall fall, as though of its own weight, all force must cease, and the neck and head allowed to resume their natural position.

If the horse do not readily lower his head on feeling the pressure on the top of it, which this tension of the snaffle reins produces, he may be taught more prompt obedience by crossing the reins of the snaffle under his chin, and drawing them tightly, so as to compress the jaw, at the same time bearing down with as much force as possible (see fig. 18). He will soon learn that the tension of the snaffle means "lower your head," and he will be quick to obey without waiting for the more painful part of the operation. By the direct flexion of the jaw we mean the relaxing of those muscles by which the mouth is shut; this will ordinarily be accomplished by the action of the curb-bit in the preceding exercise, but if the horse persist in poking out his nose, and holding the bit "in his teeth," his mouth may be forced open, in a way that he will be likely to remember, by the following process:—Stand facing the left side of the horse's head, and take the left snaffle rein in the left hand, and the left curb-rein in the right, both as near to the bit as will allow of a firm hold. Now raise the elbows, and draw the hands away from each other with sufficient strength to force the jaws apart (see fig. 19). In

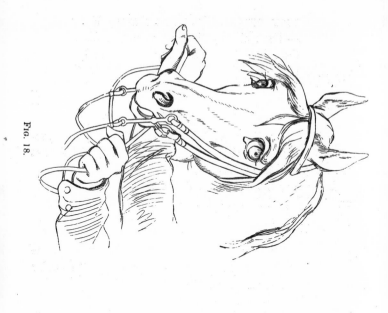

FIG. 18.

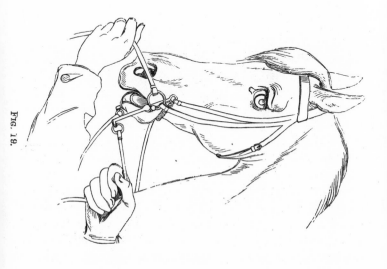

FIG. 19.

this, as in all other operations, the force applied by the trainer should be proportioned to the resistance of the horse.

LATERAL FLEXIONS OF THE NECK.—The trainer will stand by the side of the horse's shoulder, as in the flexions of the jaw. He will take the right snaffle-rein in his right hand, and draw upon it over the horse's neck, (see fig. 20,) holding the left snaffle tight enough to prevent the horse from turning his body.

As soon as the neck yields to allow the head to go round to the right, the tension of the left rein must cease. When the head is well brought round (fig. 21), the two reins should be equally drawn upon until the head assumes a perpendicular position, and until the horse evinces his lightness by champing the bit. After having held him a few seconds in this position, the head should be gently drawn back to its natural place. It is important that the horse should not be allowed to do anything of his own will, and his head should be drawn back before he tries to move it of his own accord. The flexion to the left, which should be alternated with this, is of course performed by the opposite process. When this flexion can be readily made with the snaffle, the curb-reins should be used until the least touch is sufficient to cause the horse to turn his head quite to the shoulder. This is an exercise which should be frequently repeated, even after the training of the horse has been completed, as it will serve to keep him light and submissive. It is not necessary at all times to cause the horse to bring his head entirely round; it is better occasionally to cause the head, pivoting on the neck, to be lightly turned from side to side, so that the horse shall look toward either side, and not to the rear, as in the complete flexion.

LATERAL FLEXIONS OF THE NECK—THE TRAINER IN THE SADDLE.—For this exercise the trainer should be in

11*

the saddle, holding both reins of the snaffle in his hands in such a manner as to barely feel the bit. He should then draw lightly on the rein of the side toward which he desires the horse to turn his head (see fig. 22), increasing the force as the horse increases his resistance, and always in such a manner as to control him. The horse will soon tire of struggling against the bit, the continued pressure of which causes an increasing pain, and he will sooner or later incline his head toward the side. As soon as the head is drawn well round to the side (see fig. 23), the rein of the opposite side must be drawn upon as well as the other, so as to place the head in a perpendicular position. It is very important that this perpendicular position should always be attained, as the suppling can never be perfect without it. If while the head is being drawn to one side, the horse try to avoid the pressure of the bit by turning his body round, the opposite snaffle-rein may be used to prevent him from doing so.

DIRECT FLEXION OF THE HEAD AND NECK OR RAMENER.*—The trainer being in the saddle, he will take both of the snaffle-reins in his left hand. He will then place the edge of his right hand on the reins, so as to give greater force to the tension of the left hand, and by a steady pressure he will draw upon the reins until the horse yields and drops his head toward his breast. As soon as he shows, by champing the bit, that he maintains this position without aid from the hand of the trainer, it will be sufficient to raise the right hand to reward him. If the horse try to back away from the bit, a slight pressure of the legs will suffice to keep him in his position. When he will yield to the action of the snaffle, he will do so much more readily to that of the curb-it. The curb

* By *Ramener* is meant the placing the head in a perpendicular position.

FIG. 20.

FIG. 21.

should, of course, be used with much more skill than the snaffle.

This flexion is the most important of all; the others chiefly tend to render it attainable. As soon as it can be executed with ease and promptness, as soon as a slight touch of the hand is sufficient to bring and maintain the head in a perpendicular position, the contractions of the fore part of the animal are destroyed, and its lightness and equilibrium are established.

THE HIND PARTS.—The rider, in order to direct his horse, acts upon two portions of his body,—the front and the rear. He employs for this purpose two movements,— one with the legs, which gives an impulse to the croup (the hind parts), the other with the hands, which directs and modifies this impulse, by the head and neck.

FLEXIONS OF THE CROUP AND MAKING IT MOVABLE.— The trainer, being mounted, willl hold the curb-reins in his left hand, and the snaffle-reins in his right. He will first bring the horse's head into a perpendicular position by drawing lightly on the curb. Then, if he wishes to execute the movement to the right, he will pass the left leg back behind the girths, and press it against the horse's flank, until the croup yields to the pressure. He will, at the same time, cause the left rein of the snaffle to be felt, proportioning its tension to the force which is opposed to it. The action of the rein is to combat the resistance of the horse, and that of the leg to determine the movement. The right leg should not be kept away from the horse's side during the movement, but should remain near to it in its natural position, to keep him in place and to aid a slight forward impulse, which the right side would natu- rally acquire by the rotation of the whole body about a centre, which should coïncide with the centre of gravity of the horse   The force with which the two legs are pressed against the sides should be about equal, and the trainer should bear in mind that their office is to turn the horse between them, much as one would turn a stick held between the fingers; that is, by pressing against different points of the opposite sides. This lesson should be proceeded with slowly, and so gradually as not to discourage the horse. While it is yet in its early stages, the side-long movement, which the French call the *manége de deux pistes** may be practiced as a variety. This may be accomplished after a week's practice, while the old military school did not attempt it until after several years.

BACKING.—This is an exercise which has not, until Baucher's time, been sufficiently appreciated, but which has a very great influence in the education of the horse. The trainer should first assure himself that the croup is exactly on a line with the shoulder, and that the horse is light in hand. The legs should be pressed gently against the two sides in such a way as to cause the horse to lift one of his hind legs, the snaffle being held sufficiently to prevent his advancing. An immediate pressure on the curb will cause the horse to replace his foot, slightly to the rear of its natural position. If the horse shall have turned to the right or to the left, he may be brought into place by the aid of the snaffle and the leg, and the movement of the hind parts may be repeated. This should be practiced for a time without trying to make the pupil recede to any extent, the first object being to teach him to use his hind legs with facility, while he retains his general lightness. This object being accomplished, it will soon be possible to

* " *La piste* is an imaginary line upon which the horse is made to walk When the hind legs follow the same line as the fore ones, the horse is said to go *d'une piste*, or on one line. He goes *de deux pistes*, or on two lines when his hind legs pass along a line parallel to that traced by the fore legs "—*Baucher's Dictionnaire d'Equitation.*

Fig. 22.

Fig. 23.

make him walk backward as gracefully and as easily as forward. Baucher considers this to be the best exercise of all, and its proper performance to be the best test of the horse's education.

RECAPITULATION.

Stationary Exercises—the Trainer on Foot.

1. Flexions of the jaw to the right and to the left, using the curb-bit.

2. Direct flexion of the jaw, and the depression of the neck.

3. Lateral flexions of the neck with the snaffle and with the curb.

Stationary Exercises—the Trainer on Horseback.

1. Lateral flexions of the neck with the snaffle and the curb.

2. Placing the head in a perpendicular position with the snaffle and with the curb.

3. Lateral movements of the croup, and rotation of the croup and shoulders around the centre of gravity.

4. Movement of the hind legs, and backing.

THE PACES.

The young horse, at first stiff and awkward in the use of his members, will need a certain degree of management for the development of his powers. We have by the preceding rules, acquired a means of acting on the separate parts of the horse's body. We must now facilitate his means of action, by exercising his forces together. If the animal respond to the aids of his rider, by the jaw, the neck, and the haunches; if he yield by the general disposition of his body to the impulses which are communicated to him; if the play of his extremities be easy and regular, the entire mechanism of the animal will move with perfect harmony in the different paces. It is these indisputable qualities which constitute a good education.

THE WALK is the mother of all the other paces of the horse; by it we may obtain their cadence and regularity.

Before causing the horse to advance, we should first assure ourselves that he is light in hand; that is to say, that his head is perpendicular, his neck supple, and his croup straight and plumb. The legs will then be gently closed to give the horse a forward impulse; but we should not at the same time slacken our hold on the horse's mouth, for then the horse, free from all restraint, would lose his lightness, and, by the contraction of his neck, would render powerless our efforts to manage him properly. The rider's hand should be, at all times, an impassable barrier to the horse whenever he endeavors to move his head from a perpendicular position. He will soon accustom himself to the fact that it is only within our limit that he will find ease and comfort.

So long as the horse will not keep himself supple and light in his walk, we will continue to exercise him on a straight line; but as soon as he shall have acquired more ease and stability, we will commence to make him turn to the right and to the left in walking.

THE TROT.—The rider will commence this pace very moderately, following exactly the same process as for the walk. He will maintain the lightness of his horse, not forgetting that the faster the pace becomes, the more he inclines to fall back into his natural stiffness. The hand should now be used with redoubled skill; the legs will second the hand, and the horse, kept between these two barriers, which will be an obstacle only to his faulty movements, will soon acquire, with the cadence of the step, grace, extension, and steadiness.

THE GALLOP.—In preparing the horse for the gallop, it

is necessary to render him as light as possible, in order that he will not oppose our efforts. By a pressure of the legs, the hind quarters are to be brought well under the body, and, by a simultaneous action of the hand and the legs, his fore quarters are to be raised as for a short leap. The great care of the rider during the whole time of training the horse to this pace, should be given to keeping him, as much as possible, in a light, supple, and active condition. Although a sort of gallop is the natural gait of the horse. the gallop of a well-trained saddle-horse is almost entirely artificial; and, to obtain its high action, grace, and entire subjection to the will of the rider, is more difficult than any other exercise connected with training. It is impossible for a horse to gallop well until he has been thoroughly suppled, and is in the condition to act only as he is impelled by his rider; the position of the head and the pliability of the neck must be perfect.

No horse can be said to be perfectly trained to the gallop until he can be made to lead off with either the right or the left foot, as we may desire, or change his leading foot at every step, or as often as we may choose to have him do so; not that it is often important, when a horse gallops well with whichever foot he happens to lead off with, whether he starts with the left or the right, but because his ability to change at the least hint from his rider, is an indication, and a necessary one, that he is in the proper condition as to lightness and submission. It is only by patiently applying the supplings which have been described, and by adapting them to the altered necessities of the new pace, that we can, within a reasonable time, train our pupil to a satisfactory gallop.

A great deal has been written on the subject of making a horse lead off with his right, or his left foot, as we may desire; but, after a careful perusal of all that is to be found treating on this matter, we have found no positive information about it, and believe that it is not possible to give rules for producing this result with certainty, under all circumstances; still there are very many riders who do it, although they cannot clearly tell another person how it is to be done,—just as expert swimmers, or skaters, perform with ease feats of skill which they cannot teach to others, and directions for which cannot be written. There is one principle which is easily to be understood from the foregoing instructions, which is, that a horse will, if properly handled, lift that foot first on which there is the least weight resting, and that if the preponderance of weight be changed from one leg to another, the greatest action or "leading" will be transferred to that on which the least weight is bearing. There is a certain "knack" of thus transferring the weight from one part of the horse's body to another which cannot be described, but which may soon be attained with practice.

The nearest approach to a rule for making a horse lead off with the right or left foot, at the pleasure of the rider, is the following:

To make the horse lead off with the right foot, get him well in hand, with his head in an easy position, and his hind legs well under his body and then bear the hand to the left and give an increased pressure to the right leg. This rule is not by any means infallible, but it is the best to commence with, and the young horse-trainer will soon learn to modify it, or, what is more likely, will soon acquire a supreme contempt for all rules, and will establish a communication with his horse ensuring his success.

In the gallop, the horse will sometimes change his step with the hind feet without changing in front; he is then said to be "disunited" in his gait. This is a habit of which he may easily be broken by being always made to stop and begin again regularly. The rule for correcting such a false step, without stopping the horse is, when he is leading with the right foot, to hold the rein firmly, and to press the left leg against his flank in such a way as to fix the left hind foot on the ground, and allow the other to regain its place in advance. If the horse be leading with the left foot and become "disunited," the right leg must be pressed against his flanks, as it is the *left* hind leg which has fallen behind.

THE SPURS.—Writers upon horsemanship, and teachers of the art generally, will inform you that the spur is only to be applied to the horse when it is impracticable to urge him onward with the legs, or when you would force him to advance towards some person or thing which terrifies him,—in short, only as a punishment. I undertake to say, however, that if properly used, it will be found of the greatest assistance in training the most spirited animal, even those which have not been conquered by the use of the hardest bits, guided by the strongest hands. With the aid of the spur the veriest Bucephalus will speedily be reduced to subjection, rendered gentle and promptly obedient to rule, and readily brought to a stand-still in the midst of his most frantic bounds.

The spur will also be found a valuable agent in conquering the animal's tendency to shift his centre of gravity too much towards his front or rear. In "horses of high action," the greatest amount of force resides in the hind quarters, whence their greater rapidity of movement. Precisely the reverse of this is the case with those of heavy, sluggish mood.

Having, through the instrumentality of suppling, broken up the natural forces of the horse, we should now proceed, by a judiciously blended use of the legs and hands, to concentrate them in the middle of the animal's body, the proper location of his centre of gravity. The spur should be applied adroitly and with caution; the legs being as little moved as possible, and brought together so gently as to pause within a quarter of an inch of the horse's flanks, before they actually touch them. The hand should be perfectly in unison, the reins being held with a strong grasp, so as to completely control the increased violence of movement caused by the spur. If the hand do not check this at the very moment it is given, and a struggle for the mastery ensues, we should restore the horse to complete tranquillity before attempting to resume our instructions. By pursuing this course, he may gradually be brought to endure the the severest application of the spur, without increasing his pressure upon the bit, accelerating his pace when moving, or starting when standing still.

A horse being thus far subjected, three-fourths of the task of breaking is accomplished, his forces being completely at our command, and his centre of gravity coïncident with the middle of his body, where it properly belongs, as all his forces unite at that point. Every movement being now perfectly controlled by the rider, his weight can readily be shifted when it becomes requisite.

OF LEAPING THE DITCH AND BAR.

The great desideratum is to induce the horse to undertake the leap with readiness. If the course I have directed to be pursued, for getting the natural forces of the animal under subjection to our will, have been implicitly followed, its value will be made apparent in the ease with which we shall make him clear every obstacle before him. But should he make any resistance, do not employ means to urge him on, which are likely to cause terror, such as a whip applied by another person, or loud shouts. We must gain his obedience by our own physical exertions, as these alone will give him the ability to fulfil our directions intelligently. In order, therefore, to overcome the forces which cause his resistance, we must first have brought him perfectly under the control of the legs and spur, the use of which will enable us to act directly and successfully upon them.

The bar being first kept on the ground until he crosses it without opposition, is to be raised, inch by inch, to the greatest elevation at which he can clear it, without too severe exertion. An attempt to make him do more is un· wise, as being likely to give rise to a strong disinclination for such exercises.

The bar, heretofore loose, is now to be firmly fastened in its place, that the horse, in leaping, may carefully avoid hitting it, which he might not take pains to do, did he know that a touch of his feet would remove it. Nor should the bar be so enveloped with covering as to diminish its hardness, as it is essential that he should be taught by experience the disagreeable results of an unsuccessful leap.

Before attempting the leap, the rider should be sufficiently firm in his seat to prevent his body's anticipating the movement of his steed. His loins should be supple, and his posteriors well adjusted to the saddle, so as to avoid encountering a severe shock on alighting. His thighs and legs must perfectly fit the sides and body of the horse, thus giving him ready and complete control. The hand, in its natural position, will calculate, by feeling the mouth of the horse, the amount of force with which he is approaching the bar. In this position he will bring the horse to the leap, and if he maintains his freedom of pace to the last moment, a slight resistance with the leg and hand will aid in the elevation of the fore, and the bound of the hind quarters. As the horse rises to the leap, the

grasp of the hand is to be relaxed to be again applied when
the fore legs touch the ground, lest they should sink under
the weight of the body.

We should be content with trying only a few leaps at a
time, never attempting such as are too great for the animal's powers. Horses are sometimes so much alarmed in
, this way, as to refuse thereafter to perform leaps only half
the height of those to which they have been previously
accustomed.

The reader has now been presented with a detailed account of the best manner of training horses for the saddle,
and they will be found satisfactory in proportion as he
applies them with spirit, adopting, of course, such altera-
tions as will be suggested by circumstances. Of the preliminary exercises, not one is unnecessary or unprofitable.
He who would have a thoroughly good saddle-horse should
be contented to follow M. Baucher's directions, until he is
able to prove that they are erroneous.

It is recommended that each lesson be of a half hour's
duration, that the horse have two lessons per day, and
that the training be continued for sixty days.

FULLER.S.C.

Fig. 24.

CHAPTER XVII.

HOW TO RIDE A HORSE.

IT would be useless, in this work, to enter into an argument in favor of horse-back riding. It is so inspiriting, so healthful, so enchanting,—such a truly noble exercise for both men and women,—that it pleads its own cause, and it cannot fail to commend itself to all who will master its difficulties sufficiently to fairly test its merits.

Driving is very well for invalids, and for those who are indolent, or timid, while it is often convenient for all; but a free gallop or a prancing piaffer, on a well-bred and well-trained horse, appeals so strongly to the life and spirit of all vigorous persons, while it brings relief for dyspepsia and hypochondria, and immunity from nearly every ill that flesh is heir to, that it must effect, more and more, its own adoption.

This being the case, it is deemed necessary to the purposes of this chapter only to give a detailed statement of the various practical matters connected with the art of Riding,—safely assuming that the reader will find, in the practical application of its principles, sufficient inducement for its continued exercise.

THE SADDLE.—Of the various sorts of saddles, there are only two which are sufficiently desirable for modern use to require notice in this work. These are the English hunting saddle and the Somerset saddle.

THE HUNTING SADDLE is the one which is now almost universally used for gentlemen's riding. It is smooth, hard, and close fitting, being usually covered with the best tanned hog-skin. This saddle, as used for hunting, is from sixteen to twenty inches long, according to the size of the rider, from pommel to cantle, slightly depressed in the centre, and having its flaps inclined forward, their anterior edge being furnished with a padding, which, by preventing the leg from slipping forward, gives security in the descent from a leap, or when the horse kicks badly.

For road riding the saddle may, without disadvantage, be half an inch shorter than would be necessary for hunting; and, as it is seldom necessary for the pleasure rider to assume so bracing a position as is, at times, required in the hunting-field, the flaps may be somewhat more perpendicular. Beneath, the saddle should be well chambered,—that is, it should be wide over the withers, and free from stuffing at this point, and there should be a space of at least two inches between the pads of either side to leave a free space over the horse's spine, from one end of the saddle to the other. The pads should be only sufficiently stuffed to protect the horse's back from injury, as too much stuffing, by increasing the distance between the rider and his horse, gives an insecurity to his position. On either side of the saddle, just in front of the stirrup bars, there should be a ring about three-fourths of an inch in diameter, to which to attach the breast-plate, if it should at any time be necessary to use one.

The beauty and durability of the saddle depend upon the quality of the leather of which it is made. The best quality is hard and firm, and the bristle-holes are large and clearly defined. Hog-skin varies in quality so greatly that its price ranges from ten to one hundred dollars per dozen.

The cost of such a saddle as is above described, when made in the best manner, is from thirty to forty-five dollars; good looking saddles may be bought for a very much less price, but the best ones are the cheapest, when we consider their durability, and the comfort which they ensure to the horse and rider.

THE SOMERSET SADDLE is so called, because it was invented for one of the Somerset family who had lost a leg below the knee. " It is padded before the knee and behind the thigh, to fit the seat of the purchaser, and if provided with a stuffed seat of brown buck-skin, will give the quartogenarian pupil the comfort and confidence of an arm chair. They are, it may be encouraging to mention, fashionable among the more aristocratic middle aged. The front roll of stuffing is much used among those who ride and break their own colts, as it affords a fulcrum against a puller, and a protection against a kicker. Australians use a rolled blanket, strapped over the pommel of the saddle, for the same purpose. To bad horsemen who are too conceited to use a Somerset, I say, in the words of the old proverb, ' Pride must have a fall.'"*

THE GIRTHS, of which there should always be two, should be of the best quality of webbing, of good width, and they should be supplied with very strong, long-tongued buckles.

THE STIRRUP-LEATHERS should be attached by bars closed at the rear by a clasp, (see fig. 25) acting with a spring in the manner of an ordinary knife blade. This renders the foot-hold always secure, so long as it is desirable that it should be so; and, if the rider fall with his foot fastened in the stirrup, the clip yields and allows the strap to draw out towards the rear. The best stirrup straps are usually made with the rough side of the leather outward, as being more

*" The Art of Taming Horses."

durable. They should be just long enough when let out
to their full extent, to allow the ball of the foot to touch
the stirrup when the leg is stretched down to its fullest

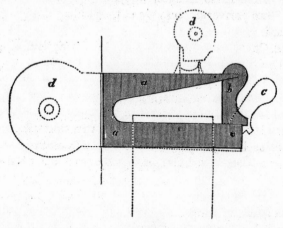

FIG. 25.

a a. The bars of the clasp.   *b.*   Is inserted like a knife-blade on a spring.
c.   The same partly open.   *d d.* The parts by which the clasp is fastened
                                                    to the saddle, and are covered by the leather.

extent. It is sometimes desirable to ride with the stirrups
thus long, and any excess of leather beyond what is required for this, will be inconvenient when riding with a
shorter stirrup.

THE STIRRUP-IRONS should be large enough to allow
the ball of the foot to pass easily through them, and not
less than 1½ inches wide at the bottom. A very light
stirrup is objectionable, as it is more easily lost by the foot
and less easily recovered, than one of medium weight.

SADDLE-CLOTHS.—These are of two sorts. The first is
that which is attached to the rear of the saddle, and the
office of which is to protect the rider's coat from being
soiled by the perspiration of the horse. They are voted
" slow" by modern riders.

The second form is a heavy felt cloth, or a folded blanket, which is put on the horse's back under the saddle, and which greatly protects the horse from injury by its friction. It is of further use in absorbing the perspiration of the horse, thus preventing the pads of the saddle from becoming hard.

THE CRUPPER is too familiar to need description. It is of use only on such horses as are, from their straight shoulders and low withers, unfit for the saddle. All well-bred saddle-horses are so high in the withers that there is no danger of the saddle slipping forward.

THE BREAST-PLATE OR HUNTING MARTINGALE is of use only on such very highly bred horses as, from their high withers and small, round barrels, may "run out of their saddles" in ascending steep hills. It consists of a strap which passes about the neck, and is attached to the girths beneath, having on either side, at a distance of about nine inches below the top of the withers, a ring, from which pass short straps to the breast-plate rings of the saddle.

MARTINGALES are of three sorts:—the running martingale, which has two rings through which the reins are passed; the standing martingale, which is buckled to both rings of the bit; and the cavesson martingale, which is buckled to the nose-band of the bridle. The object of the standing martingale and of the cavesson martingale, is to keep the horse's head always in position, and they are but poor substitutes for a proper rein-hold. Except for unskilful riders on fretful horses, their use is to be deprecated as unnaturally constraining the movements of the horse.

The running martingale is scarcely ever more desirable, though with horses which have a habit of rearing, or of throwing up their heads, it may be used as a last resort. But in all cases the straps should be sufficiently long to allow the rings to go quite up to the buckles when the horse's

12

head is in a perpendicular position, and the reins should be supplied with buttons to prevent these rings from being caught on the buckles of the reins.

THE BRIDLE should be of white or russet leather, of good quality, and it will be more satisfactory if its buckles are of polished steel and detachable (that they may be easily cleaned), rather than covered with leather, and sewed fast to the bridle. Covered buckles are usually so weak as to easily get out of order. The bridle should be, for elegance, as plain as possible, and it may have either single or double head-straps, according to the sort of bit which has to be used. Some persons use a nose-band, buckled sufficiently short to prevent the horse from opening his mouth to its full extent, but it is possible so to train a horse as to render this unnecessary.

THE BIT.—As to the form of the bit, it is the opinion of many that there should not only be a different bit for each sort of "mouth," but that there should be various bits to suit the varying temper of the same horse. Baucher, who is high authority, insists, on the contrary, that one sort of bit is sufficient for all horses, and for all occasions. He recommends a particular form of the *bit and bridoon bridle.* (See Baucher's chapter.) The snaffle should be small, and not long. The curb-bit he describes thus: "Branches straight, six inches long from the eye of the bit to the extremity of the branch; the canon, or that part of the bit which acts against the bars of the mouth, is three-fourths of an inch in diameter; the width of the port at the bottom is two inches."

The "Pelham" bit, (see fig. 26) a combination of the snaffle and the curb, if of sufficiently large size, is more elegant in its appearance, having but a single head-piece, and is very effective. The "Hanovarian" (see fig. 27) is a powerful variation of the Pelham bit, and in the hands of a practiced horseman has an excellent effect on the horse's action. There are few horses which can be satisfactorily

FIG. 26.—The Pelham Bit.

idden with the plain snaffle-bit—such as is represented in figure 28.

FIG. 27.—The Hanovarian Bit.

a Ring pieces for the attachment of the head stall made movable (as at *b*), to prevent interference with the action of the curb-chain.

THE PULLEY BRIDLE can be useful only when it is necessary to ride a pig-headed, stiff-necked brute, whose peculiar fancy is for taking the bit between his teeth, and running like mad, without a moment's warning.   For ordinary

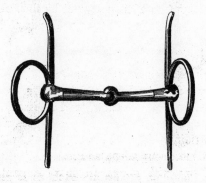

FIG. 28—The plain Snaffle-bit.

use, it acts as a plain snaffle, but, if the horse try to run away with it, a stout pull on the rein which passes through the ends of the bit and over the top of the head, will effectually *gag* him and bring him to terms.   It is much better than the saw-edged, jaw-breaking devices in use in some parts of the world, and, for special uses, it is desirable; but for a gentleman's saddle-horse it would be absurd, inasmuch as no horse fit for saddle use would attempt any prank which Baucher's bit, with its 6-inch leverage, would not speedily check.

SPURS.—The best form of spur is the old-fashioned sort known to the trade as the "hunting-spur." This sets over the heel, and is fastened by a strap around the instep. The more fashionable form at the present time, is the spur which is either screwed fast to the heel of the boot, or which is fastened to it by a spring which fits into a socket made in the heel. The points of the spur should be filed off, so that they cannot prick the horse too severely; in ordinary riding they are used only as reminders.

The use of the spurs, as directed in the chapter on Baucher's method of training, adds greatly to nearly every effect of the motions of the legs, and by their skilful application, it is possible to make the well-trained horse seem a portion of ourselves.

THE DRESS.—The riding dress for gentlemen, in this country, where there are no riding or hunting clubs, and where there is no special fashion for riding costume, may be anything that is appropriate to the season, convenient, and not easily injured by the frequently recurring mishaps incident to riding. Tight breeches, with the boots worn outside, are most convenient, and least subject to accident; but pantaloons, with straps, are more elegant, and sufficiently convenient.

MOUNTING AND DISMOUNTING.

MOUNTING.—1. Walk up to the horse in a quiet, confident way, pat his face and neck, and speak to him gently; then, standing opposite his left shoulder, fix the reins in the left hand, and with the right hand separate a portion of the mane and wind it around the thumb of the left hand. Then facing the horse's rump, hold the stirrup in the right hand and put the left foot firmly into it; now hop around so as to face the saddle, and lay the hand on the right side of the cantle; raise yourself in the stirrup, and throw the right leg well over the horse's back, without bending the knee As soon as you touch the saddle, loose the hold of the mane, but be careful that, in finding the right stirrup, your efforts produce no reäction on the bit, which should be held only tight enough to cause the horse to stand quietly. Or,

2d. Approach the horse as before, step back so as to

face the saddle, take the curb-rein lightly in the right hand
and lay that hand on the right side of the cantle of the
saddle; with the help of the left hand place the foot in
the stirrup, and then, taking a portion of the mane in the
left hand, place yourself in the saddle, as before directed,
raising the right hand to clear the right leg, and letting go
of the mane and taking hold of the curb-rein with the left
hand as the right rises from its position on the cantle to allow the leg to pass over. This method of mounting is less
formal and more graceful than that first described, but it
requires a certain degree of skill and good horsemanship to
enable one to perform it, without taking too strong a hold
of the horse's mouth.

These are methods of the schools, and it is convenient to be able to employ them at pleasure; but the following directions by Baucher will enable one to mount more
easily and more quickly:

Approach the horse's shoulder, take the reins in the left
hand, and then take in the same hand a portion of the
mane firmly, but in such a manner as not to tear the hair
from its roots. Place the right hand on the pommel of
the saddle, passing the four fingers inside the pommel and
laying the thumb on the outside; spring lightly and raise
yourself upon your wrists. As soon as your middle has
reached the height of your hands, throw the right leg
over the croup, without touching it, and place yourself
lightly in the saddle.

These directions all apply to mounting from the left side
of the horse; for mounting from the right or off side, they
should, of course, be reversed.

There is no right or wrong side of the horse from which
to mount, and the rider should be able to mount from
either side, indifferently.

DISMOUNTING.—In leaving the saddle, it is customary, as

it is easy, to dismount by simply reversing the first direc
tions given for mounting,—thus: having the reins and
whip in the left hand, take hold of the mane, withdraw
the right foot from the stirrup, lay the right hand on the
pommel of the saddle, and throw the right leg backward
over the horse's rump, being careful not to touch him with
the spur. As the leg descends to the horse's side, move the
right hand from the pommel of the saddle to the cantle;
lower the right leg to the ground and take the stirrup in
the right hand, so that the foot may be withdrawn without
throwing the stirrup against the horse's flank.

A less dignified but more graceful mode of dismounting is the following: disengage both feet from the stirrups,
place both hands on the pommel of the saddle, lean slightly
backward, and then throw the body forward, bringing the
weight on the wrists; continue the spring, so as to bring
either leg over the horse, landing on either side at pleasure, dropping close by his side and keeping hold of the
reins over his withers.

THE SEAT.—On this subject Nimrod says: "It was well
observed by Don Quixote, in one of his lectures to Sancho,
that the seat on a horse makes some people look like gentlemen, and others like grooms; but a wonderful improvement has taken place within the last half century in the
seat on horseback of all descriptions of persons, effected
chiefly by the simple act of giving the rider a few more
inches of stirrup-leather. No gentleman now, and very
few servants, are to be seen with short stirrups, and, consequently, a bent knee, which, independently of its un-
sightliness, causes uneasiness to the horse as well as to his
rider,—whose knees being lifted above the skirts of the saddle deprive him of the assistance of the clip by his thighs
and legs. The short stirrup-leather, however, was adopted
with the idea of its giving relief to the horse although a

moment's consideration would have proved the contrary, and for this reason : the point of union between a man and his horse, as well as the centre of action, lies just behind the shoulder blades, which, as must be apparent to every one, is the strongest part of the horse's body, and where the sack of wheat or flour is placed by the farmer or miller. With short stirrup-leathers, the seat of the rider is thrown farther back on the saddle, instead of being exactly in the centre of it, and consequently his weight is thrown upon the part approaching the loins,—the weakest part of the body, and very easily injured. From the same mistaken notion was the saddle formerly placed nearly a hand's breadth from the shoulders, which, of course, added to the mischief."

In military riding, the stirrup-straps are nearly as long as they can be reached by the ball of the foot. In cross-country riding, on the contrary the strap is considerably shortened and the foot is placed home,—that is, the stirrup is carried in the hollow of the foot. This gives greater security to the seat, and lessens the risk of loosing the stirrup in leaping. The seat, in pleasure-riding, should be a compromise between these two. Various directions are given for the length of the stirrup, such as that the stirrup should hang opposite the ankle joint when the leg is extended downward ; that the leg should be extended, the toes raised as much as possible, and the stirrup adjusted to the position of the ball of the foot, when so placed ; or, that when the ball of the foot is in the stirrup, the rider can, keeping his ankle still bent, so raise himself as to just clear the pommel. Practically, the best direction is, for the rider to carry his feet in the position that is most comfortable to him, provided that it does not greatly vary from any of the foregoing, and that it does not cause his seat, in riding, to be behind the middle of the saddle. The proper position of the stirrup and the depression of the heel are represented in fig. 29. The foot must always be carried *nearly parallel to the horse's body, turning out the toe but very little.* The great essential of any seat on horseback is, to have it perfectly secure, natural, and unrestrained. Baucher gives the following directions for acquiring a good seat. He recommends for the purpose a quiet old horse:

The pupil being in the saddle, the instructor will examine his position in order to detect those parts which most require suppling. The pupil will first expand his chest, and retain himself some time in that position. He will next move his head to the right, or to the left, without a corresponding motion of the shoulders. The chest, arms, and head having become properly suppled, he will remove one of his legs as far as possible away from the saddle, and afterward replace it in such a manner as to take a firm clip with his knees and thighs. The leg must be entirely under the control of the pupil, and must be gradually replaced, not allowed to fall back of its own weight. The thighs and knees preserving their adherence to the saddle; the legs must be swung like a pendulum, the heels being raised to the height of the cantle of the saddle. The pupil should hold in either or both hands, weights of from ten to forty pounds, and should continue this practice until he can do it without affecting the security of his seat. The instructor should push the pupil from his seat to one side or to the other, and should watch that he regains it by the use of his hips and knees only. The hands, and consequently the shoulders and whole upper portion of the body, should remain motionless during this movement. In all of these exercises the pupil must have in view the necessity for guiding his horse independently of the means which keep him in his position, and never endeavoring to strengthen his position by his hold of the reins. It is a useful prac-

12*

tice for the pupil to get upon his knees, and subsequently upon his feet in the saddle, while holding weights in his hands.

THE HANDS.— The position of the hands, in riding, is a matter of the utmost importance, as on the delicacy and firmness of the touch depends very much the rider's ability to make his horse entirely submissive to his efforts. In cross-country riding, and in all cases where great care is necessary, the reins of each side should be held in the hand of that side. (See fig. 30.) This manner of holding the reins is always the safest, and, as a gentleman in riding is not obliged to use his right hand for a sword, as are military men, there is no reason why he should not use it in such a manner as to give him the best possible control of his horse's mouth.

With all strange or unruly horses, in turning to the right draw on the right rein, and to the left on the left rein. If you find that your horse is so delicately trained that he can be turned by the least pressure of the rein against either side of his neck, it will often be convenient to hold the reins together in the left hand. Baucher, in his *Manège* riding, holds the curb-reins together in his left hand, and the snaffle-reins together in his right. An alternate tension on the two reins keeps the horse more sensitive to the bit. As it is the almost universal custom among good riders in this country to ride with the reins in the left hand only, and as those deviating from this custom would be considered awkward, such persons as desire a reputation for skilful riding should hold their reins as is represented in Fig. 31. The right hand, in which the whip is firmly held, may rest on the hip, or hang by the side. The left hand should be held with the thumb upward and pointing toward the horse's ears, and with the little finger near to the pommel of the saddle and directly above it. This enables one to hold

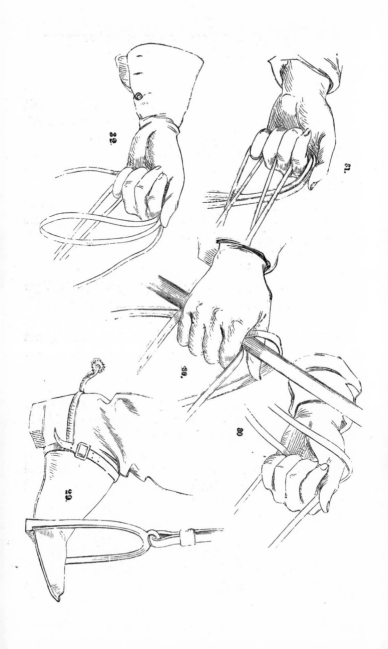

the elbow close to the side. The old custom of turning the knuckles upward, without giving more power, throws the elbow away from the side, and gives the rider an ungraceful appearance. If the horse has been trained as described in the chapter on Baucher's method, he may be best ridden with the curb-rein alone; the rein of the snaffle, being slackened only a few inches, may be easily drawn up at pleasure when it is necessary to give the horse a more firm support.

"Lightness of hand," about which much is said, is really a *firmness;* and, except with delicately formed and perfectly trained horses, a light hold of the bit is not only dangerous, but is injurious to the perfect action of the horse. On the road the rider should always maintain his horse's head in a perpendicular position; this requires the rein to be drawn to a certain point, at which it should be constantly kept, unless it be necessary to slacken the pace. The horse will soon learn that it is only within this limit that he can be free from the pain caused by the pressure of the bit, and, by keeping his mouth just within it, he will render the hold a light one; but, should he attempt to pass beyond it, he should find his rider's hand as firm and unyielding as iron. When in this position the horse is extremely sensitive to the least movement of the rider's hand, and by an awkward motion he may be thrown upon his haunches, or at least interrupted and confused in his gait.

THE LEGS.—The legs are no less important in guiding and assisting the horse in his movements than are the hands, for his changes of direction, and indeed his every action is no more dependent on his fore parts, which are controlled by the hands, than on the hind parts which are controlled entirely by the legs. A uniform pressure of both legs tends to bring the horse's hind feet forward, or to give a forward motion to his body. The pressure of

one leg, placed behind the girths, tends to turn the crou
around the fore legs from that side. An equal pressure of
both legs differently placed, and delicately aided by the
hand, tends to turn the horse around his centre of gravity,
and, by a combination of these aids, which require as much
practice in the management of the legs as in that of the
hands, the horse, in his movements, may be made entirely
submissive to the will of his rider. The legs have still another office, in enabling the rider to displace his weight so
as to throw more weight on one side of the horse than on
the other, and to cause him to raise the legs of the side
from which the weight has been removed. The rider
should carefully avoid distressing his horse by an unnecessary pressure of his thighs.

THE PACES.

THE WALK is so simple a gait that it is only necessary to
say of it that, except when adopted as a resting or breathing time for a weary horse, it should be performed with
animation, the head being kept in position, and the action
made lively and firm; this should especially be the case
when the object is to perform a slow journey, or simply to
exercise the horse. After fast travelling on the road, it is
at times desirable to allow the head to drop, and the whole
muscular system to become relaxed; but this should be
only for a sufficient distance to enable the horse to recover
from temporary exhaustion, and it should never be allowed
on rough ground with any horse, nor even on the smooth-
est ground with such as are inclined to trip. The rider
may suffer his own body to drop into an easy position, but
he must be ready instantly to regain his firmness in case
of a false step.

THE TROT is the *fashionable* gait in this country, though

it is less easy to the rider and to the horse than a well-gathered canter; and it is for both of them an artificial gait, and both will need much practice before they will be able to perform it gracefully. On the part of the horse, there is too frequently a tendency to bear heavily on the bit, and to trot with a low, reaching step. This always causes a contraction of the neck and jaw, and usually an irregular motion of the hind parts, which is far from being either easy or elegant. No matter how fast the trot may be, the animal should always preserve his lightness and freedom of action, maintaining a perfect suppleness and a uniformity in his step.

Military men, and the riders of the French school, practice what the English very properly term 'riding hard,' or sitting close to the saddle, while the English and very many American riders rise in the stirrup at each step of the horse. The latter is certainly the most easy for both horse and rider. This opinion is sustained by Nimrod, who writes as follows: "It is indeed to the disuse of this practice in France, and other parts of the continent, where rising in the stirrups is never resorted to, even on the hardest trotting horses, that is to be attributed the rare occurrence of persons riding any distance, at a quick rate, for pleasure. To this peculiar system in our horsemanship are we indebted, also, for our rapid style of posting, as without it post-boys could not endure the fatigue the action of a horse creates, especially in hot weather, over a fifteen miles stage, at the rate of ten or twelve miles an hour, without a moment's intermission; whereas, by means of it, he performs the task with comparative ease and comfort. The objection to it on the part of foreigners lies in the fancied inelegance of the motion, which we consider not worthy of an argument; but of this we are certain, that what is called 'riding hard,' that is, *not* rising in the stir-

rups in the trot, nor leaning any weight on them in the
gallop or canter, must be extremely distressing to the
horse."

If the novice attempts riding hard, he should avoid
leaning back too much, as this, by throwing the weight
near to the horses coupling, must always be distressing
to him. The proper position is to incline a very little
backward, enough to bring the shoulders over the cantel
of the saddle, or nearly so.

In rising in the stirrups one should lean a little forward,
and the motion should be only enough to break the shock
of the horse's step. The feet should be carefully kept in
a line with the horse's sides, as close as possible to his
body, and the swaying motion which they are likely to
take should be avoided. One should be able to ride in
this manner without the least support from the reins. In
slow trotting, as indeed in all slow riding, the reins may
be held together in the left hand, if the rider be acquainted with his horse, and is sure that he is not inclined to trip.

THE GALLOP AND CANTER.—While the gallop and canter are entirely different paces, the former being a succession of short leaps, and the latter a movement of the front
and hind legs successively, the transition from one to the
other is so gradual that it would be difficult to exactly fix
it, and the style of riding in both paces is very much the
same.

The horse being light in hand, and the rider being easy,
yet secure, in his seat, it will only be necessary to observe
a few important directions, such as the following:

The hand or hands, having a proper hold of the reins,
should be so held that the body is not twisted out of its
proper position; that is, supposing the reins be held together in the left hand, the left shoulder should not be thrown
forward, but both shoulders should be placed as nearly as

possible at right angles with the line of travel. If the horse lead with the left foot, his body will be inclined a little to the right, or if he lead with the right foot it will be inclined a little to the left. In either case, the rider should face the direction in which he is going, rather than the direction of the horse's body.

As there is more motion on that side of the horse which is leading, the rider's foot of that side will be more inclined than the other to sway with the horse's step; this should as far as possible, be avoided, as inelegant and insecure. The body of the rider should be perpendicular,—or, in the language of Baucher, every part of the body should rest on the part next below it, and the weight should be thrown somewhat into the stirrups, as being less fatiguing to the horse than when borne entirely by the seat.

The thighs should in all cases grasp the horse, but not with so much power as to render him uncomfortable,—a frequent error with strong men.

In the gallop the motion of the horse is very much increased, and there is proportionately greater necessity for the observance of the foregoing suggestions.

For further information concerning the different paces, the reader is referred to the chapter on Baucher's system of training horses for the saddle.

THE PACE, or AMBLE, is a gait which is not recognized in the art of Equitation, and which demands no special attention here, inasmuch as particular instructions with regard to it are not required after what has been said on the general subjects of the "Seat," "Hands," etc.

While pacing horses are in active demand for the saddles of middle-aged beginners, and although the gait has the sole and questionable advantage of being " as easy as a rocking-chair," it may not be amiss to say that the sidling movement and boring mouth of this class of horses, and the necessarily *swagging* seat of their riders, exclude the gait from the *manège*.

To an accomplished horseman, pacing is either painfully swinging or painfully dull. So long as his horse moves forward in a direct line he can preserve a safe, elegant, and comfortable seat, no matter how high the action; but when to the forward movement there is added a swaying from side to side, such a seat is impossible; and, indeed, all works on horsemanship, only teach the means for correcting this gait as a vice. Still, as many of the readers of this work may have reason, on account of timidity or physical weakness, to prefer pacing horses, their attention is called to the superior advantages of that particular variety of the gait called "Racking."

A true *pacer* moves the two feet of each side at the same time, and his action is neither so safe nor so pleasant as that of the *racker*, whose feet are set down one after the other in regular one-two-three-four time.

TURNING.—In turning the horse, in any pace, the rider should recollect that he is not simply to pull him round by the head, as this will invariably induce a contraction of the neck or of the whole body. The legs should be held sufficiently close to the sides to keep the horse's hind legs well under him, and the leg on the side from which it is desired to turn should be carried back of the girths at the same time that the head is drawn toward the side; this will cause the horse to turn gracefully, and to retain his lightness.

THE HALT.—There is one principle which must be borne in mind, in making a sudden halt from a rapid pace; that is, that if the hind legs are under the body, when the horse stops, they receive their share of the shock, whereas, if they are not so placed, the whole shock comes on the fore-legs, and a sudden halt becomes dangerous, or disagreeable. In halting from the gallop, touch the horse gently, but steadily, with the spurs when the hind legs are forward, and immediately follow this movement by a tension of the hand. If the rein is drawn *before* the spurs are used the hind legs cannot be controlled, and the horse stops only after a series of bounds, which are as uncomfortable to the rider as they are ungraceful. The instant halt, from an ordinary gallop, may, with a well-trained horse, be effected without difficulty.

Skilful riding is, if the expression may be allowed, an *acquired instinct*, and written instructions can give but an imperfect idea of the manner in which an accomplished rider is enabled to make his horse entirely subservient to his will, holding him, between his hands and his legs, ready to obey his least suggestion, and powerless to oppose his wishes; yet this is not a difficult acquirement for any person who will devote himself with zeal to his own and his horse's education.

HINTS FOR SPECIAL CASES.

In riding over hard ground, the horse should be kept to a trot, or a very gentle canter, as the concussion of the gallop is very severe on the hoofs and legs; strains, inflammation in the feet, break down, and, worse than all, quarter-crack, are frequent penalties of a disregard of this suggestion. The friction of hard roads on the shoes often renders them so hot as to injure the hoof.

When a piece of turf or soft road offers, the pace may be with safety extended to a sharp gallop without much danger of accident.

In riding over miry ground, the horse should be taken firmly between the legs, and the body should be inclined slightly backward, to prevent a fall forward in case of his stepping on a very soft spot.   As the hind feet are placed very nearly in the tracks of the fore feet, and as they are put down less perpendicularly, there is comparatively but little liability of the horse's falling on his haunches, and if he should do so, the fall would not be very dangerous to the rider.

The management of *shying* horses is considered in the chapter on Rarey's Method of Horse-taming.

If the horse be a kicker, recollect that he cannot kick to do any harm so long as his head is kept in the proper position, and that he may be prevented from striking out by the use of the curb, which will cause him to raise his head, in which position excessive kicking is impossible.

Some horses rear badly; they may generally be prevented from doing so by being touched in either flank with the spur, just as they commence to rise.   It may also be prevented, in some cases, by the rider's leaning well back in the saddle, and then throwing his weight suddenly forward, as soon as the fore feet leave the ground.   This creates an opposition which the horse had not calculated on when he took his spring, and brings him to his feet, or at least will prevent the horse from falling over backward.

LEAPING OR FENCING.—In the chapter on Baucher's method, there are given directions for teaching the horse to leap.   The rider will best take *his* first lessons in cautious and unobserved practice.   Very small ditches, and after them, very low fences should be "carried," with a well-trained, or very active horse.   The first landing from ever so small a leap, if it be really a leap, and not a scramble, is usually made with the rider on the horse's neck, or, at least, very far forward on the saddle; but the *knack* of the thing is soon acquired, and with the aid of coolness and courage, the novice will, after a few slight mishaps, find it easy to keep well down in his seat, and to land in such a manner as to jeopardize neither his own neck, nor his horse's fore legs.

Instead of the usual lengthy directions for leaping, we insert only the following suggestions, believing that the art is to be acquired only by practice, and that the experience of each individual, bought at the cost of a few mishaps, will be of more value than a volume of detailed instructions.

In going at a leap hold the reins in both hands, keeping them rather low, and steadying the horse by a uniform but not too tight hold of his mouth, reducing the speed to enable the horse to gather his hind legs well under him to take the spring.

As soon as he rises, give him the reins, and be ready to hold him at the moment of landing,—but be careful not to interfere with him until he has fairly touched the ground; a nervous grasping of the reins, such as is natural to the beginner, will almost inevitably bring him to grief.

All *high* leaps should be approached slowly, and those which require a long distance to be covered, should be ridden to at a gallop.

In approaching a water leap, take a firm hold of your horse's head, and, having made up your mind to jump it, do not let him swerve to the right nor to the left; the time for indecision has passed, and the leap must be taken at all cost, or *that* horse will never face water again.

Be careful never to lead your horse to a leap which you are not sure that he can cover, except in a case of absolute necessity; he will then, if necessary, go to severe leaps with confidence, and with a good chance of "carrying" them.

Do not try to *lift* your horse at his leaps. You might as well try to lift yourself by your boot-straps. If your horse need animating by whip or spur, let it be done before you approach the leap. Any interference on the part of the rider, at the time of leaping, is more likely to do harm than good. In descending from the leap, throw the shoulders and body well back, to prevent a fall forward. Confine yourself entirely to the standing leap, until both you and your horse can perform it properly. This will render the flying leap always easy and safe; but if the horse be first taught the flying leap, he will acquire the bad habit of *rushing* at his fences.

Do not disgust your horse by making him leap repeatedly over the same place; rather lead him to believe that the leaps are taken from necessity.

It is generally best not to ride to the bank of a ditch to examine it, and then turn to run at it; if it lie in your way, and you are pretty sure of its character, either take it on faith and *go at it*, or don't attempt it at all; any indecision will render your horse nervous, and lessen his ability to leap safely.

THE ART OF FALLING.—"He that will venture nothing, must not get on horseback," and every horseman must expect, sooner or later, to be thrown. Nimrod says: There is an art in falling, as well as in preventing falls. This consists in getting clear of the horse as soon as possible. If thrown over the horse's head, put out one, and if possible, both hands, to prevent the shock from being received by the head;—a broken collar bone is better than a broken neck.

If the horse falls, the rider should roll away from him as soon as he possibly can, lest in his struggle to rise again he strike him with his legs or head. Instead of losing hold of his reins, and abandoning his horse to his own will, as the man who is flurried at this time invariably does, he keeps them in his hand, if not always, perhaps in nine cases out of ten, and this secures his horse. It was the remark of a gentleman who was, from his desperate system of riding, and despite of his fine horse-manship, known to have had more falls than any other man during the time he hunted in Leicestershire, that nothing had so low an appearance as that of a man running on foot over a field, calling out, "stop my horse." In case of a severe fall, if surgical aid cannot be immediately obtained, drink a wineglassful of *strong* vinegar and water; its revulsive effect on the circulation will delay inflammation.

RIDING WITH LADIES.—If the lady with whom you are to ride is a good horsewoman, and her horse is perfectly trained, your responsibility is a light and pleasant one, involving only those usual attentions in mounting and dismounting which suggest themselves. Any unnecessary interference with the lady, or her horse, or excessive solicitude for her safety, must, to a woman of good sense, be annoying, and may not unfrequently be the cause of accidents. As, however, a lady is never so well prepared, from her mode of dress, natural timidity, and inferior strength, for the exigences of an accident, or a contest with a frightened horse, you should always be watchful of her horse, without appearing to be so, especially when passing vehicles or unusual objects on the road.

If the lady be inexperienced, or her horse badly trained, an increased responsibility rests upon the gentleman; and here coolness and good judgment on his part are requisite. If the lady be timid he must inspire her with confidence, not by ridiculing her fears, but by a quiet consideration of her wishes and solicitudes, even when they are the result of a foolish timidity. She will then receive his assurances that "there is no danger," with a reliance upon his judgment which she could not otherwise feel.

If, on the other hand, as is very often the case she be

over-confident of her own skill or the good disposition of the horse, keep a vigilant eye upon her, but do not unwisely show your own anxiety, or utter cautions which will only tempt her to a greater display of her own fearlessness, with a laugh at your advice. At the proper moment you may suggest the danger you see, giving her the reasons for your apprehensions.

The instructions for assisting the lady in mounting will be found in the chapter on Ladies' Riding, and comprise all that is necessary on that topic.

If you are to ride with a lady under circumstances which render it probable you will have to assist her, or on thoroughfares where many vehicles will be met, ride on the left side of her; but if otherwise, it is well to consult her preferences as to which side you shall take. There is no rule to be prescribed on this point, though the advantages of riding on the left side may be stated as follows:

You have the right hand nearest to her, to render her any assistance, if required. On the other side your bridle-hand, which is comparatively inefficient for this purpose, is the only one you can conveniently use.

Any disarrangement or entanglement of the skirt can be corrected by the gentleman, and is less liable to be observed by passers-by.

The left side being the one on which all carriages pass, you ride between them and your lady's horse.

Conversation is much more easily carried on, as the lady can, with less exertion, turn her face toward the gentleman.

If the saddle turn, or any accident render it necessary to lift the lady from the saddle, the left side is always preferable.

The objections to riding on this side are, that an awkward rider, or horse, may hurt or incommode the lady's feet, and that it is sometimes desirable to the lady to adjust her dress when she would prefer the gentleman to be on the other side.

In rapid riding, keep near to your lady, but do not crowd her; the horses' heads should be equally advanced, but when about to pass a vehicle you may ride slightly forward, to be more sure not to press her feet in turning out, and to be in a better position for assisting her.

If it become necessary, in an extremity, to lift the lady from the saddle, direct her to remove her leg from the pommel, and to take the reins in the right hand; then hug your left foot close under your horse's side, to strengthen your position and to move him as close to her as possible; hold your reins in the left hand, pressing the back of the knuckles against the left side of the pommel of your saddle, for a fulcrum, and then grasp her with the right arm firmly around the waist, and lift her on to your right thigh; turn your horse sharply around to the right, that her's may not kick her on finding himself free.

The lady should keep a firm hold of her reins until she begins to leave the saddle, when she should drop them and grasp your horse's mane, at the same time disengaging her foot from the stirrup. During the whole operation the gentleman must be firm and decided, and must studiously avoid feeling, and consequently communicating to his companion, the least alarm.

CHAPTER XVIII.

LADIES' RIDING.

WRITTEN BY A LADY.

LEARNING TO RIDE—THE SIDESADDLE—THE GIRTHS—THE STIRRUP—THE BRI-
DLE—THE MARTINGALE—THE BIT—THE DRESS—MOUNTING AND DIS-
MOUNTING—THE POSITION—THE HANDS—ACCIDENTS.

EVERY lady should learn to ride; not at a mature age,
when her frame has become exhausted by a sedentary life,
and consequent ill health; nor even when, her school-days
being over, she is thought to have leisure for wholesome
exercise; but in childhood, when her will is strong and
her body obedient to it. Particularly in our large cities,
too little care is given to the physical culture of young
girls. Their minds are engaged, not often with energetic
mental work, but with idle thought for dress and show;
while no other exercise is taken than a measured daily
walk, and occasional dancing and waltzing.

Where household labor is disdained, and no opportunity can be afforded for floriculture or any other agreeable
out-door occupation, there is no substitute so good as
horseback riding. But for the country girl it becomes
indispensable. Not her health, perhaps, but her happiness
demands it. No woman ever rides so well as one who
from childhood has loved her pet colt. She has chased
him, perhaps, for hours around a 'ten-acre lot:' and when,
his frisky mood over, she has been able to take him coax-
ingly by the mane and lead him to a mounting place, great
was the triumph of her wild ride. And no training or
care can give the freedom and skill of this youthful prac-

Fig. 33.

tice. When, at length, she is able to bridle and saddle him, her seat may be somewhat faulty, and her use of the reins awkward, but these faults are easily remedied, and are certainly atoned for by her freedom and fearlessness. Besides, no one can fully enjoy riding who does not both love and admire the noble animal which she rides; and the quick intelligence of the horse yields ready obedience to the hand and voice of a woman who has learned lovingly to control him. His affectionate nature yields to her the mastery, often more readily than to a stronger power.

Well mounted on a strong, spirited horse—with a wide country before her—on a clear, cool day—with a love for all the beauty around her, of the noble animal beneath her, and glowing with the bounding life within her, a lady capable of enjoyment is certainly prepared for it then. The first gentle pace of the horse starts the warm blood in her veins, and as both become excited, the glow tingles to the very finger-tips. The close-clinging to the horse, the slight reliance upon stirrup and bit, and the generally light proportion of rider to steed, give a feeling of being possessed of the powers of a new life, of riding upon the whirlwind, and yet controlling it with a word.

This combination of a sense of weakness and of power, as every woman knows, is her greatest delight, and is the secret of many an enjoyment which she attributes to other causes. If a quieter mood possess the rider, there is no such pleasant manner of strolling over a wide extent of country, otherwise inaccessible. The discovery of new paths and openings in woods and hilly country, where momently changes are succeeding each other in the pano-rama, affords delights which are not attainable in any other way. Even hundreds of miles of travel are more pleasantly accomplished in the saddle than in any other manner, even by ladies; provided always that they be

13

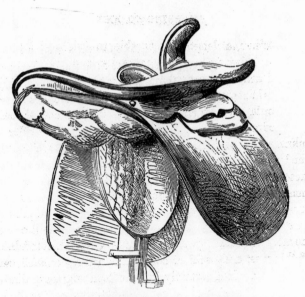

Fig. 34.—Ladies' Saddle without the right-hand horn.

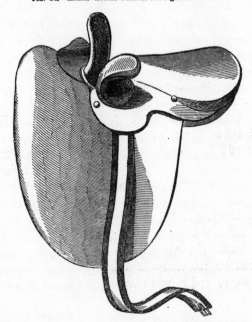

Fig. 35.—The reverse view of the above, showing the Leaping-horn.

[290]

well attired and well mounted. Then the companionship of friends is infinitely more sweet under the exhilerating influences of active exercise, fresh air, and keen physical enjoyment. What so gay as a party of high-spirited equestrians? The emulation of riders and horses adds a new element of enjoyment, while the beauty of every fair rider is enhanced not only by the glow of pleasurable excitement, but by the contrasts of color and form which each may present, in her habit and her horse. Companies of gentlemen and ladies, in full hunting suits, bounding in all the excitement of a race over a smooth stretch of road, or better still, over wide meadows, in eager chase, present one of the most beautiful sights imaginable. Of the healthfulness of this most delightful of accomplishments too much cannot be said. But certainly its benefits must greatly diminish when it is resorted to, merely to strengthen the body. If a lady be recommended to ride for her health, let her first seek for the *delight* of riding, for nothing is more tiresome than being heavily jolted in a lady's saddle, or more wearisome than being quietly ambled over the ground by a small, spiritless pony.

To ensure ease, elegance, and enjoyment in riding, many things are requisite. We enumerate as follows:

THE SIDESADDLE. — The following, by Mr. Rarey's English editor, is sensible, and to the point:

"Ladies' saddles ought invariably to be made with what is called the leaping-horn, or crutch, at the left side. (See figs. 34 and 35.) The right-hand pommel has not yet gone out of fashion, but it is of no use, and is injurious to the security of a lady's seat, by preventing the right hand from being put down as low as it ought to be with a restive horse, and by encouraging the bad habit of leaning the right hand on it. A flat projection is quite sufficient. This will be quite clear to you, if, when sitting in your chair, you put a cylinder, three or four inches in diameter, between your legs, press your two knees together by crossing them, in the position of a woman on a sidesaddle. Besides, when a man clasps his horse, however firmly, it has a tendency to raise the seat from the saddle. This is not the case with the sidesaddle seat: if a man wishes to use a lance and ride at a ring, he will find that he has a firmer seat with this kind of sidesaddle than with his own. There is no danger in this side-pommel, since you cannot be thrown on it, and it renders it next to impossible that the rider should be thrown upon the other pommel. In case of a horse leaping suddenly into the air and coming down on all four feet,—technically, "*bucking*,"—without the leaping-horn there is nothing to prevent a lady from being thrown up. But the leaping-horn holds down the left knee, and makes it a fulcrum to keep the right knee down in its proper place. If the horse in violent action throws himself suddenly to the left, the upper part of the rider's body will tend downwards, to the right, and the lower limbs to the left: nothing can prevent this but the support of the leaping-horn. The fear of over-balancing to the right causes many ladies to get into the bad habit of leaning over their saddles to the left. This fear disappears when the hunting-horn pommel is used. The leaping-horn is also of great use with a hard puller, or in riding down a steep place, for in either case it prevents the lady from sliding forward.

"But these advantages render the right-hand pommel quite useless, a slight projection being all-sufficient (see fig. 35); while this arrangement gives the habit and figure a much better appearance. But every lady ought to be measured for this part of the saddle, as the distance between the two pommels will depend partly on the length of her legs.

" When a timid, inexperienced lady has to ride a fiery horse, it is not a bad plan to attach a strap to the outside girth on the right hand, so that she may hold it and the right-hand rein at the same time without disturbing her seat. This little expedient gives confidence, and is particularly useful if a fresh horse should begin to kick a little. Of course, it is not to be continued, but only used to give a timid rider temporary assistance. I have also used for the same purpose a broad tape passed across the knees, and so fastened that in a fall of the horse it would give way."*

The prejudice of many American ladies, especially in the country, against the third horn of the saddle, is purely the result of habit. Having always been accustomed to the old style of saddle, they experience a restraint in the first use of the leaping-horn, which suggests a dangerous confinement of the limbs, and they seem to fear that they could not easily disengage themselves from it, in case of accident. This fear is groundless; they could, in no case, get off on the right side, and in dismounting to the left, the leg is simply lowered away from it, so that it can, in no sense, be considered an obstacle to jumping off from the horse. The mere fact that it prevents that worst of all accidents—being thrown on to the left horn in case of the horse falling—is an unanswerable argument in its favor, and no lady, who has become accustomed to its use, would be willing to dispense with it.

THE STIRRUP.—English ladies very often ride with the ordinary open stirrups, and it is not clearly apparent why the custom is not universal. Except in very cold weather, the slipper can have no advantage, and in very warm weather it must be uncomfortable. As, however, the slip-

* "The Art of Taming Horses," &c. From this work we have also taken the suggestion for some of the cuts which embellish these "Hints."

per is almost universally used in America, two cuts, representing the most fashionable forms, are here introduced.
Figure 36, is the ordinary slipper, with a small pad

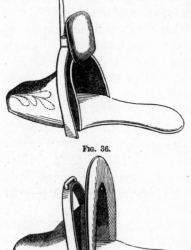

buckled over the iron,
to protect the ankle.
In fig. 37, a French slipper, the ancle is more
effectually protected by
the projection and turn-
ing up of the upper edge
of the slipper, so as to
entirely separate the
iron from the ancle.

FIG. 36.

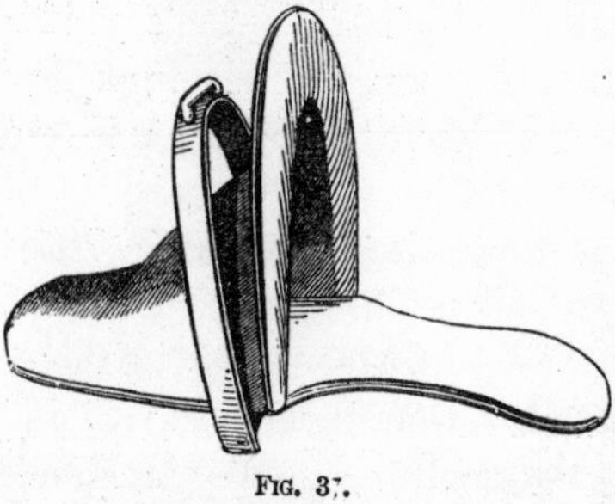

GIRTHS.—The ladies'
saddle should be sup-
plied with three girths,
—two under both flaps,
as on gentlemen's sad-
dles, and one *under* the
near-side flap, and *over*
the off-side flap. They
all draw up on the off

FIG. 37.

side, and on horses which require to be girthed to suffocation, the two under ones should be made tight at the
stable, and again after the lady has mounted, and then the
outer girth should be drawn taut, confining the flap on the
off side. Well-bred horses have high, sharp withers, around
which it is impossible for the saddle to turn, and do not
require excessively tight girthing. If a lady *hang* on the
near side-horn of her saddle, no amount of girthing will
prevent the saddle from bearing hard against the withers.

The girths should be of a modest color, and of the best
quality of English webbing.

THE BRIDLE.—The bridle for a lady's horse should be

perfectly neat and simple. The head-stall and reins should always be made of the most pliant of leather. It is well to have the two reins made of different material, or of different size, that they may be readily distinguished. It is indispensable that a lady should know when her horse is well bridled and well saddled, and she should study the adjustment of bit and buckle.

The martingale is often adopted for show, rather than use. A lady's horse, properly broken, will bend to the hand without it, and where not absolutely required, it is far better dispensed with. This remark applies particularly to the nose or standing martingale; for, should a horse make a false step, half his power to recover himself is destroyed by the manner in which his head is confined by it. The objection to the ring-martingale is not so great but one of this kind can only be used on the snaffle-rein and is of very little service.

THE BIT.—Ladies should always use either the Pelham bit (fig. 26), or the bit and bridoon, which is a combination of both snaffle and curb. Its arrangement is shown in figure 13. There are many sorts and sizes of these bits. Some are very light and elegant, being intended especially for ladies' use. Ornamental frippery should find no place in any part of a lady's riding outfit, and it is peculiarly inappropriate for the bit, which should be, in all cases, as strong and effective as possible. There is no bit in the world which, while it does not annoy a nervous horse, gives such absolute control over an obdurate brute as this very Baucher bit elsewhere described. Its large, smooth canon is easy in the mouth, and the great length of the branches affords a leverage which is especially necessary to riders of little strength.

THE WHIP, an essential element of the lady's riding outfit, should be stiff and substantial, without being heavy.

It may be lightly made, and finished with delicate ornament, and often becomes a gem in the lady's costume. It is needed not so much to punish the horse or to animate him, as to control his movements by its pressure against his flank, as the gentleman controls his horse by a pressure with his right leg.

THE DRESS.—"Few ladies know how to dress for horse exercise, although there has been a great improvement, so far as taste is concerned, of late years. As to the headdress, it may be whatever is in fashion, provided it fits the head so as not to require continual adjustment, often needed when the hands would be better employed with the reins and whip. It should shade from the sun, and, if used in hunting, protect the nape of the neck from rain. The recent fashions of wearing the plumes or feathers of the ostrich, the cock, the pheasant, the peacock, and the kingfisher, in the riding hats of young ladies, are highly to be commended.

The hair should be arranged in the firmest manner possible. If suited to the style of the lady, it may be plaited at the back and looped across, in a manner which will support the hat and present a very comely appearance. Or it may be found pleasanter to turn all of the back hair to the top of the head, where a high hat is used. All loose arrangements of the hair, except short curls, when they are natural, should be avoided. But few hair-pins should be used, and those long and firmly woven into the hair.

Ladies' habits are usually made too long; if the extra length be turned to a heavy hem at the bottom, it will be found much more likely to stay well down over the feet, which is all that is required; weights are unnecessary and cumbersome. A foot longer than an ordinary skirt will be found sufficient, if the material be suitable. Light cloth will be found the most appropriate for the skirt, if the color be becoming and sufficiently dark. For country riding it may be bordered a foot deep with leather. A habit of the same should be worn in winter, adapted in shape to the figure of the lady. If she be short and plump, the more closely it fits the figure the better, particularly the sleeves, which should never be large. If she be slight, the dress may be opened in front and the sleeves loosened at the wrist, with white linen chemisette and sleeves. No basque, or a very slight one, should be worn, nor anything else which will flutter in the wind. No ornament is needed. A good effect of color and form is all that is seen or that is desirable.

"The fashion of a waistcoat of light material for summer, revived from the fashion of the last century, is a decided improvement, and so is the over-jacket, of cloth or seal-skin, for rough weather. It is the duty of every woman to dress in as becoming and attractive a manner as possible; there is no reason why pretty young girls should not indulge in picturesque riding costume so long as it is appropriate.

"Many ladies entirely spoil the set of the skirts by retaining the usual *impedimenta* of petticoats. The best dressed horsewomen wear nothing more than a flannel chemise with long, colored sleeves, under their trousers.

"Ladies' trousers should be of the same material and color as the habit, and if full, flowing like a Turk's and fastened with an elastic band round the ankle, they will not be distinguished from the skirt. In this costume, which may be made amply warm by the folds of the trousers, plaited like a Highlander's kilt,—fastened with an elastic band at the waist,—a lady can sit down in a manner impossible for one encumbered by two or three short petticoats. It is the chest and back which require double folds of protection during, and after, strong exercise."

If ladies prefer, a quilted skirt, not too full, may be worn. It should be lined with silk or glazed muslin, and will be found no impediment. Long boots are a great comfort and protection in riding long distances.

All ladies who desire that riding should be to them a healthful exercise, must take great care that their dress be perfectly easy in every part, particularly over the chest and around the ribs. Let the boots be easy, and their gloves, which should be leather gauntlets, large and soft, and all elastic bands very loose.

MOUNTING.—The lady in mounting should, if convenient, be assisted by two persons ; one to hold the horse,— standing directly in front of him, and holding by the check pieces of the bridle, above the bit,—and the other to assist her to her seat. Having taken the reins and whip in the right hand, she will stand with her face towards the horse's head, and with her right hand on the left pommel of the saddle. In the left hand she will hold her skirt, in such a manner as to enable her to raise it clear of the ground. The gentleman will stand, facing her, and opposite to the horse's shoulder, with his left hand holding by his mane ; this steadies the horse when the lady springs. The gentleman will now stoop and take the lady's left foot, which has been raised fifteen inches from the ground, in his right hand, clasping it firmly under the instep. The skirt having been raised to clear the foot, is now dropped, and the lady places her left hand on the gentleman's right shoulder, giving a spring to straighten the left knee. During this spring the gentleman will simply keep his hand still, supporting the lady's weight, but not raising her until the knee is fairly straightened, when he may lift her to the required height, but without trying to push her over on to the saddle. She will find her seat more easily without such assistance, which would often tend to throw her over the horse, rather than

13*

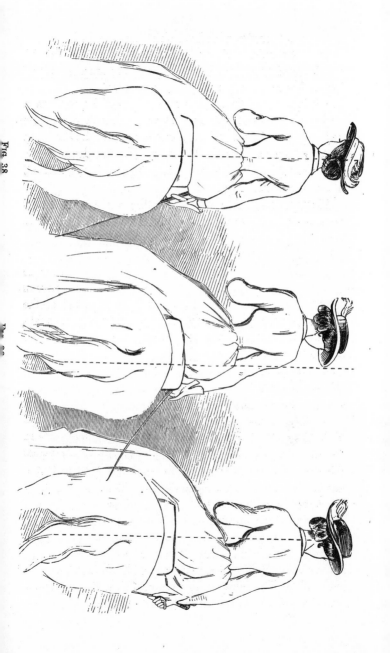

Fig. 38

on his back. Being seated with her right hand still on the pommel, the lady will, with her left hand, adjust the folds of her skirt. She will then remove her hand from the pommel, and place her right knee over it; when the gentleman will place her foot in the stirrup, and then aid her in taking proper hold of the reins and whip. When this is accomplished, the attendant at the horse's head steps out of the way, and the lady assumes the control. Fortunately, the operation is less tedious than its description.

DISMOUNTING.—A lady dismounts with perfect ease. After the groom has taken his place in front of the horse and secured him, by releasing her hold upon the bridle and stirrup and lifting her right leg over the pommel, which she now holds with the right hand, while the left, on the shoulder, or in the hand of her gallant, affords her sufficient support in slipping to the ground.

THE POSITION.

THE SEAT IN THE SIDESADDLE.—The lady should, by exercises similar to those recommended for gentlemen, endeavor to acquire a perfect independence of the rein-hold in the security of her seat. She should be able to lean far to the right or to the left, or lie back on the horse's haunches, or forward on his neck, and to regain her position without disturbing her seat in the saddle, and without holding by the reins. With the use of the leaping-horn it will be more easy for her to attain perfection, in this respect, than it will be for the man, who must depend in a great measure on the clip of his legs.

We introduce a series of cuts to show the difference between good and bad positions in the sidesaddle. Fig. 38 represents the proper position, the figure being erect, directly over the horse's spine, the shoulders at an equal height. and the elbows near the sides. Fig. 39 shows a more common faulty position, the weight of the body being placed far to the left, and supported by the horn. This position is taken from a fear of falling to the right, and is most distressing to the horse, while it makes the lady look as though hung on a peg at his side. In fig. 40, the last described ungraceful position is attempted to be avoided by a lady who takes her seat in the proper place on the sad-dle, and at that point, her courage failing her, bends her shoulders far to the left, by a combination of curves more remarkable than beautiful.

The fear which occasions these faults will in a great measure disappear if the leaping-horn be adopted.

The spine should be perpendicular over a line running lengthwise through the centre of the saddle, and the right leg, by which the weight should be mainly supported, should lie as far from the right as the construction of the saddle will allow. The right leg, from the knee down, should lie close to the saddle, rather than be pressed hard against it. Care should be taken to keep the foot turned to the right; otherwise the lady can have no firm hold, and it will break one of the most graceful lines of her flowing skirt.

It is also important that the stirrup be not too short. It should be of such a length as to raise the left thigh lightly against the leaping-horn, while the heel is very slightly depressed below the level of the ball of the foot. The leg can then be either borne hard against the horn, or lowered slightly away from it at pleasure.

THE HANDS.—It is believed by many that a good seat is all that is required to make a good rider, and it is un-doubtedly of vast importance to the fair equestrienne. But this excellence can be more easily obtained than the proper use of the hands. However strange it may seem, a " heavy " hand is found quite as common among ladies as gentlemen, though this is more from lack of decision and energy than from any other cause. Practice alone can ensure a delicate hand, unless it be a natural gift. Some hints towards holding the reins properly will assist materially.

Ladies, particularly those with very small hands, will often find it burdensome to hold their reins both in one hand, as is universally taught in our riding-schools. For young riders it is best to use both hands, pulling the right rein when they wish to go to the right hand, and the left when they wish to go to the left. It is better for new beginners to ride with one bridle and two hands, than with two bridles and one hand: it ensures a square seat, and gives that power which can only be dispensed with when great skill is acquired. A man has the power of turning a horse, to a certain extent, with his legs and spurs; a woman must depend on her reins, her whip, and her left leg. The best way for a lady is, if her hand be light, to knot up the snaffle and let it rest within her reach, in case of accident to the other rein. Or, if her touch be not delicate enough for the curb, let her hold it lightly and depend on the snaffle. In this case the snaffle should be taken on either side of the second finger of the bridle hand, and the curb on either side of the little finger. Reverse the order, if it is desirable to use the curb. Two reins are certainly more safe, and sufficient practice will enable a lady to use them with perfect ease. She should be able to shift them instantly to the right hand, without slackening her pace, in case of disarrangement of her skirt, or other accident.

Ladies, whose hands are sufficiently large, may ride with the four reins gathered in the left hand, keeping the elbow close to the side, and the thumb pointed upward, as recommended for gentlemen; but usually with ordinary reins, only the snaffle, or the curb-rein,—as the case may

be,—can be held gathered, and the otner must lie across
the hand (fig. 32). When two reins are held in each hand
they should be arranged as in fig. 33, but the whip should,
usually, be dropped and allowed to hang by its cord from
the wrist, as the two reins are quite enough for a lady's
hand, and this double hold of both reins is not often necessary at a time when the whip is called for.

The Whip and the Left Heel are valuable aids to a lady
in the saddle. By a proper use of them she is enabled to
retain a much freer hold upon her reins. Particularly in
stopping and turning they are invaluable. Also, in starting,
the pressure of the leg and whip should be applied to
bring the horse up to the bit. In making the turn he
must be kept well up, and be assisted both by a steady feeling of the outward rein, which should only be relaxed
enough to admit of an easy inclination of the horse to the
side to which he is to turn, and, by a stronger pressure of
the outward aid,—the leg or whip,—to keep the haunches
from falling too much out. Care must be taken at all times
to make the step steady, and not by a sudden or violent
pull upon the reins, which often causes some horses to rear,
and injures others. The use of the reins, the heels and the
whip might be enlarged upon indefinitely; but only the
nicest care and minute observation can teach the lady the
rare art of perfect management.

ACCIDENTS.—Ladies, of course, should never ride horses
which are in any manner vicious. But the best animals
are not faultless, nor the most sure-footed always reliable.
The lady should therefore be prepared for critical situations.
Perhaps the most common fault is shying. If a horse is
known to be afraid of any object, his attention may often-
times be diverted by turning away his head or speaking
kindly to him; also, rather than to oppose him, he may
often to much better advantage be humored in his whims,

and even be compelled to continue them after he is tired; thus, if he turn short round, make him turn in the same direction half a dozen times. If he refuse to go forward compel him to go backward.

Stumbling is more often a habit or an infimity than an accident. Where it is accidental, it is generally in a young horse, who will probably recover himself without danger to the rider; but, on the slightest intimation, she must throw her body back, and by raising her hands raise his head and assist him to regain himself. The greatest danger a lady encounters is the possibility of her horse rearing very high; when she should be sufficiently self-possessed to slacken his rein and throw the whole weight of her body forward, being always ready to rise the moment the horse comes to the ground. With proper watchfulness of eye and hand, a well-seated lady will always be prepared for any emergency. Above all things be chary of an improper use of the whip.

Remember that with a long skirt about her feet, and with little experience in such exercise, it is always unsafe for a lady to leap from her saddle. She can tell at once, on mounting, if her saddle is not securely girthed, so that only inexcusable neglect will admit of its turning. So long as the saddle is in its place, and the horse on his feet, a lady should *never* leave him under any circumstances unless he be rearing badly, and an attendant be at hand to receive her; if the saddle turn entirely off from the horse's back, or, if he has fallen and cannot recover himself, a lady may disengage herself quickly, but carefully. In a runaway, her place is close down in the saddle, holding the four reins low on either side, and giving an alternate tension to the curb and snaffle, steadying her horse in the road and saving her strength to force him to run long after he would gladly stop.

CHAPTER XIX.

HOW TO DRIVE A HORSE.

THE ART OF DRIVING—PLEASURE DRIVING—HOW TO HOLD THE REINS—DRIV-ING A PAIR—FOUR-IN-HAND DRIVING—DRIVING WORKING HORSES—PLOW-ING—THREE-A-BREAST.

WHEN the colt is once made to understand what is required of him, in both double and single harness, his after education depends on the skill and patient perseverance of his driver. The art of driving, whether for pleasure or work, demands a clear understanding of the requirements of each particular case, and attention to every motion of one's horse. Pleasure horses are required to travel actively, evenly, safely, and with as much *style* as possible, while work horses are required to throw their weight into the collar, and with a steady, even pull, without swerving to the right or to the left, and without fretting or noticing what is going on about them, to keep up a uniform motion of their load, at no time losing the assistance of its momentum, and never unnecessarily wasting their strength by a sudden rapid pull. The ability of the horse to assume one or the other of these characters depends even less upon his own nature than on the manner in which he is driven.

In PLEASURE DRIVING the seat should be rather high, so that one may easily see over the dash-board of the carriage, but low enough for a direct pull on the bit when it is necessary. The feet should be firmly planted (avoiding an ungraceful or studied attitude,) in such a manner as to give strength to the pull, and security to the position, in

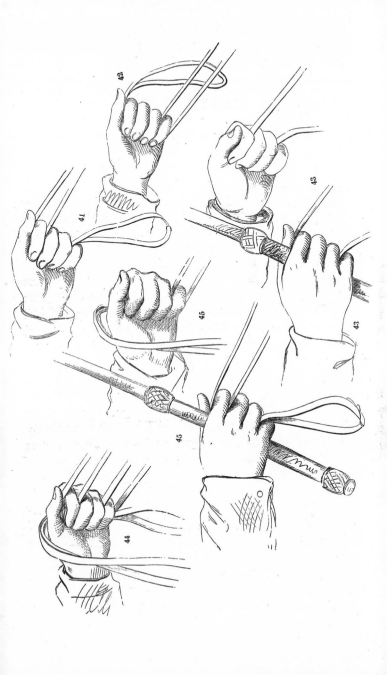

case of a sudden jolt of the carriage. The legs and hips should be as firm and immovable, and the upper part of the body should be as free and flexible, as possible, the principle being borne in mind, as in the case of riding on horseback, that while the seat should be perfectly secure, this security should not imply the least support from the reins, nor the least inability to do whatever may be necessary with the head or arms.

The eyes of the driver should be always on his horses, yet always about him. While he should see every strap and buckle within eye-shot, every movement of the horses' ears, every toss or shake of their heads, and every step that they take, he should also see every vehicle coming toward him, every object by the roadside, or elsewhere, which can possibly frighten his team, and every stone or uneven place in the road on which they are likely to step, or which may come in the way of the wheels. To sit in this manner, and to be thus watchful while driving a pair of lively horses, and at the same time to appear perfectly at ease, is no small accomplishment; still it may be attained by practice, and is essential to elegance in driving.

The manner of holding the reins should depend on circumstances. They may be both held in the left hand in either of the following ways, the hand being held with the thumb upward:—

First. Let the off rein pass over the fore finger, and the near rein between the fore and middle fingers, the thumb pressing on the off rein to keep it in place, and both reins passing out between the ring and little fingers, as shown in fig. 41; in this way they can be held very securely.

Second. Let the near rein pass under the little finger, and the off rein between the ring-finger and little finger, both ends being brought out between the thumb and fore finger, falling over the knuckles, and being secured by the pressure of the thumb, as is shown in figure 42; this is a lighter hold than the former, and is better for driving perfectly trained horses which require only the least touch to bring their heads into the proper (perpendicular) position. It is more fatiguing than that first described, with horses which are at all hard on the bit.

When it is desirable to hold the reins in both hands, the off rein may be taken in the right hand, by passing the fore finger under it, and allowing it to fall down through the hand, and out between the ring and little fingers; this will admit of the hand being opened to take the whip. (See fig. 43.) The rein in the left hand may remain in the same position as before. If it be necessary to strike a severe blow with the whip, the rein should be passed into the left hand, and quickly regained after the blow has been struck; this manner of holding the reins will give the greatest possible power over the team. The whip should be taken from its socket only when there is occasion to use it, and it should be returned as soon as it has become unnecessary. While held quietly in the hand it should lie horizontally across the near rein, and pointing over the whiffle-tree on the near side.

Driving a single horse is not at all difficult, and it requires only a good hand, a good temper, and a watchful eye. The horse's mouth should be lightly felt, that he may be supported if he trip; and especially in going down hill, the driver should sit with his feet well braced and his hand ready to support the horse in a false step, which, if at all, is most likely to occur at this time.

Driving a pair of horses requires much more skill and care. It is thus described by Stonehenge:

"IN DRIVING A PAIR, the great art consists in putting them together so as to draw equally, and to step together.

To do this well, the horses must match in action and temper, two slugs being much better than a free-tempered horse with a slug; because, in this case, the whip applied to the one only makes the other more free, and as a consequence it is impossible to make them draw equally. In some cases where two horses are exactly equally matched, the coupling-reins must both be of equal length; but this is seldom the case; and when they do not do an equal amount of work, the coupling-rein of the free one must be taken up, and that of the idle horse let out. In watching the working of the two horses the pole-pieces should always be the guide; and if both are slack, with the end of the pole steady, and neither horse shouldering it, the driver may rest contented that his horses are each doing their share; if, however, the pole is shouldered by either, that horse is a rogue, and is making the other do more than his share, keeping the pole straight by the pressure of his shoulder, instead of pulling at the traces. On the other hand, if either horse is pulling away from the pole, and straining at the pole-piece, he is doing more than his share, and his coupling-rein must be taken in accordingly. Sometimes both shoulder the pole, or spread from it, which are equally unsightly habits, and may generally be cured by an alteration of the coupling-reins of both horses, letting them out for shouldering, and taking them in for its opposite bad habit. The reins are held in the same way for double-harness as for single. In driving a pair, it should always be remembered that there are two methods of driving round a curve, one by pulling the inside rein, and the other by hitting the outside horse, and these two should generally be combined, graduating the use of the whip by the thinness of the skin of the horse. In all cases the whip is required in double harness, if not to drive horses when thoroughly put together, yet to make them pull equally; and there are very few pairs which do not occasionally want a little reminding of their duties. A constant change from one side to the other is a prevention of those tricks and bad habits which horses get into if they are kept to one side only. The coachman should, therefore, change them every now and then, and back again, so as to make what was a puller from the pole, rather bear towards it than otherwise when put on the other side."

There is a certain animation of manner on the part of the driver which, without being noisy or demonstrative, keeps a team lively and cheerful at work, while another driver would not be able to get them to nearly so good a pace with even more labor to himself, and more fatigue to them. To attain this correspondence with one's horse should be the object of every person who attempts to become a fine driver. No such influence can be had over a horse which is not light in hand, and sprightly in his action,—that is, in the condition which is best and most easily attained by the suppling for the saddle described in the chapter on that subject. Some of the advantages of this are, that it gives the horse more style,—that is, a higher, more graceful step, a better carriage of the head and tail, and generally a more lithe appearance. It has considerable influence in causing the horses of a double team to step together in measured time. This must of course depend very much on their relations as to size and form, but it will do more than any other mode of training to equalize their steps, as it renders them very sensitive to the least action of the hand, and as the trotting of one horse will produce a slight reäction on the hand, it must have an equal effect on the mouth of the other horse with which the hand is equally connected.

FOUR-IN-HAND DRIVING.—With respect to coupling four-horse teams, the heads, particularly those of the wheel-horses, should not be too closely confined. It looks well to see them with their heads close together, running boldly up to their bits; but if you confine them too tightly, they cannot apply all their power to the collar.

Wheel-horses should, in this respect, have more liberty than their leaders, not only on account of the pole, but to enable them to "quarter their ground" and bring themselves into a proper situation to hold back in going down hill, which they cannot do if their heads are confined. When the leaders' heads are well together, they are much easier driven; the least motion of the wrist will affect their mouths, and of course they are much safer on their feet; for, on the least false step they make, the support of the coupling-rein is immediately felt; without this, they would be down before they could receive assistance from the coachman's hand.

Of the two reins used for coupling, one must be uppermost at the crossing; that one should be buckled to the horse that carries his head highest, otherwise he will be constantly annoying his partner's mouth.

All attempts at directions for curbing coach-horses must be vain, and can only be regulated by their mouth, temper and disposition.

Horses with hard dead mouths require the greatest skill and management to draw tolerably, and should not be curbed up tightly, as that will tend to increase the difficulty. To ride or drive horses with pleasure and advantage, you must have a light finger and play with their mouths with skill and humor. Some horses have a trick of getting the check of their bit into their mouths; this is very dangerous, and should be prevented by a washer or round piece of leather.

The most dangerous horse in a team is a stiff-necked one, which, in going down hill, instead of inclining his head towards his partner, and throwing out his quarters so as to hold back the coach, twists his head another way, looking over one shoulder, and with the other shouldering the pole or his partner. When you have one of this sort you can do nothing with him by pulling up, but must whip his mate up to him, and if that does not answer, cross the road quickly with the leaders, to prevent running off to the side to which he is pushing.

If your horses are nervous and fidgety, they will not bear being confined too tightly at first starting, but must be humored and allowed some length of chain, particularly if the road be rough and full of ruts. When there are no breechings the horse requires to be nearer to the pole, or in holding back his collar will get too far forward, unless restrained by a false martingale. Some coachmen object to breechings as being troublesome to horses in hot weather, but they are almost indispensable in hilly countries, as they enable the horse to hold back with less strain on his back and legs, and add greatly to the security of both team and vehicle.

The draft of the leaders will be greatly equalized by crossing the inside traces, fastening that of the near horse to the whiffle-tree of the off side, and that of the off horse to the near whiffle-tree.

The great art in driving four-in-hand is to favor the peculiarities of the different horses of the team. It is not often that all four will draw equally at all times, nor is it desirable that they should do so. By allowing first one and then another to slacken his pull, the team will be able to do more in a day than if all were always pulling. Some horses will naturally draw at their best on starting off, and will work with less energy after a few miles, while others will hang back at first, and come in to their work as they get warmed up. By consulting their inclinations, the driver may economize the strength, and preserve the temper of his team, so as to secure a greater amount of work with less effort than if he kept the sluggard up to the bit from the start, and restrained the early ardor of the more spirited animal.

If your horses have a fancy for working in a peculiar manner, or at a particular stage of the journey, you will derive an advantage from consulting that fancy as far as practicable. Fig. *d* shows the manner in which the reins may be held in the left hand, and fig. *e* the manner in which the off reins may be taken in the right hand, for more careful driving. When the reins are all held in the left hand, the right may be laid on any one or more of them as occasion may require.

In turning corners, draw the leaders around first and let the wheel horses follow as nearly as possible in their tracks—not turn at the same time.

On ascending ground, the leaders should do more than half of the work, to compensate the wheel-horses for their extra effort in holding back when going down hill.

DRIVING WORKING HORSES differs from pleasure driving, as much as does its object. One desideratum in pleasure driving is a certain style and a regard to appearance, while teaming or business driving has for its main object the best economy of the strength of the team, and its application to the performance of labors. It is true that a teamster may have a just pride in the appearance and style of his team, but this should always be subordinate to their usefulness, and the main problem which he has to solve is, how to turn a certain amount of invested capital, and a certain amount of hay and grain to the best account, in performing the work in which he and his team are employed. To accomplish this, having the horses fed in a manner to give them the greatest possible strength and health, and so groomed that their systems are in the best condition for appropriating the nutriment of their food, he should keep the following rules always in view:

First.—The load should be just what the horse or the team can move steadily along, being neither so light that they are occupying their time in going over the road with less than they can draw, nor so heavy that they must over-tax their strength to draw it, or stop to take breath and to recover from the effects of too hard a strain; in short, they should do all that they can do comfortably, never much less, and never any more.

Second.—Horses will work better if they are kept well up to the bit, not sufficiently to pull on it, but just enough to feel its effect and to receive its support in case of a false step, than when allowed to become negligent and careless in their gait.

Third.—When there are two or more horses in a team, they should be so harnessed as to draw exactly alike. This requires them to be of uniform dispositions, and in equally good training; any deviation from this will cause one horse to do more, and another less, than his share of the work.

Fourth.—Working horses should never be whipped while drawing, except it is absolutely necessary; and then they should not simply be tapped, but smartly punished in a manner that will cause them to understand and to recollect that their driver really means that they shall work, and work properly.

Fifth.—If necessary to stop to rest before going up a hill, let the halt be at a little distance from the foot of the hill, that they may not get in the habit of stopping just at the foot of every hill which they encounter. When they are fully rested and prepared to go on, let them move vigorously, but do not allow them to *rush* at the hill; they would in such a case lose more in wind than they would gain in impetus. If possible, go moderately up every hill without stopping, recollecting that it is much harder to start a load against a hill, than it is to keep it in motion after it is started. At the top of every difficult hill, either stop the team or let them walk slowly for a few rods, until they have recovered from the effects of the extra exertion.

Sixth.—At all times, and especially in difficult places, or when first starting with a heavy load, the driver should carefully avoid exciting his team by crossness or impatience, but should hold them steadily by the bit, and talk to them in a quiet and determined manner, endeavoring to keep them cool and resolute, pulling evenly and steadily until they start their load, without making a sudden jump at it, as many nervous horses are inclined to do. Such a movement is very likely to disconcert the other horses, and it exhausts the strength more than ten times the effort properly expended.

Seventh.—In descending a hill, especially if there be no break or drag on the wheels, the team should be so held back that the wagon never gets an increasing speed, and the pole should be kept in an exact line with, and not diagonally across, the wagon.

Eighth.—The team should never be so hardly driven as to become *blown* (where it is possible to avoid it), nor should they ever be allowed to become indolent, or careless in their gait. They should always be active and willing, but never impatient to do more than is clearly within their powers.

A road team, well kept, and driven according to the above directions, will last longer, keep in better condition, and do more work than horses managed by the ordinary system, and in the hands of persons who are either not able or not willing to give any thought to the matter.

14

These directions apply to all sorts of teaming, whether with drays or trucks in towns, or with farmers or manufacturers' wagons on country roads.

The proper driving of stage and omnibus horses is a combination of the essential points of pleasure and team-driving. The team should still be kept cool and resolute, and very free from impatience, and they should at the same time be held so well in hand that they can, at a moment's warning, be either stopped or turned suddenly out of their course. They should also be able to start from a halt steadily, and without loss of time. As it is important that their pace should seldom degenerate into a walk, their trot should be uniform, and not excessively fast; and unless the horses are only required to go very short stages, they should not travel faster than from six to eight miles per hour, according to their load.

PLOWING.—Plowing on rough ground, with horses which are fit for anything else, is, at best, a painful necessity. There is occasionally to be found a stylish carriage team, or a pair of fast trotters which will work like oxen at the plow; but generally horses of spirit will become impatient under the frequent interruption caused by stones, or by the frequent turning necessary in small fields, while the harness generally used for this work is neither comfortable nor complete. In large fields, free from obstructions, horses may very properly be used, as they are more pleasant to work with than oxen; but in rough work the latter are preferable, being by temper and structure much better adapted to such work than horses.

Horses are frequently driven to the plow with the single line, or with a pair of lines fastened to the outer rings of each horse's bit, the inside rings being connected by a short line passing from one to the other. This will do very well for quiet, well-trained animals, in good ground;

but with horses at all inclined to be unruly or impatient, or working in soft or stony ground, we should use the same sort of reins as in driving on the road, thus giving a fair hold of each horse's head.

Horses used for this work should be taught to stop instantly at the word, to start promptly and together, and to pull evenly. The team should be brought quickly around

FIG. 41.—Whiffle-tree for plowing three-abreast.

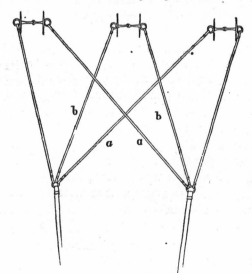

FIG. 42.—Lines for plowing three-abreast.

at the turns and headlands, and made to take their places as actively as possible for the new furrow; but they should not be started, if at all blown, until they are fully ready to go to the end of it without stopping, unless, indeed, it be a very long, or a very hard one.

It is the opinion, apparently a good one, of the best farmers of the present day, that no two horses are strong enough to turn such a furrow as is necessary for the proper cultivation of the soil, and they recommend that three or four be used. Assuming this to be the case, it should be remembered that three horses working abreast will pull nearly as much on a plow as will four geared in the ordinary way,—that is, the third horse, from being fastened within three or four feet of the plow, would have nearly as much power to draw it as would two horses drawing it from a distance of from fifteen to twenty feet.

Fig. 41 represents the best form of whiffle-tree for three horses plowing abreast. Fig. 42 is an arrangement for the lines for plowing with such a team, which will be found effective for horses which are inclined to pull irregularly, before being sufficiently broken, but as soon as they understand it, the lines marked a and b may be dispensed with. Indeed, intelligent horses will soon learn to work entirely without lines. The writer had a three-horse team which he trained to plow by the word in less than a month, so that they would work perfectly well without lines on the shortest turns. There are few horses which will not become irregular in their working without the assistance of the lines.

CHAPTER XX.

THE taming of horses by the process which is herein detailed is now exciting much attention, from the fact that
it has recently been practised with great success in London
and other foreign cities by Mr. John S. Rarey, of Ohio;
and it is now popularly known as "the Rarey system,"
although it is claimed to have been known from time im-
memorial to the trainers of circus-horses, both here and
in Europe.

J. S. Rarey was an Ohio farmer, and his family connections still reside near the city of Columbus. He has been
from his childhood a horse-breaker of some reputation
among his neighbors, and even when he had first developed
his present system he very quietly practised it in the more
unsettled parts of the country, extending his travels even
to Texas. He taught his system to others for a small fee,
and wrote a pamphlet some six years ago, which he gave
to his pupils, but which was kept by them under a promise
of secrecy. This is the only book ever published by Mr.
Rarey, but one of his pupils in England has written a very
readable little volume* on this system, and other matters
of interest to the horseman. From this English work this

---

* The art of Taming Horses, by J. S. Rarey, &c., by the Hunting corres-
pondent of the Illustrated London News. London: George Routledge & Co.

chapter has been compiled, and we believe that it is the best exposition of this system for subduing vicious horses, and for overcoming the fears of timid ones, that has yet been presented to the public.

The subjugation of vicious horses has been a great desideratum ever since horses were first ridden by man, but, until very recently, there has been no knowledge of a rational means for rendering them docile or tractable. The plans hitherto adopted have generally been too much according to the directions of a Norfolk trainer, of the time of Queen Elizabeth, who wrote as follows:

"If your horse does not stand still, or hesitates, then alrate him with a terrible voyce; and beat him yourself with a good sticke upon the head between the ears; and then stick him in the spurring place iii or iiii times together, with one legge after another, as fast as your legges might walk: your legges must go like two bouncing beetles."

The most celebrated horse-tamer before Rarey's time was an Irishman, named Dan Sullivan, known as the "Irish whisperer," who would, after a half hour's private interview with the most vicious horse, bring him out perfectly tamed,—so long as he himself used him; but he would not remain docile in the hands of other persons. Sullivan pretended to have got his secret from a poor soldier, who revealed it as an Indian charm. The secret was given by Sullivan to one of his sons, but it is not now known. Probably it was not capable of a general application.

All other methods of taming very vicious horses, so far as we have any information, have been based on cruelty and harsh treatment, and they were never entirely successful.

The mere reading of these directions is not sufficient to make horse-tamers of all who choose to try a hand at it; they are merely a stepping stone, and an introduction to a series of processes which they sufficiently illustrate, which can be carried into effect, only by the aid of experience.

The success of Mr. Rarey in England was such as but few of any calling have attained, he having made in a few months, over one hundred thousand dollars in subscriptions to his lectures, and having gained the acquaintance of many of the best people in the kingdom. In London he tamed a Zebra, an animal hitherto considered untamable, so that he could ride him as he pleased. He also tamed Cruiser, the most vicious stallion in England, " who could do more fighting in less time than any other horse in the world," and who for a long time had to be fed through a barred helmet. It was considered as much as any man's life was worth to attend to him.

There were many other very remarkable instances of the success of Mr. Rarey's attempts to tame horses that were so violently vicious that all previous efforts to subdue them had failed.

In bringing a horse to that state in which he obeys without resistance the will of man, we have to overcome— *First, his fear* of the presence and actions of man. *Second, his anger,* or an instinctive resentment, of which the unbroken horse makes as unmistakable an exhibition as any other animal, or even man himself. *Third, his waywardness,* or the natural desire for liberty of action and impatience of restraint : and we must supplant these passions by—*First, affection for his master,* that instinct so strong in the dog and elephant, and traceable in some other animals. *Second, a fear* of the chiding or chastisement of his master, united with the conviction that the only way to avoid or escape it is by obedience. *Third, an interest in, or ambition for,* the labors to be performed : the last is most clearly seen in the eagerness of the nobler bloods for the race, the chase, or even for the battle.

The means which are adopted for accomplishing this are —*First,* familiarity with the presence of man under circumstances which convince him of man's kind intentions. A colt accustomed to be handled and kindly treated, will be easily trained to the harness, or at least rendered in some degree manageable when grown. *Second,* some system which shall demonstrate to the horse the superiority of man, and his power to overcome him physically. Of this we have instances in the capture and subduing of wild elephants in India, of wild horses on the plains of America, and it has been the method of breaking refractory horses, in all times and among various nations. The mounting by a strong rider, who holds the painful thong or bit in the mouth of the horse, and urges him to his greatest endeavors to remove his burden, until, weary and exhausted with vain efforts, he is submissive, is a process long known to savage and civilized horsemanship. Subsequently the horse must gradually be made to understand the language of words and signals by which his master would communicate to him his wishes, and the training is complete.

We must not, however, overlook one all-important element which has not often been taken into account, and never fully explained—the magnetic influence which a fearless man has over all inferior animals ; an influence much stronger in some persons than in others. It is well known that all animals, even those most wild and ferocious, instinctively regard man with feelings different from those exhibited toward other beings; and although they meet him for the first time, in their own haunts, where they have reigned supreme, they show great dread of, and rarely begin an attack upon him. This proves a recognition of man's position, which in their domesticated state develops into a wholesome fear, mingled with a dependence upon him; and instances are by no means rare, where, with the most vicious horses the calm, firm demeanor of a man or woman has quelled resistance, when strength and violence had failed.

The contest between the horse and his master will be more or less violent and protracted, in proportion to the strength and disposition of the horse, and the nature of the means used, or the skill of the horseman.

In this system all the requirements here stated are supplied, by means so simple that almost any one may apply them, and it is so efficacious as to leave scarcely a wish for anything more or better.

At no stage of the contest is there any, even *temporary advantage* gained by the horse, to relieve the hopelessness of the struggle, and it permits the comparatively quiet position of the master, while the horse is engaged in the most desperate efforts, every one of which brings him more inextricably into difficulty, while every submission brings him relief, until, upon his final abandonment of all effort, he lies helpless but comfortable upon the ground, and the soothing attentions of his master convince him that no harm is intended him; and to complete the triumph he wins his gratitude and affection by releasing him from his difficulties. In approaching a vicious animal Mr. Rarey brings most distinctly to his aid the magnetism before alluded to, which courage and unflinching firmness will always enable us to exercise upon the Horse.

As an essential principle the horseman should always bear in mind that he can accomplish nothing if he allows himself to lose his temper or to become afraid of his horse.

14*

INSTRUCTIONS FOR PRACTICE.

If you are not well accustomed to the handling of unbroken and spirited horses, your first subject for practice should be a comparatively quiet horse. After you have repeatedly laid him down as directed, you can try others more difficult until you can at length undertake those that are vicious and even untamable by other methods.

PREPARATIONS.—Supply yourself with a *strong surcingle*, to be buckled around the horse at the girth; *a strap*, as

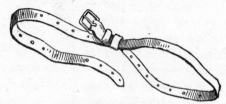

FIG. 48.—Strap with buckle.

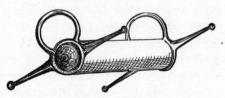

FIG. 49.—Wooden gag-bit.

represented at Fig. 48, made of good stout leather an inch and a quarter wide and three feet or more in length, having a loop by which to form a noose, and a strong buckle; a *second strap*, without a buckle, but with a loop made by doubling over one end of the strap and sewing it strongly. This strap should not be less than five feet in length. A *common bridle*, with stout reins and bit, will answer for ordinary horses, but for vicious animals inclined to bite, a *wooden gag-bit*, as in Fig. 49, is used by Mr. Rarey. A long *buggy whip*, with a good cracker, should be kept near at hand. If you intend to ride the horse after his lesson, your saddle should be accessible, or be handed to you at the right time. If there is danger of the horse hurting his knees, a *pair of knee-pads* should be provided (Fig. 50), the body of which (*b*) is made of felt; *c* is a leather shield; *a* is the strap, with a buckle, and for a part of its length is of Indian rubber, to give it elasticity.

FIG. 50.—Knee-pad.

THE ENCLOSURE.—Horses have been trained by the expert, on the open ground, where soft and free from stones, &c.—or in a barn, or bullock yard, well supplied with straw or tan,—being sure that there are no beams or posts against which the horse or his trainer may be hurt. It is far preferable to have a suitable enclosure about 30 feet square, the fence so high that the horse cannot see over it, and the floor covered a foot deep with straw, tan, or saw-dust. It is of importance that the horse should see or hear no person or object beyond the enclosure, to distract his attention. If the horse is very vicious, the enclosure may have a half-door by which a gradual acquaintance with the horse may be formed. It is better that even with the worst horses but one person should enter the enclosure with the animal.

TO STABLE THE HORSE.—Mr. Rarey gives some excellent hints for the stabling and haltering of the colt or horse, which it is undesirable to repeat here, but the points to be observed are :—never to frighten or run after him; patiently follow him around the pasture or field until he enters the enclosure you intend for him, or by leading a steady horse into the stable gradually entice the colt to follow; do not throw up your arms, or halloo at him, but by gentle methods accomplish your object.

To APPROACH THE HORSE.—Enter the stable or enclosure quietly, and if the horse shows signs of fear, stand at the entrance without moving until he shows no uneasiness; then approach him a step or two, and if he is again afraid, stop a few moments. Again step toward him, stopping whenever he appears alarmed. Your arms should be stationary, the right hanging by your side, and the left hand projected toward the horse, but not at full length. Approach him toward the shoulder, and if he moves a little forward or backward, step cautiously more to the right or left. When you are within reach he will turn his head to smell your hand; do not move it at first, but encourage him to touch it with his nose; gradually touch his head and neck, stroking him the way the hair lies, speaking all the time in a gentle tone, repeating the same words as " Ho ! my boy," " Pretty boy," " Nice Lady," &c. The accustoming the horse from the first, to the sound of the voice, is deemed of great importance.

After you have caressed your horse a little, take your halter in your left hand and walk slowly up to him. After again rubbing and soothing him, put the end of the strap around his neck, slowly get his nose into the halter and buckle it. The halter should have a long strap or rope, so that if he wish to walk to the opposite side of the stable he can do so. Do not tug at the halter, but gradually begin to control him by pulling him to one side : never go before and attempt to pull him after you. When he is somewhat accustomed to the halter, a suitable bridle, as

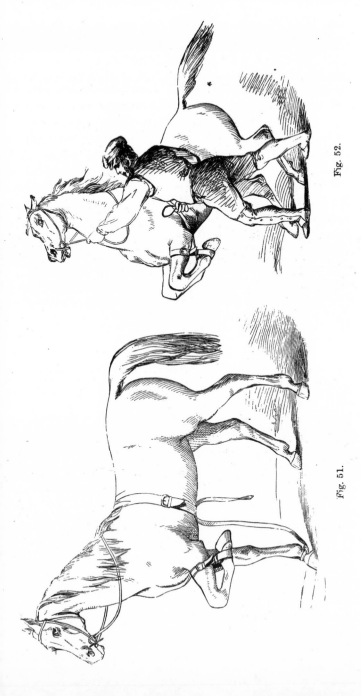

Fig. 52.

Fig. 51.

previously described, should be put on him before proceed
ing further in the process.

TYING UP THE LEG.—With ordinary horses this is not
a difficult feat, after the preliminary steps, but in some
cases even Mr. Rarey himself has taken two hours before
he could accomplish it. Soothing, gentle means are the
only ones to be used, such as rubbing and handling the
legs, until you can take up the foot as if for shoeing. Then
put the noose of strap, Fig. 48, around the left fore leg, just
below the fetlock, and draw it snug. Raise the foot and
pass the strap around the fore-arm, and buckle it. If the
horse is to be laid down on the left side, the buckle should
be on the inside of the leg, so that it can be easily reached
when he is down. You may now handle or go about your
horse with more freedom, as he cannot kick, and will not
be able to run very fast. It is well to lead him about for
some time, in this condition, before proceeding further.
Fig. 51 represents the horse at this stage of the proceedings.

LAYING THE HORSE DOWN.—Next, the surcingle is
to be buckled on, and the second strap is put around
the right fore-leg, below the fetlock, drawing the noose
tightly, and passing the end through the surcingle,
as in Fig. 51. The horse is now made to hop, and the
moment he moves his right leg the strap is drawn tightly,
so as to bring the leg in the same position as the other.
This will cause him for a moment to come upon his
knees, when the strap may have another turn around
the surcingle to secure it. The struggle now commences. He rears on his hind legs, and springs violently
about, so that some agility is required to keep up with
him, but you are merely to follow him about, guiding
him as well as you can, so that he does not injure himself, keeping close to his side, just behind the shoulder,
holding the bridle in the left hand, and the end of strap

No. 2 in the right. See Fig. 52. This demands more self-possession than strength, as boys, and even ladies, have successfully laid down large horses, and few or no serious accidents are recorded. The struggle rarely continues longer than from five to ten minutes, and no horse has been known to hold out for more than fifteen minutes.

It is not necessary to oppose the horse by violently pulling on the bridle, but merely use the reins to steer him away from the walls of the enclosure; or, if he be obstinate, he may be compelled to walk backwards until he is tired out. When he finally sinks forward on his knees exhausted, you can, by pulling the off rein firmly, bring him over upon his left side. If he make a second attempt at resistance, so much the better, as his subjugation will be more complete after he gives up.

When completely subdued and upon his side, begin to caress and soothe him, rubbing his head, neck and legs, speaking kindly to him as you move about him, and he should be repeatedly stroked and handled wherever he is disposed to be "touchy." Any articles he is inclined to fear may be brought to him, and placed upon him, such as a Buffalo robe, umbrella, saddle, or harness. Mount him yourself quietly, to convince him you will do him no harm. After all resistance has ceased, you may remove his straps, and continue the rubbing and your soothing attentions. If he attempt to rise, you may hold him down by the head, or by doubling up a fore leg, as at first, but if he is too quick for you, do not contend with him, but let him rise, and again tie his feet, and lay him down. After working with him thus for an hour, encourage him to rise, and, after an interval of a few hours, repeat the lesson; indeed, two or three lessons per day may be advantageously given to an obstinate animal. After each, and whenever he shows submission, reward him by caresses, soothing words, or a lock of hay. This wins for you his gratitude and affection, and with a little pains, he will readily follow you and obey your call.

VICES AND BAD HABITS.

REARING.—This is a vice which is not very common, at least in a dangerous form. It can generally be prevented by the use of the martingale.

Another good preventive, in the case of saddle-horses, is, when the horse is about to rise, to touch him with the spur, on one side only; this will cause him to stop to lift the hind leg on that side, and if he persists in his attempt the spurs may be used vigorously, first on one side, and then on the other, but not so fast as to prevent the horse from raising his hind legs alternately, as he is spurred. The least touch of the curb bit will cause some vicious and badly trained horses to rear, while those which have been thoroughly trained, as by the system of Baucher, will rear slightly, to a great height, or not at all, as their rider may desire; but it is obvious that horses so delicately trained should not be ridden by unskilful persons, lest the awkwardness of the rider should cause unexpected curveting.

KICKING.—It is impossible for a horse to kick, while one of his fore legs is strapped up, as we have described; and if a horse has the habit of kicking in harness, he may be driven a few times with only three legs to walk on. We may, after that, have a strap, long enough to reach to the hand when in the wagon, fastened around the pastern of the near side fore leg, and passing through a ring in the harness. We now drive the horse slowly, and, at the first laying back of the ears, jerk up the foot, and leave him powerless to kick. In this manner this worst of all vices, in harness horses, may be effectually and permanently cured.

PULLING BACK ON THE HALTER.—This is a vice which has probably arisen from the horse having, at some time, broken a weak halter in a fit of impatience. The only safe cure for it, and this is not always successful, is to tie the horse with a very strong halter, which it will be impossible for him to break; finding that his efforts are futile, he will, after a time, usually desist from pulling,—though some incorrigible brutes will try every new halter as soon as they are fastened, and will break it if possible.

SHYING is a most dangerous vice, the treatment of which is thus described by Stonehenge:

Shying is sometimes the effect of fear, and sometimes of vice; and there are many horses which begin by the former and end with the latter, in consequence of misman-agement. The young colt is almost always more or less shy, especially if he is brought at once from the retired fields where he was reared, to the streets of a busy town. There are, however, numberless varieties of shyers, some being dreadfully alarmed by one kind of object, which to another is not at all formidable. When a horse finds that he gains his object by turning round, he will often repeat the turning without cause, pretending to be alarmed, and looking out for excuses for it. This is not at all uncommon, and with timid riders leads to a discontinuance of the ride, by which the horse gains his end for the time, and repeats the trick on the first occasion. In genuine shying from fear, the eyes are generally more or less defective; but sometimes this is not the cause, which is founded upon a general irritability of the nervous system. Thus, there are many which never shy at meeting wagons, or other similar objects, but which almost drop with fear on a small bird flying out of a hedge, or any other startling sound. These are also worse, because they give no notice, whereas

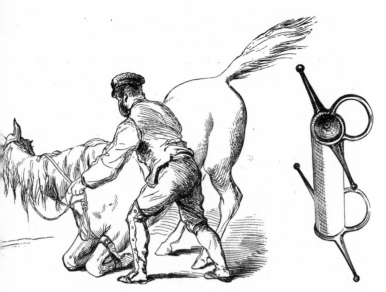

Fig. 53.

Fig. 54.

the ordinary shyer almost always shows by his ears that he is prepared to turn.

For shyers the only remedy is, to take as little notice as possible, to make light of the occurrence, speak encouragingly, yet rather severely, *and to get them by the object somehow or other.* If needful, the *aid* of the spur and whip may be called in, but not as a *punishment.* If the horse can be urged to go by the object at which he is shying without the whip or spur, so much the better; but if not, he must be compelled to do so by their use. Whenever fear is the cause of shying, punishment only adds to that fear but where vice has supplanted fear, severity should be used to correct it. As a general rule the whip need never be used, unless the horse turns absolutely round, and not then unless there is reason to suspect that he is pretending fear. If only he will go by the object, even with 'a wide berth,' as the sailors say, he may be suffered to go on his way unpunished; and nothing is so bad as the absurd severity which some horsemen exercise after the horse has conquered his reluctance, and passed the object. At this time he should be praised and patted, with all the encouragement which can be given; and on no account should he be taught to make those rushes which we so commonly see on the road, from the improper use of the whip and spur. If punishment is necessary at all, it must be used beforehand; but it often happens that the rider cannot spare his whip-hand until the shying is over; and then, in his passion, he does not reflect that the time is gone by for its employment.

BAULKING OR JIBBING.—This is one of the most provoking vices of the horse, and it can be successfully combatted only by a man of the most imperturbable temper. The least sign of vexation only increases the evil, and makes the animal more and more troublesome each time that he refuses his work.

The writer has known a thick-headed, quick-tempered Irish driver to fly into a passion and beat or otherwise abuse his horse, on the least symptom of baulking, until the animal became absolutely worthless from a confirmation of the habit.

As a rule it may be stated, that horses baulk from nervousness, or unsteadiness of disposition, if not, indeed, from an over-anxiety to perform their work. Nervous, well-bred horses are more susceptible to the influences which induce baulking, than are colder blooded, more indolent ones. A high-mettled horse, when carelessly driven, will start suddenly against his collar, fail to start his load, draw back from the pain which the concussion causes, rush at it again, and again draw back, until it becomes impossible for his driver to steady him in his collar for a dead pull. Add to this a smart cut with the whip, and a fiercely spoken word,—with perhaps a blow over the nose, or a stone in the ear,—and every fear or vicious feeling of the horse will be called into action, and he becomes entirely unmanageable, requiring to be left for an hour or two in his position before he gets sufficiently calm to be coaxed to move. There may, occasionally, be a horse which cannot be made to draw steadily by the most careful treatment, but the cases are exceedingly rare in which gentle treatment, and firmness,—a patient persistence in mild, authoritative command, and judicious coaxing,—would not either prevent the formation of the habit, or cure it, when formed.

The prevention of baulkey habits lies with the driver. If he jump on to his load, gather up his reins carelessly, flourish his whip or call out wildly to his horse, he will be very likely to start him forward with a jerk which will be of no avail to move a heavily laden wagon. The horse thus commences to baulk at a heavy load, and, after a certain amount of such treatment, he will refuse to draw any thing except under the most favorable circumstances. Let any man driving a strange horse, with a load which he is not *perfectly sure* that he can start easily, proceed according to the following directions, and he may be certain that if the animal be not already a "jibber" he will not make him so, and that if he is one he will have the best chance for getting him along without trouble: He should slowly examine the harness and wagon (partly to accustom the horse to his presence), gather up the reins gently, speaking to the horse to prevent his starting, get quietly into his seat, and then, if possible, get control of the horse's mouth before allowing him to move, so that when he does step off it may be only at a slow walk. If by a forward movement of the hands he can be made very gradually to press against the collar, and if the whole operation is performed in a cool and unexcited manner, there will be little difficulty in bringing him to a dead pull, from which he will recoil only if the load is a serious tax on his strength.

If you fail in the first attempt, wait until your horse has become quiet, and until you have recovered from your own vexation, and then try again. It may be necessary to have the assistance of one or two persons, to start the wagon from behind, but they should not push it until the horse is fairly against the collar.

To cure the habit of baulking is not an easy matter, and it is possible only by the kindest treatment. If the horse show fear by his excited manner, or by looking about him wildly, that he is expecting a blow, you may be sure that he has received hard usage under similar circumstances, and that he must be convinced by caresses and kind words that you will treat him gently. You must recollect that the horse cannot understand your language, and that, while he is confused, he will misinterpret every sign that you make to him. He has an idea of your superior power, and in his fear that you will exercise it, as bad drivers have done before, to his injury, he will not, at once, feel confidence in your kind intentions. He *must* feel this confidence, whether it take an hour or all day to convey it to him, before you can do anything to cure him of his trick. If you have him harnessed to a light wagon, on a smooth road where it will afford but little resistance, you may, by repeated trials, convince him that it is a simple and easy matter to draw it, and you should continue to exercise him from day to day with the same light load, and afterward increase it gradually, until you have trained him to a quiet manner of starting, or of going up a hill or elsewhere where he has been accustomed to baulk.

By the same gentle treatment you may start a horse or a team that have baulked under the driving of another person. Request the driver and all spectators to go to the side of the road, and then unfasten the check-reins, hang the reins where they will be easily accessible, but so that they may lie loosely on the horses' backs, caress them and allow them to look about and convince themselves that no harm is being done. When they have become properly quiet, go to their heads and stand directly in front of the worst jibber of the team, so that his nose may come against your breast if he start. Turn them gently to the right, without allowing them to tighten their traces, and, after caressing them a little, draw them, in the same way, to the left. Presently turn them to the right, and, as you do so, bring them slowly against their collars and let them go.

CHAPTER XXI.

RACING.

BY RACING, in the proper acceptation of the term, is meant a trial of speed between *running* horses. Match-trotting, although more in vogue in this country, is less intimately connected with the science of breeding horses, which it is one of the objects of this work to discuss.

With the moral bearing of the subject of horse-racing we have nothing to do. It is used as a means for improving the breed of horses, and this result is certainly attained, for there can be no doubt that more capital is devoted, and more attention given, to the raising of thorough-bred horses than could be expected to take this channel if no such remunerative market for fine horses existed. It is true that the thorough-bred horse is frequently of but very little practical use for anything but racing and breeding, but as a getter of horses for all kinds of ordinary work, whether for the saddle or harness, he is not only unequalled, but almost indispensable, since without him we could not have for any kind of work so good an animal as it is possible to get by an infusion of thorough blood. Even if it were probable that thorough-bred horses would be raised in perfection without the stimulus of racing, there would be no means for ascertaining which of them was the best for transmitting the two important qualities of speed and bottom (or endurance); no other test would so fully make known these qualities.

To give the reader an idea of the manner in which horses are trained for racing, and of the management of the race itself, we condense the following account from the best writers on the subject, in England, (where horse-racing is a national pastime, Parliament adjourning on the day of the great Derby race at Epsom,) and from the rules of the English "Jockey Club." A careful study of the manner in which horses are trained for racing cannot fail to give some valuable suggestions as to keeping working and pleasure horses in a proper condition for the performance of their labor.

Training-stables are necessarily located near a good piece of ground upon which to exercise the horses. This should be, if possible, of such a character that it will never get either very soft in wet, nor very hard in dry weather. A piece of deep old turf, on land which is thoroughly well drained, either naturally or artificially, is best for the purpose. The stables themselves should be roomy, and well ventilated; and it is desirable to have them rather dark than light, as the horses get the necessary amount of light in taking their exercise, and as they will be more ready to take their feed, and to rest themselves after hard work, in tolerably dark stables. The best form for the stable is probably a compromise between stalls and loose boxes which keep their inmates entirely secluded,—that is, large stalls, about ten feet in length and six feet in width, closed at the rear with a door which can be locked, when it is desirable to allow the horse to move about at pleasure in his apartment, and boarded up only to a height of six feet; the remaining space, from the top of the partition to the ceiling, which should be from ten to twelve feet from the floor, being supplied with iron bars, which will allow the horses to see each other; and which will make the stable generally warmer in winter, and allow a better circulation of air in summer. A cheap arrangement of shutters, to entirely close up the barred space, will confine the heat to the stables which are occupied.

Training establishments are usually supplied with saddles, of various forms, weights, and sizes; bridles; bits, of every form; rollers, straps, knee-caps and boots, and clothing in every conceivable variety; also with the simpler remedies for the ordinary ailments of horses in training. Before the training commences the horse should be examined as to his health, form, and temper, as well as to his pedigree. This examination is one of the most responsible duties of the trainer, and its object is to put him in possession of as many facts as possible as to the points of strength and weakness of the horse, whether acquired or inherited. By the deductions therefrom made, he decides in what way it is best to treat his subject so as to develope his powers, with the least risk of injuring his health or disposition. The average length of time required for training is about six months, during which the horse undergoes three different stages of treatment, the object being to remove all unnecessary fat from the external and internal parts of the body, to put the heart and lungs in the best condition for the performance of their functions, and to give, by means of exercise and nutritious food, the greatest possible amount of strength and endurance.

The first preparation, as far as exercise is concerned, consists mainly of walking, which removes excess of fat, and gives hardness and endurance to the legs. After it has been continued for from two to four weeks, according to the condition of the horse, he has his first *sweat*, which is given by galloping him moderately, under heavy clothing; if it be desirable to greatly reduce any part of the body in particular, as, for instance, the neck or shoulders, these parts are more heavily laden with blankets than the rest of the body. Immediately after the perspiration has begun to flow freely, the horse should be well scraped, and then rubbed dry, by four boys working as rapidly as possible. During the first preparation an occasional short gallop is allowed, to vary the monotony of the work, but it must be only a very gentle one; and toward the last these may be somewhat increased, if the horse is evidently in condition to bear the extra work without being put back in his training. The sweats are continued at intervals during the whole time of the first preparation, this matter being decided by the trainer from his knowledge of the character of the horse. Light doses of physic are also given, from time to time, as they may be required.

During the second preparation, the feed, which was eight quarts of oats per day at first, is raised to ten quarts; the sweats are more frequent, and the gallops are more frequent and more severe, the object being to improve the wind as well as the legs and muscles.

In the third or final preparation, the work is made more severe, the feeding is managed with the utmost care, being small in quantity and highly nutritious. The water, as well as oats and hay (all of which must be of the very best quality), should be given in such a way as to produce the best results.

The stable must at all times be kept scrupulously clean. Every circumstance which can possibly have an influence on the condition of the horse is taken into the account, and faithfully regarded. The sweats, at first, are gross and lathery, but towards the last they are little more than water. From this fact the progress of the horse's training may be approximately ascertained. The legs are hand-rubbed, at least fifteen minutes each, every day.

During the whole time of training there is a great liability to all manner of accidents and diseases, and the trainer finds, in the treatment of such cases, no small part of his labor, while nothing can be more vexatious than to see a horse, whose final preparation is in the full tide of successful experiment, thrown out of the race by a casualty, such as "breaking down," or "Curb."

LAWS OF RACING.

The following are some of the rules of the Jockey Club of England:—

"THE AGE of all horses is taken from the 1st of January.

"IN CATCH WEIGHTS any person can ride without going to scale. A FEATHER WEIGHT is defined to be 4 stone, but the usual declaration must be made if the jockey intends to ride more than that weight.

"A MAIDEN horse or mare is one that has never won. AN UNTRIED stallion or mare is one whose produce has never started in public.

"JOCKEYS MUST RIDE their horses to the usual place of weighing, and he that dismounts beforehand, or wants weight, is distanced, unless he is disabled by accident, in which case he may be led or carried to the scale. If a jockey fall from his horse, and the horse be rode in from the place where the rider fell by a person of sufficient weight, he may take his place the same as if the rider had not fallen. (At Newmarket, jockeys are *required* to weigh before as well as after the race.)

"EVERY JOCKEY IS ALLOWED 2 lbs. above the weight
15

specified for his horse; but should any horse carry more than 2 lbs. above his weight without having declared it, he will be considered distanced, although he came in first.

"HEATS.—For the best of the plate, when three heats are run, the horse is second which wins one heat. For the best of the heats, the horse is second that beats the other horse twice out of three times though he do not win a heat. When a plate is won by two heats, the preference of the horses is determined by the second heat. When a plate is given to the winner of the best of three heats, a horse must be the actual winner of two heats, even though no horse appear against him for both or either of the heats. When three horses have each won a heat, they only must start for a fourth. In running heats, a dead heat goes for nothing, and all the horses may start again, unless it be between two horses that had each won a heat. Horses drawn before the plate is won are distanced. No distance in a fourth heat.

"FALSE DESCRIPTION.—No horse will be deemed the winner of any race which shall be proved to have run under a false description; the disqualification to remain in force until his pedigree be ascertained and recorded. No objection can be made after the lapse of twelve months from the time of running.

"ALLOWANCE OF WEIGHT to the produce of untried horses or mares must be claimed at the time of running. Extra weight and allowances for not winning are not accumulative unless particularly specified. Extra weights for running are enforced up to the time of running.

"FICTITIOUS NAME.—When any person enters a horse, or subscribes, under a fictitious name, or in the name of a person not fully identified at the time, he will be considered in all respects as the owner of the horse, and as the subscriber to the stake. The stewards of the Jockey Club have power to call upon a nominator to produce testimony that the horse named is not the property, either wholly or in part, of any person whose name appears in the list of defaulters; and if he fail to do so, they may cause the nomination to be erased.

" EXAMINATION OF MOUTH.—When the age or qualification of a horse is objected to, either before or after running, the stewards have power to order the examination of the horse's mouth, by competent persons, and to call for such evidence as they may require, and their decision is final. The person requiring the horse's mouth to be examined, at Newmarket, must pay the expenses of such examination, unless it should prove that the horse is of the wrong age, in which case the Jockey Club will pay it.

" FRAUDULENT OWNERS, &c.—If a horse shall run, or be brought to run, for any race, in England or elsewhere, and shall be proved not to be of the age represented, the Jockey Club have power to disqualify for ever the owner, or part owner, trainer, groom, or person having the care of such horse at the time, from running or training any horse where the rules of the Jockey Club apply, and from being employed by any member of the Club. And any horse thus fraudulently entered or run, is for ever disqualified for running in any race whatever.

"NON-PAYMENT OF STAKES.—No person can start a horse for any race, either in his own name or that of any other person, unless both the owner and namer shall have paid all former stakes and forfeits before the time fixed for starting for the first race. This rule extends to forfeits due elsewhere than at Newmarket, provided a notice of them be delivered by ten o'clock in the evening preceding the day of running.

" DEFAULTERS.—No person in arrear for stakes or forfeits, after application for payment, and no person notoriously a defaulter in respect of bets, can enter and run in his own name, or in that of any other person, any horse of which he is wholly or in part owner. And to prevent any evasion of this rule, the stewards have power to call upon the nominator to procure satisfactory testimony that such is not the case, and on failure of such proof may cause the nomination to be erased; and the nominator will be held liable for the stakes or forfeits thereon. And no horse trained by any groom or person thus in default, or in any way under the care of a person in default, will be permitted to start. Should any horse, coming under the above regulations, be mistakingly permitted to start, he will not be considered a winner, though he should come in first; and the subscriber will have to pay the whole stake, as for a beaten horse. (This rule does not apply at Newmarket, but at most of the principal races elsewhere.)

"LIABILITIES OF SELLERS AND PURCHASERS.—When a horse is sold with his engagements, the seller has not the power of striking the horse out; but, as the original subscriber remains liable for the forfeits, he may, if compelled to pay them, place them on the forfeit-list, as due from the purchaser to himself; and both the purchaser and the horse remain under the same disabilities as if the purchaser had been the original subscriber. In all cases of private sale the written acknowledgment of both parties that the horse was sold with the engagement is necessary to entitle either buyer or seller to the benefit of this rule.

"FORFEITS MAY BE PAID.—When a person has a horse engaged in the name of another party, who may be on the list of defaulters, he may, if he pay this forfeit, start his horse, leaving the forfeit on the list, and substituting his own name for that of the person to whom it was previously due. He may take the same course in respect to forfeits not on the list.

" NON-DECLARATION OF FORFEITS.—When a person takes a nomination for a stake, in which the forfeit is to be declared by a particular time, and does not declare forfeit by the time fixed, he takes the engagement on himself, and his name will be substituted for that of the original subscriber."

The following is Admiral Rous' scale of standard weights for ages:—

HALF A MILE.

Age.	April 1.		May 1		June 1.		July 1.		Aug. 1.		Sept. 1.		Oct. 1.		Nov. 1.	
Years.	st.	lb.	st.	lb.	st.	lb.	st.	lb.	st.	lb.	st.	lb.	st.	lb.	st.	lb.
2	5	2	5	7	5	12	6	1	6	3	6	5	6	7	6	8
3	7	5	7	7½	7	10	7	13	8	0	8	1	8	1½	8	2
4	8	7	8	7	8	7	8	7	8	7	8	7	8	7	8	7
5, 6, and a.	8	9	8	8	8	7½	8	7	8	7	8	7	8	7	8	7

T. Y. C., OR SIX FURLONGS.

Age.	April 1.		May 1		June 1.		July 1.		Aug. 1.		Sept. 1.		Oct. 1.		Nov. 1.	
2	4	9	4	13	5	3	5	6	5	8	5	10	5	12	6	0
3	7	2	7	4	7	6	7	7½	7	9	7	10	7	11	7	12
4	8	7	8	7	8	7	8	7	8	7	8	7	8	7	8	7
5, 6, and a.	8	13	8	12	8	11¼	8	11	8	10½	8	10	8	9	8	8

ONE MILE.

Age.	April 1.		May 1		June 1.		July 1.		Aug. 1.		Sept. 1.		Oct. 1.		Nov. 1.	
2	4	2	4	4	4	7	4	10	4	13	5	2	5	4	5	5
3	6	12	6	13	7	1	7	4	7	6	7	7	7	8	7	9
4	8	7	8	7	8	7	8	7	8	7	8	7	8	7	8	7
5	9	0	8	13¼	8	13	8	12½	8	12	8	11¼	8	11	8	10
6 and a.	9	1	9	0	8	13½	8	13	8	12	8	11½	8	11	8	10

TWO MILES.

Age.	April 1.		May 1		June 1.		July 1.		Aug. 1.		Sept. 1.		Oct. 1.		Nov. 1.	
2	0	0	0	0	0	0	0	0	4	2	4	7	4	9	4	11
3	6	3	6	7	6	12	7	0	7	2	7	5	7	6	7	7
4	8	7	8	7	8	7	8	7	8	7	8	7	8	7	8	7
5	9	2	9	1½	9	1	9	0½	9	0	8	13	8	12	3	11½
6 and a.	9	5½	9	5	9	3½	9	3	9	2	9	1½	8	13	8	12

THREE MILES.

Age.	April 1.		May 1		June 1.		July 1.		Aug. 1.		Sept. 1.		Oct. 1.		Nov. 1.	
2	0	0	0	0	0	0	0	0	0	0	0	0	4	0	4	4
3	6	0	6	4	6	8	6	11	6	13	7	0	7	2	7	4
4	8	7	8	7	8	7	8	7	8	7	8	7	8	7	8	7
5	9	4	9	3	9	2	9	1½	9	1	9	0½	9	0	9	0
6 and a.	9	8	9	6½	9	6	9	5	9	4	9	3	9	2	9	1

FOUR MILES.

3	5	10	6	0	6	4	6	7	6	9	6	10½	6	12	7	0
4	8	7	8	7	8	7	8	7	8	7	8	7	8	7	8	7
5	9	6	9	5	9	4	9	3	9	2½	9	2	9	1½	9	1
6	9	11	9	9	9	8½	9	7	9	6	9	5	9	4	9	4
aged	9	13	9	10	9	9	9	7	9	6	9	5	9	4	9	4

Mares to be allowed 5 lb. from April to June 1st; 3 lb. from June 1st to September 1st: 2 lb. from September 1st to November. Geldings allowed 3 lb. throughout the year.

The stone is 14 lbs.

HANDICAPPING.

By handicapping is meant an adjustment to the different horses entered for a race of such different weights as will equalize their powers, and give them all equal chances for winning the race. The person who makes the adjustment is called the "handicapper," and it is his duty to inform himself of the character of each horse, of the running that he has previously made, of his age, and in short of every circumstance which can effect his running in the race in view.

Although very much in vogue, it is a system which encourages more dishonesty than any other connected with the turf, inasmuch as it offers a premium for fraud, by making it appear, to the "handicapper," at least, that one's horse is a poor one, when he is quite the reverse. The means by which this is accomplished are as many and as dishonorable as they are notorious. A horse will, at times, be made to lose every race for a whole season, in order that in a "handicap" race, for which he is being prepared, he may be weighted as lightly as possible, and that then, with the extra power which has been kept in abeyance, he may easily win a prize which repays ten-fold the losses of the early part of the season. The whole system has done more to bring discredit on the racing of horses than anything else connected with it, especially in England, where handicapping is much more general than in this country. Without it, it is possible to make horse-racing respectable; with it, it will be more difficult than ever to divorce it from the fraud and rascality which it is said to foster.

The speed of the best race-horses is from $13\frac{1}{2}$ to 14 seconds per furlong, or from 1 m. 48 s. to 1 m. 52 s. per mile.

CHAPTER XXII.

VETERINARY HOMŒOPATHY.

THE HOMŒOPATHIC treatment of disease is based on the discovery of Hahnemann, and its fundamental principle is:

"In order to cure a disease, select such a remedy as is capable of producing a similar malady in a healthy person, and of such a remedy prescribe only a small dose."

Without any discussion as to the truth of this theory, there is a sufficient reason for the preparation of this chapter, in the fact that a large and intelligent class of persons prefer this system of practice, and there can be no doubt that it is as well adapted to the diseases of animals as to those of the human family.

The practice of Veterinary Homœopathy has been popularized by several valuable works, to two of which we are much indebted in the compilation of this chapter—"The New Manual of Veterinary Homœopathic Medicine," by J. C. Schœfer, translated by Ch. J. Hempel, M. D., and "The Hand Book of Veterinary Homœopathy," by John Rush,—published by Wm. Radde, N. Y. The reader is referred to these works for the treatment of complicated cases.

The remedies used in homœopathic treatment should be prepared with the greatest care, and are usually in the form of liquid solutions. They can be purchased at present only at certain places in large towns; but as they may be kept for a very long time, and are not expensive, and as a very small quantity will suffice for years, it will be found most convenient to procure sets of the remedies, which are neatly put up in boxes. The following list of medicines will be found sufficient for the ordinary diseases of the horse. The first column gives the names which are used in the prescriptions, the second gives the abbrevia ions with which the bottles are labelled, and the third gives the English signification of the Latin terms.

LATIN.	ABBREVIATION.	ENGLISH.
Aconitum napellus,	Acon.	Wolf's bane.
Ammonium muriaticum,	Am. mur.	Muriate of ammonia.
Antimonium crudum,	Ant. cr.	Antimony.
Arnica montana,	Arn.	Leopard's bane.
Arsenicum album,	Ars.	Arsenic.
Belladonna,	Bell.	Deadly nightshade.
Bryonia alba,	Bry.	White bryony.
Calcaria carbonica,	Calc. carb.	Carbonate of lime.
Campora,	Camph.	Camphor.
Cannabis sativa,	Can. sat.	Hemp.
Cantharides,	Canth.	Spanish fly.
Carbo vegetabilis,	Carb. veg.	Vegetable.
Causticum,	Caust.	Caustic.
Chamomilla,	Cham.	Chamomile flower
China,	Chin.	Peruvian bark.
Cina,	Cin.	Wormseed.
Colchicum autumale,	Colch.	Meadow saffron.
Colocynthis,		
Conium maculatum,	Con.	Hemlock.
Dulcamara,	Dulc.	Bittersweet.
Euphrasia officinalis,	Euphr.	Eye bright.
Hepar sulphuris,	Hep.	Liver of sulphur.
Hyoscyamus niger,	Hyoc.	Henbane.
Ipecacuanha,	Ipec.	Ipecacuanha root.
Kali carbonicum,	Kal. carb.	Carbonate of potash.
Lycopodium,	Lyc.	Clubb moss.
Mercurius corrosivus,	Merc. cor.	Corrosive sublimate.

15*

Mercurius solubilis,	Merc. sol.	Soluble mercury.
Mercurius vivus,	Merc. v.	Quicksilver.
Natrum muriaticum,	Nat. mur.	Kitchen salt.
Nitrum,	Nitr.	Saltpetre.
Nux vomica,	Nux. v.	Vomic nut.
Opium,	Op.	White poppy.
Phosphorus,	Phos.	Phosphorus.
Platina,	Plat.	Platina.
Pulsatilla,	Puls.	Meadow anemone.
Rhus Toxicodendron,	Rhus t.	Sumach.
Sabina,	Sab.	Savina.
Secale cornutum,	Sec.	Spurred rye.
Sepia,	Sep.	Cuttle fish.
Silicea,	Sil.	Silex.
Spongia marinatosta,	Spong.	Burnt sponge.
Squilla maritina,	Squil.	Sea onion.
Stramonium,	Stram.	Stinkweed.
Sulphur,	Sulph.	Brimstone,
Thuja occidentalis,	Thuj.	Tree of Life.
Veratrum album,	Verat.	White hellbore.
Tartarus emeticus,		Tartar emetic.
		Nitric acid.
		Phosphoric acid.
		Tincture sulphur.

The remedies being in a liquid form, the best means of administering them to the horse is, to put six drops on a small piece of bread, or on a wafer of flour paste, and to raise the horse's head a little, "press down the tongue to one side, and pull it out as far as may be, and then place the wafer as far back as possible; after which the mouth is held closed with the hand, in order to compel the animal to swallow the wafer." Schœfer says: In some cases the dose has to be repeated; but all useless and improper repetitions should be avoided. If no change of any kind should take place after the first dose, this is a sure sign that the medicine had been improperly selected, and that a second dose of the same remedy would not do any more good than the former had done. In this case we have to review the symptoms a second time, and to select a different remedy. If the first dose should produce a favorable change in the symptoms of the disease, and this change should again be followed by an aggravation, it is proper to give a second dose of the same remedy. If the symptoms should become aggravated after the first dose, we should not all at once resort to a different remedy; for this aggravation might be what we have termed homœopathic aggravation, which would soon be followed by a favorable reaction. In all very acute diseases that run a rapid course, and after one, two, or four weeks, terminate in death or recovery, such as Glanders, Pleura, Pneumonia, et cetera, the dose should be repeated every five, ten, or fifteen minutes.

In such dangerous maladies, the first dose is often followed by a visible improvement, which soon ceases, however: this is the time to repeat the dose, and a second dose may then be eminently useful. In chronic diseases that run a long course, the medicine may be repeated every day, or every two, three, or four days. In such cases the rule is, likewise, not to interfere with an incipient improvement by giving another dose of the same or some other remedy.

If the improvement stops, the medicine may be repeated, and if no improvement at all should set in after a reasonable lapse of time, another medicine may be chosen. Among the class of chronic diseases we number all nervous and mental diseases, lingering fevers, etc. An improper remedy does not produce any very injurious effects; for a homœopathic remedy only acts upon a disease to which the medicine is really homœopathic: otherwise the smallness of the dose is such that the medicine cannot possibly affect the organism. All that we have to do is, to give another remedy, and endeavor to avoid mistakes for the future. Homœopathic remedies may be applied externally in the case of burns, and other injuries. We use principally Arnica, Symphytum, and Urtica-urens, from twenty to thirty drops in a half pint of water, and this mixture to be applied to the part according to directions.

A proper diet in the case of sick domestic animals is of great importance. All applications, quack medicines, etc., that might interfere with the regular treatment, have to be avoided. Injections of water mixed with a little salt on soap are allowable. The usual feed may be continued. * * * * * * * Half an hour, at least, should elapse, between the feeding and taking of the medicine.

On the treatment of the sick animal, Rush says :

Treatment of a sick animal. As soon as an animal is discovered to be unwell, let it be immediately placed in a house by itself; this is necessary both for the welfare of the sick animal and for the safety of the others. The house that the animal is placed in ought to be warm, well-lighted and ventilated, and above all, kept scrupulously clean. Let the person who attends to the wants of the animal be very cautious to approach in a quiet manner, never make any unnecessary noise, or do any thing that would tend to irritate the animal when in a state of health.

With regard to diet. In acute diseases no food whatever ought to be given until improvement has taken place, and even then only in a sparing manner ; the articles of diet most suitable are bran, oats, hay, carrots, Swede turnips, and green food, either grass or clover.

The bran may be given either dry or wetted, whichever way the animal prefers it.

Oats may be given mixed with the bran, either raw and crushed, or whole and boiled.

It is necessary to keep the animal without food or water half an hour before and after administering the medicine.

Repetition of the dose. In acute diseases it is necessary to repeat the dose every *five, ten, fifteen,* or *twenty* minutes.

In less acute diseases, every *two, four, six,* or *eight* hours.

In chronic diseases, once in *twenty-four* hours is sufficient.

REMEDIES FOR SPECIFIC DISEASES.

MANGE.

The principal medicine to be used in this disease is *Sulphur*, of which six drops must be given every day for two or three weeks; afterwards the following medicines will be found useful—*Arsenicum, Sepiœ,* and *Rhus toxicodendron*.

Arsenicum, if the hair falls off and the skin becomes loose and flabby, or if there are ulcers with hard red edges.

Dose.—Six drops night and morning.

Sepiœ, if the parts affected are tender, and the animal shrinks when touched, or if there are white-looking blisters, filled with a watery fluid.

Dose.—Six drops night and morning.

Rhus toxicodendron, if there are hard elevated patches or scabs that do not fall off of themselves, and if taken off, others soon form in their places.

Dose.—Six drops three times a day until better.

FARCY.

REMEDIES. *Aconite, Arsenicum, China, Rhus Toxicodendron,* and *Thuja Occidentalis*.

Aconite, if accompanied with fever, in which case the

swelling is hot and painful, the animal refuses to eat, is restless, and moves about from place to place.

DOSE.—Six drops or twelve globules, three or four times a day.

Arsenicum and *China* alternately, if the swelling is cold.

DOSE.—The same as prescribed for Aconite.

Rhus toxicodendron, if with the hot swelling there is great stiffness of the limb.

DOSE.—Six drops or eight globules, morning, noon and night.

Thuja occidentalis, if there are any pimples or hard patches, or if the animal frequently stretches the limbs, and a crackling noise is heard at the same time.

DOSE.—The same as recommended for Rhus toxicodendron.

GREASE.

REMEDIES. *Thuja occidentalis, Secale cornutum, Arsenicum, Mercurius vivus,* and *Sulphur.*

Thuja occidentalis, both internally and externally, if there are bluish or brownish excrescences, which bleed on the least touch, and there is a discharge of fetid ichor.

DOSE.—Six drops three times a day; at the same time the parts may be bathed with the strong tincture night and morning.

Secale cornutum and *Arsenicum* may be used in alternation, if there is a watery swelling or dark looking ulcers, with fetid discharge.

DOSE.—The same as directed for Thuja occidentalis, internally.

Mercurius vivus, when there are numerous small ulcers that discharge a thick matter, and bleed when touched.

DOSE.—Six or eight drops twice a day.

It is necessary to give a dose of *Sulphur* once a week during the treatment, and keep the legs clean by washing them with warm water.

FOUNDER.

REMEDIES. *Aconite, Bryonia, Veratrum, Arsenicum,* and *Rhus toxicodendron.*

Aconite, if there is inflammation, the animal stands as if rooted to one spot, the breathing is hurried and interrupted, the breath is hot, and the pulse accelerated.

Dose.—Six drops every one, two or three hours.

Bryonia, complete stiffness of the limbs, with swelling of the joints.

Dose.—Six drops every two hours.

Veratrum, if it is brought on by violent exercise.

Dose.—The same as directed for Bryonia.

Arsenicum, if it is caused by bad or heating food, or after a cold drink when overheated.

Dose.—The same as directed for Aconite.

Rhus toxicodendron, if there is much pain in the feet, and the animal is very stiff in his movements.

Dose.—Six drops or eight globules three times a day ; at the same time the limbs may be bathed with a solution of Rhus, externally, twice a day.

HIDE BOUND.

REMEDIES. *Arsenicum, Antimonium crudum, Mercurius vivus,* and *Sulphur.*

Arsenicum, if there are hard scurfy patches about the skin, coldness of the skin, general emaciation, loss of strength.

Dose.—Six drops or six globules three times a day until better.

Antimonium crudum, if there are rough scales on the skin, coat very rough, loss of appetite, and excessive thirst.

Dose.—Six drops in a little water night and morning.

Mercurius vivus, if the animal has fits of shivering, the

hair falls off from various parts and leaves the skin of a dull leaden color, voracious appetite or unnatural appetite, eating of dirty litter and even dung.

DOSE.—Six drops or six globules night and morning.

Sulphur, as an intermediate remedy, may be given twice a week during the whole treatment.

DOSE.—Six drops in a little water.

THRUSH.

This disease is of frequent occurrence, where proper care is not taken as regards cleanliness, by allowing the horse to be continually standing on moist litter or in his dung, whereby the frog becomes soft and tender, and there is a discharge of fetid pus and matter from the cleft of the frog. For the cure of this disease cleanliness is requisite, and to place the animal upon a dry or sandy bottom.

REMEDIES. *Tincture sulphuris, Phosphoric acid, Squilla,* and *Arsenicum.*

Tincture sulphuris is considered most specific for this disease.

DOSE.—Six drops night and morning until better.

Phosphoric acid is useful, especially if the preceding remedy has been of little benefit.

DOSE.—The same as of Tincture Sulphur.

Squilla, if there is a fever or inflammation of the parts.

DOSE.—Four drops twice a day until the inflammation is subdued.

Arsenicum, if the discharge is very fetid, and there is lameness, the foot very hot and painful.

DOSE.—Six drops three times a day.

MEGRIMS.

REMEDIES. *Aconite, Belladonna, Arnica, Opium,* and *Sulphur.*

Aconite will be serviceable, and may always be given, especially if during an attack the horse falls down and then tries to get up again without succeeding.

DOSE.—Four drops every hour until relieved, after which it may be repeated at longer intervals, increasing them until the horse is entirely cured.

Belladonna, if the animal turns quickly round, falls down and continues alternately to struggle and lie quietly.

DOSE.—The same as directed for Aconite.

Arnica, if the disease is supposed to arise from mechanical injury.

DOSE.—Six drops every one, two or three hours, according to the severity of the case.

Opium, if the animal lies in a stupid state as if dead.

DOSE.—The same as directed for Arnica.

The medicine ought to be given two or three times a day, for a week after an attack, to prevent its recurrence, finishing with a dose or two of *Sulphur* in the same manner as directed for the other remedies, only at longer intervals.

INFLAMMATION OF THE BRAIN.

REMEDIES. *Aconite, Belladonna, Veratrum,* and *Opium.*

Aconite, in the very commencement of this disease, if the pulse is accelerated, fever, congestion towards the brain, rapid breathing, and trembling of the whole body.

DOSE.—Six drops every twenty minutes until several doses have been taken, or the more violent symptoms subdued, after which the next remedy should be taken into consideration.

Belladonna, if the animal has a wild, staring, fixed look, dashes furiously and unconsciously about, which is indicative of violent congestion of the brain.

DOSE.—Six drops put upon the tongue every fifteen or thirty minutes. until the violence of the attack is subdued.

Veratrum, if the legs and ears are icy cold, with convulsive trembling of the whole body, or where there is a reeling, staggering motion, and the animal plunges violently and falls down head foremost.

DOSE.—The same as directed for Belladonna.

Opium, if after the paroxysms the animal remains motionless, with fixed, staring eyes, the tongue of a black or leaden color.

DOSE.—Six drops every half, one or two hours, according to circumstances.

CARTARRH, OR COMMON COLD.

REMEDIES. *Aconite, Nux vomica, Dulcamara, Rhus toxicodendron, Bryonia, Arsenicum, Mercurius vivus,* and *Pulsatilla.*

Aconite will be useful in the beginning of the disease, if there is fever and heat of the body, restlessness, short hurried breathing, violent thirst, urine fiery red, and the discharge from the nose impeded.

DOSE.—Six drops or six globules every three hours until better.

Nux vomica, if during the prevalence of north-easterly winds, and if the mouth is dry, tongue coated white, an offensive earthy odor emitted from the mouth, and a thin watery or thick bloody discharge from the nose.

DOSE.—Six drops or six globules twice a day.

Dulcamara, if the attack was brought on from exposure to wet, and the animal is dull and drowsy, the tongue coated with a thick sticking phlegm.

DOSE.—The same as directed for Nux vomica.

Rhus toxicodendron. if short dry cough, great accumulation of mucus in the nose, without being able to discharge it, obstructed respiration, frequent sneezing, and restlessness.

Dose.—Four drops or six globules three times a day.

Bryonia, if there is difficulty in breathing, dry spasmodic cough, swelling of the nose, profuse coryza, or crusts of hardened mucus in the nose.

Dose.—The same as directed for Rhus toxicodendron.

Arsenicum, if the discharge from the nose continues too long, is acrid and corroding to the nostrils, dry cough, sneezing, with discharge of watery mucus from the nose.

Dose.—Six drops twice a day.

Mercurius vivus, in the first stage of the disease, if there is swelling of the nose, profuse coryza with much sneezing.

Dose.—Six drops or six globules three times a day.

Pulsatilla, if the cough is loose, discharge of greenish fetid matter from the nose.

Dose.—The same as directed for Mercurius vivus.

COUGH.

REMEDIES. *Dulcamara, Nux vomica, Squilla, Bryonia, Ammonium muriaticum, Drosera, Pulsatilla,* and *Lycopodium.*

Dulcamara, if it follows cold, especially if the cold comes on from wet, and there is a discharge from the nose.

Dose.—Four or six drops three or four times a day until better.

Nux vomica, if the cough is dry, and the cough comes on when first leaving the stable.

Dose.—The same as directed for Dulcamara.

Squilla, if the animal makes a groaning noise before coughing, and the whole body shakes from coughing.

Dose.—Four drops or six globules two or three times a day.

Bryonia, if the cough is of several weeks' standing, and worse from motion.

Dose.—Six drops night and morning.

Ammonium muriaticum, if the horse appears to be choked or about to vomit, loss of flesh, the skin sticks to the ribs.

Dose.—Four drops every three hours until improvement is manifest.

Drosera, if the cough is of long standing, worse at night when the animal lies down.

Dose.—Six drops night and morning.

Pulsatilla, if the animal is timid and easily frightened, or if with the cough there is a bad smelling discharge from the nostrils.

Dose.—Four drops or six globules every three hours.

Lycopodium, if the cough is excited or worse after drinking, and comes on in fits, coughing a great many times in rapid succession.

Dose.—Six drops three times a day.

Attention ought to be paid to diet in this disease; no inferior food should be given, such as the animal must eat a large quantity of to keep itself alive; but whatever is given should be good, and that moistened with *cold* water; carrots are very good, either raw or boiled.

SORE THROAT.

REMEDIES. *Aconite, Mercurius vivus, Belladonna, Spongia, Lycopodium,* and *Sulphur.*

Aconite, if there is much fever, accompanied with dry heat of the skin, the parts affected inflamed and red, violent thirst, and difficulty in swallowing.

Dose.—Four drops every two hours, until the febrile symptoms have ameliorated, after which give the next remedy.

Mercurius vivus, if there is much saliva in the mouth, enlargement and swelling of the glands of the neck, difficult deglutition, symptoms worse toward night.

Dose.—Six drops or eight globules three times a day until better.

Belladonna, if there is difficulty in breathing, shrinking when the throat is touched, as the slightest pressure causes a choking sensation, difficulty of swallowing, especially fluids, which are returned through the nose.

Dose.—The same as directed for Mercurius.

Spongia, if the breathing is very difficult, accompanied with a rattling kind of sound, the animal has an anxious countenance, turns his head from side to side and appears to be suffocating.

Dose.—Four or six globules every two hours.

Lycopodium, if the animal sweats, and the swelling is most under the jaw, the membrane inside the nose and lips yellow, the mouth smells very badly.

Dose.—Six drops night and morning until better.

Sulphur, in obstinate cases, if the swelling is extensive, painful constriction with difficult deglutition.

Dose.—The same as of Lycopodium.

INFLAMMATION OF THE LUNGS.

REMEDIES. *Aconite, Phosphorus, Bryonia, Belladonna, Tartar emetic, Hepar sulphur, Mercurius vivus, Ipecacuanha, Rhus toxicodendron, Squilla,* and *Sulphur.*

Aconite, in the very commencement, if there is much fever, quick and full pulse, thirst, hurried respiration, dry heat of the skin. It is considered the sheet anchor for this disease, as well as for all cases of inflammation, if it is resorted to immediately at the commencement of an attack.

Dose.—Four drops or six globules every fifteen, twenty or thirty minutes, until some amelioration of the most violent symptoms takes place, which may generally be seen at the end of two or three hours; it may then be administered at longer intervals, in alternation with the next following remedy.

Phosphorus may be used in alternation with *Aconite*, when the more violent febrile symptoms have been subdued.

Dose.—Four drops or six globules every one, two or three hours, according to the violence of the symptoms.

Bryonia, if the breathing is difficult, especially if with each respiration there is heard a grunting sound.

Dose.—The same as directed for Phosphorus.

Belladonna, if the breathing is hurried, and a rattling noise is heard in the throat, short dry cough occasioning a spasmodic constriction of the throat and chest.

Dose.—The same as directed for Phosphorus.

Tartar emetic, if the breathing is short and difficult, cough coming on in paroxysms, irregular, almost imperceptible pulse; it is especially useful if hepatization is supposed to have commenced.

Dose.—Four drops or six globules every three or four hours.

Hepar sulphur, frequent deep breathing, with wheezing, expectoration of tenacious mucus, as if tubercles or abscesses had formed.

Dose.—Six drops three times a day.

Mercurius vivus, if there is much discharge, dry cough, oppressed breathing, pulse feeble, frequent sweating.

Dose.—The same as prescribed for Hepar sulphur.

Ipecacuanha, if the breathing is rapid and anxious, rattling noise in the throat when breathing, eyes red and inflamed.

Dose.—Six drops every one, two or three hours, according to the violence of the case.

Rhus toxicodendron, if there is oppression and heaving of the chest in breathing, the nose red, inflamed and painful to the touch, and the animal has his legs widely separated.

Dose.—The same as directed for Ipecacuanha.

Squilla, violent painful cough, breathing quick and anxious, constant desire to urinate.

Dose.—Four drops or six globules every three hours.

Sulphur, rattling in the chest on breathing, relieved by expectoration, cough dry, with discharge of lumpy, greenish mucus as if abscesses had formed.

Dose.—The same as directed for Hepar sulphur.

The animal must be debarred from food till the violence of the disease is abated, and then it ought to be sparingly given for some time. Cold bran mashes, carrots, and a little sweet hay may be given. After a day or two, if all goes on favorably, a few oats may be allowed; cold soft water, frequently refreshed, should be constantly kept within reach of the horse.

If the legs are cold, they must be rubbed with the hands, and flannel bandages applied; the usual practice is to use straw or hay bands, but these are too cumbrous, and frequently irritate the animal, and consequently do more harm than good.

INFLUENZA.

REMEDIES. *Aconite, Mercurius vivus, Belladonna, Arsenicum*, and *Bryonia.*

Aconite is generally required to commence the treatment with, if the disease assumes an inflammatory character, and there is fever, dry cough, violent sneezing, and running from the nose.

Dose.—Four drops or six globules every three hours.

Mercurius vivus, if with the sore throat there is profuse secretion of saliva, the animal sweats, watering of the eyes and intolerance of light.

Dose.—Six drops three times a day.

Belladonna, if the head is affected, the eyes prominent and inflamed, inability to swallow, especially fluids.

Dose.—The same as directed for Aconite.

Arsenicum, if there is great weakness, general heat of the body, loose evacuations, sometimes bloody, discharge of bloody matter from the nose, great thirst.

Dose.—Four or six drops three times a day.

Bryonia is useful, if the febrile symptoms do not give way after using *Aconite,* and the discharge from the nose stops, and the breathing becomes affected.

Dose.—The same as directed for Aconite.

COLIC OR GRIPES.

REMEDIES. *Aconite, Arsenicum, Nux vomica, Opium, Chamomilla, Colchicum, Cantharis, Hyoscyamus,* and *Colocynth.*

Aconite, in the commencement if there is dryness of the mouth, the ears are either hot or cold, breath hot, pulse accelerated.

Dose.——Four drops or six globules every fifteen or thirty minutes, according to the urgency of the case, if no relief is obtained after the third dose, proceed then with the next remedy.

Arsenicum, if the disease depends on indigestion, food of bad quality, drinking cold water when heated, or if it is caused by a constipated state of the bowels, in which case it is considered to be specific.

Dose.—Six drops every half, one or two hours.

I have succeeded in curing a great number of cases

with these two medicines; I generally, after giving two or three doses of *Aconite*, give *Arsenicum* and *Aconite* alternately.

Nux vomica, is useful for colic from constipation, when the animal walks slowly round, and then lies or falls down suddenly, bloated appearance of one or both flanks.

Dose.—The same as directed for Arsenicum.

Opium, if *Nux vomica* fails to remove the constipation, or if the excrements are very dry, hard and dark colored nearly black, and the animal lies stretched out as if dead.

Dose.—Four drops or six globules every one, two or three hours, according to the urgency of the case.

Chamomilla, if the bowels are relaxed, the animal is very restless, frequently lying down and getting up; an attack of pain soon followed by an evacuation, swelling of the abdomen, extremities cold, especially the ears.

Dose.—Six drops every one or two hours, according to the severity of the case, until better.

Colchicum, if the disease is caused by green food, and there is flatulent distension of the abdomen, protrusion of the rectum, the animal strikes at his belly with his hinder feet.

Dose.—The same as directed for Chamomilla.

Cantharis, if there is a troublesome retention of urine, and the animal often places himself in position to pass urine, but only succeeds in passing a few drops; if this remedy does not relieve, give *Hyoscyamus*.

Dose.— The same as directed for Chamomilla.

INDIGESTION.

REMEDIES. *Antimonium crudum, Ipecacuanha, Nux vomica, Arsenicum, China, Silicea,* and *Sulphur.*

16

Antimonium crudum, if there is total loss of appetite, rough staring coat, evacuations watery and stinking, craving for drink.

DOSE.—Six drops or ten globules night and morning.

Ipecacuanha, if there is aversion to food, or vomiting of food and mucus, stools green and fetid.

DOSE.—The same as of Antimonium crudum, or they may be given alternately.

Nux vomica is useful, if it arises from cold in the spring of the year, and there is constipation, or the animal stands in a stupid, drowsy state for hours together, without changing his position.

DOSE.—The same as prescribed for Antimonium crudum.

Arsenicum, if the derangement of the stomach is of long standing, the skin becomes hard in different places, with or without diarrhœa, but it is more particularly indicated when the stools are watery or bloody.

DOSE.—Six drops once or twice a day according to circumstances.

China, if it is a young horse that has been overworked, especially if there is much debility and loss of appetite.

DOSE.—Four drops or six globules three times a day until better.

Silicea, if the animal sweats from the least exertion.

DOSE.—The same as directed for China.

Sulphur may be given as an intercurrent remedy in any stage of the disease.

DIARRHŒA.

REMEDIES. *Bryonia, Arsenicum, Sulphur, Chamomilla, Pulsatilla, Dulcamara, China, Carbo vegetabilis,* and *Colocynthis.*

Bryonia, if there is alternately diarrhœa and constipation, or if brought on by sudden changes of temperature, especially from heat to cold.

Dose.—Six or eight globules every three or four hours.

Arsenicum, if it is the result of green or unwholesome food, and the discharges are watery, with or without pain.

Dose.—The same as directed for Bryonia.

Sulphur and *Arsenicum* may be given in alternation if the evacuations are bloody and very offensive; also in chronic diseases.

Dose.—The same as directed for Bryonia.

Carbo vegetabilis, if the discharges are very offensive and approach putridity.

Dose.—Six drops or eight globules every four or six hours.

Chamomilla, if there is swelling of the abdomen, evacuations greenish, and the animal is restless.

Dose.—The same as directed for Bryonia.

Pulsatilla, if the evacuations are frequent and full of air bubbles, flatulent state of the bowels, aversion to food.

Dose.—Six drops or eight globules three or four times a day.

Dulcamara, especially in summer, if it has been brought on by taking cold after getting wet, and the evacuations are watery, accompanied with colic.

Dose.—The same as directed for Pulsatilla.

China, if the diarrhœa is of an intermittent character.

Dose.—The same as the preceding remedy.

Colocynthis, if approaching dysentery, with colic, and the evacuations consist of slime and blood.

Dose.—Six drops every one, two or three hours, according to the violence of the case.

INFLAMMATION OF THE BOWELS.

REMEDIES. *Aconite, Arsenicum, Rhus toxiccdendron, Colocynthis, Nux vomica, Cantharis,* and *Arnica.*

Aconite is the chief remedy to be depended upon in this disease, and should be frequently administered till a calm is established, which generally takes place in about an hour.

DOSE.—Six drops or eight globules every ten or fifteen minutes, until relieved.

Arsenicum, if after the use of *Aconite* some symptoms still remain, especially if the disease has been produced by green food, or by drinking cold water when heated.

DOSE.—Six drops every half, one or two hours, or at longer intervals, if the disease is not very violent.

Rhus toxicodendron, if the extremities are alternately hot and cold, with sweating of the belly, and a frequent discharge of urine.

DOSE.—The same as directed for Arsenicum.

Colocynthis, if *Arsenicum* does not remove all the symptoms, especially if it is accompanied with colic, and there are bloody evacuations.

DOSE.—Six drops or eight globules every half or one hour.

Nux vomica or *Opium*, if after the disease is cured there remains a constipated state of the bowels.

DOSE.—Six drops night and morning.

Cantharis or *Hyoscyamus*, if there is retention of urine.

Arnica will be useful in very obstinate cases, if the discharges are very fetid, frequently small stools consisting only of slime.

DOSE.—Six drops every one or two hours, until better.

WORMS.

REMEDIES.   *Cina, Sulphur,* and *Mercurius solubilis.*

Cina, if there is a discharge of worms, violent itching of the parts, causing the animal constantly to rub.

DOSE.—Six drops or eight globules three times a day.

Sulphur, discharge of lumbrici, with hard stool.

DOSE.—The same as of Cina.

Mercurius solubilis, if there is violent heaving of the flanks, discharge of large worms, soreness of the anus.

DOSE.—Six or eight drops twice a day.

Then there are the ascarides, small dark or red worms; these sometimes exist in immense quantities, and hundreds are often voided at one time.

REMEDIES. *Cina, Digitalis, Stramonium, Sulphur*, and *Arsenicum*.

Cina, symptoms similar to those indicating its use in lumbrici.

DOSE.—The same as above stated.

Digitalis may be given if the animal wastes away, and there is diarrhœa.

DOSE.—Six drops twice a day.

Stramonium is useful if the horse rubs himself behind.

DOSE.—The same as of Digitalis.

There are several other varieties of worms; but the symptoms are too complicated to be treated from any directions that can be given; but generally *Cina* and *Sulphur* will be found beneficial. I have also seen great improvement from a dose or two of *Arsenicum*.

INFLAMMATION OF THE KIDNEYS.

REMEDIES. *Aconite, Arnica, Dulcamara, Cantharis, Cannabis*, and *Mercurius vivus*.

Aconite in the beginning, if the animal is very uneasy, and the urine is fiery red, depositing a thick muddy sediment.

DOSE.—Six drops two or three times a day.

Arnica, if it is the result of an injury.

DOSE.—Six drops or eight globules night and morning.

Dulcamara, if it supervenes after exposure to wet.

Dose.—The same as of Arnica.

Cantharis, if there are frequent and painful emissions of bloody urine, in small quantities, trembling of the hinder extremities, which are wide apart, and the back arched.

Dose.—Six drops three or four times a day, until relieved.

Cannabis, if there is violent straining; the animal is very restless, paws the ground, and strikes at the abdomen with his feet.

Dose.—The same as directed for Cantharis.

Mercurius vivus, if the animal sweats and the discharge of urine is profuse.

Dose.—The same as directed for Cantharis.

A GLOSSARY OF DISEASES.

ALBUGO, - - - - Partial dimness of the corner of the eye, with whitish spots.

ANCHYLOSIS, - - - Loss of motion in joints; bones grown together, or ligaments contracted.

AMAUROSIS, - - - A sort of blindness called "glass eyes."

BLOOD SPAVIN, - - An enlargement of the sac which contains the lubricating fluid of the hock joint.

BLOODY URINE, - - An emission of blood, more or less mixed with urine.

BOG SPAVIN, - - - An aggravated form of blood spavin.

BONE SPAVIN, - - - A bony enlargement of the lower part of the hock joint on the inner side of the leg.

BOTS, - - - - - The larvæ of the gad-fly. The eggs are deposited on the horse's hair, and after he licks them off, and swallows them, they are hatched in the stomach, where they adhere to its surface.

BREAK-DOWN, - - - Rupture of the sheath which confines the back tendon of the leg.

BROKEN KNEES, - - Injury to the knees from falling. The skin is broken, and, at times, the joint is opened.

BROKEN WIND, - - Rupture of the air-cells of the lungs; heaves.

BRUISE OF THE SOLE, Injury, and consequent inflammation of the sensible, or inner sole, caused by pressure of a badly fitting shoe, of gravel between the shoe and the foot, &c.

CAPPED HOCK, - - A swelling of the point of the hock, behind, caused by an enlargement of a sac containing synovial fluid, as in blood spavin.

CATARACT, - - - - A disease of the eye.

COLIC, SPASMODIC, - A spasmodic action of the muscular coat over certain parts of the intestines, without a corresponding activity of the whole. It produces an irregularity in the passage of the food through the intestinal canal, and causes great pain.

COLIC, FLATULENT, - An inflation of the bowels by gas emitted by the fermentation of undigested food.

CONTRACTION OF THE
FOOT, - - - - - A drawing together of the back part of the foot, and an accompanying reduction of the size of the frog.

CORN, - - - - - A bruising of the sensible sole, and an accompanying rupture of its blood-vessels at the angles, between the wall of the foot and the bar.

CURB, - - - - - An enlargement of the back part of the hock, three or four inches below its point, and a strain of the ligaments of the tendon, or a rupture of its sheath.

DIABETES, - - - - Excessive urinating.

DISTEMPER, - - - - An epidemic catarrhal fever.

ENTERITIS, - - - - Inflammation of the external coats of the stomach.

FALLING IN OF THE
FOOT, - - - - - A depression of the front part of the wall of the foot, caused by the descent of the coffin-bone in *pumiced feet*.

FALSE QUARTER, - - A more or less complete separation of the hoof as it grows down from the coronet. The result of injury to the coronet, or of neglected quarter, crack, or quittor.

FARCY, - - - -   Obstruction of the absorbent vessels, whose duty it is to remove useless matter from the various organs. It is a stage of *Glanders*.

FISTULA IN THE WITHERS, - -   A bad sore, resulting from neglected saddle-galls on the withers.

FISTULA IN THE POLL, Poll evil; a troublesome ulcer on the top of the head.

FOOT, CANKER IN, -   A growth of fungus matter (proud flesh) between the horn and sensible part of the foot.

FOUNDER, ACUTE, -   An inflammation of the laminæ of the foot, originating in too hard work, or in cold.

FOUNDER, CHRONIC, -   This is a species of founder, insidious in its attack, and destructive to the horse. It produces less severe lameness than acute founder.

FOOT, INFLAMMATION OF, - - - - -   Acute founder.

FOOT, PRICK IN THE, -   A wound of the laminæ by a badly driven nail, or the penetration of sharp substances to the sensible sole, or frog.

GALL, - - - - -   Abrasion of the skin by the saddle or harness.

GLASS EYE, - - - -   See AMAUROSIS.

GLANDERS, - - - -   A contagious disease, peculiar to horses, asses and mules. It commences with a slight discharge, generally from one nostril, but sometimes from both, and terminates in a complete obstruction of the absorbent vessels, which produces death.

GREASE, - - - - -   An inflammation of the skin of the heels, which renders them dry and hard, and causes them to crack.

GRIPES, - - - - -   See COLIC.

16*

GROGGINESS, - - - A weakness, and tottering condition of the fore legs, accompanied, usually by a knuckling over of the fetlock joint.

GUTTA SERENA - - See AMAUROSIS.

HEAVES, - - - - See BROKEN WIND.

HEMATURIA, - - - See BLOODY URINE.

HERNIA, - - - - A protrusion of the intestines, through a natural or artificial opening in the belly; rupture.

HIDE BOUND, - - - Dryness and unyielding condition of the skin, accompanied by a staring coat.

ITCH, - - - - - See MANGE.

JAUNDICE, - - - - The introduction of the bile into the general circulation. It is accompanied by a yellow appearance of the skin when visible.

LAMPAS, - - - - - A swelling of the gums or bars of the mouth.

LAMINITIS, - - - - See FOUNDER.

LARYNGITIS, - - - Inflammation of the upper part of the windpipe.

LOCKED JAW, - - - A constant spasm, and rigidity of all of the voluntary muscles. Usually fatal.

LUXATION, - - - - Partial displacement of the bones of a joint.

MALLENDERS, - - - Scurfy eruptions on the inside of the knee of the fore leg.

MANGE, - - - - - A pimpled eruption on the skin, with increasing scabs.

MARASMUS, - - - - A decay or wasting of the whole body.

MEGRIMS, - - - - A determination of blood to the head, causing temporary unconsciousness, and often causing the horse to stagger or fall.

MOON BLINDNESS, - See OPHTHALMIA.

NASAL GLEET, - - An increased and thickened discharge from the nostrils.

NASAL POLYPUS, - - A tumor hanging by a nick from the lining of the nostril.

NAVICULAR DISEASE, Inflammation, or anchylosis (growing together) at the joint formed by the coffin-bone and the lower pastern-bone, in connection with the navicular-bone.

OPHTHALMIA, - - - An inflammation of the eye which recurs at regular intervals, and terminates in total blindness of one or both eyes. It is sometimes called "Moon blindness."

OVERREACHING, - - Striking the fore legs with the shoe of the hind foot in travelling.

PALSY, - - - - - A suspension of the nervous influence over the muscles.

POLL EVIL,- - - - An inflammation at the top of the head, resulting from a bruise or gall of that part.

PUMICED FOOT, - - A foot of which the sole, in consequence of disease, descends to a level with or below the wall of the hoof.

QUITTOR, - - - - A deeply seated ulceration in the foot, resulting from a neglected or badly treated wound.

QUIDDING THE FOOD, Dropping the partly chewed food ; an indication of sore throat.

QUARTER CRACK, - - See SAND CRACK.

RABIES, - - - - - Hydrophobia.

RINGBONE, - - - - A bony enlargement of the pastern near the foot.

ROARING, - - - - Noisy inspiration, resulting from an obstruction of the air passages of the throat or lungs.

RUPTURE, - - - - See HERNIA.

RUPTURE OF THE SUS-
PENSORY LIGAMENT,   Breaking of the ligament by which the *sesa
moids*, two small bones on the back part of
the pastern-joint are kept in place.

SALLENDERS, - - - Scurfy eruptions on the inside of the hock-joint
of the hind leg.

SAND CRACK, - - - A separation of the laminæ of the hoof, forming
a crack up and down its wall; when it occurs
in the front part of the hoof it is called " toe
crack ;" when on one side, " quarter-crack."

SCOURING, - - - - Looseness of the bowels.

SITFAST, - - - - - A hardened integument on the back, resulting
from an obstinate saddle gall.

SPAVIN, - - - - - See BONE SPAVIN.

SPEEDY CUT, - - - A wound on the inside of the fore leg, near the
knee, made by the striking of the shoe of the
opposite foot in fast travelling.

SPLINT, OR SPLENT, - A bony enlargement on the side of the leg below the knee or hock.

STAGGERS, - - - - See MEGRIMS.

STALING, PROFUSE, - An excessive discharge of urine.

STRANGLES, - - - A disease, sometimes called " colt distemper."
A tumor forms under the jaw, and breathing
is rendered difficult ; in time the tumor breaks
and the patient recovers.

STRANGURY, - - - "Inflammation or spasmodic affection of the
neck and bladder."

STRING HALT, - - - A sudden jerking up of one or both of the hind
legs, not entirely involuntarily, but to a
greater height than is natural, or than is intended by the horse.

SURFEIT, - - - - A disease much resembling *mange*, but usually
commencing on the neck. It arises in, or is
accompanied by, a closing of the pores of the
skin of the affected part.

TETANUS, - - - - Locked jaw.

THICK-WIND, - - - Laborious breathing, resulting from a diminished capacity of the lungs after disease.

THOROUGH-PIN, - - A sort of wind-gall, or swelling upon the hock, and between the cord and the bone. It can be pressed through from side to side.

THRUSH, - - - - A softening of the frog of the foot, accompanied by an offensive discharge of pus.

TOE CRACK, - - - See SAND CRACK.

TREAD, - - - - - A wound of the coronet, inflicted by other feet.

WARBLES, - - - - Lumps in the back, resulting from neglected saddle-galls.

WASHINESS, - - - Looseness of the bowels.

WATER-FARCY, - - Local dropsy in the cellular membrane, resulting from general debility.

WHEEZING, - - - - Asthmatic breathing.

WIND, BROKEN, - - See BROKEN WIND.

WHIRLBONE LAME-
NESS, - - - - - Lameness of the hip-joint.

CHAPTER XXIII.

CARRIAGES.

IN a country where riding in carriages is an almost universal custom among those who can afford to keep a horse,
the selection of a carriage, and the manner of taking care
of it, are subjects of no small importance.

The vehicle, as soon as it rises above the condition of a
"business wagon," and is constructed with a view to comfort, or elegance of appearance, and assumes the character
of a "carriage," becomes an article of luxury, although
by no means a useless one; and its selection is a question
which should exercise both the judgment and the taste of
the purchaser.

No carriage can really look well if it does not look serviceable. If for heavy work, it must be strong and
appear strong, without appearing heavy or unwieldy. If
for light work, it can hardly appear too light; for it is so
generally known that delicately-made carriages may be
very strong, that the light appearance does not convey
an idea of weakness. If the carriage be intended to make
a rich display, it will be most beautifully finished when
most richly decorated. If to be used by persons of mod-

est and retiring habit, it will be most beautifully finished when it exhibits great simplicity, or an entire absence of decoration. A royal state carriage, and a simple coupé are both beautiful, though widely different. The simple vehicle will usually be the most elegant, and the error, if any, should be on the safe side.

The style of carriages in the United States is, for all descriptions, much lighter in appearance and in reality, than in England. Something is undoubtedly sacrificed on the score of strength and durability to this taste, but as it cannot be supposed that Young America will, for this generation at least, be content to drag about heavy lumbering carriages of the European style, we may find some compensation for the sacrifice in the fact, that what is lost in wear of the carriage is gained in horse-flesh, and in the speed and despatch with which our business, and even our pleasure-driving is accomplished,—while we may justly pride ourselves on having arrived more nearly at the maximum of strength for a minimum weight of wood and iron, than any other people.

Economy and safety demand that the purchaser assure himself that the carriage is sufficiently strong, and well made for the service for which it is required. If intended for use on city pavements or in stony districts, it must be of the best possible quality of material and workmanship, and a little extra weight in the wheels and axles is desirable. In all streets paved with stone, there are so many inequalities, and so many unyielding obstacles to the smooth moving of the wheels, that a single stick of unsound wood will usually soon make itself known, a bad tire will most likely be broken, a bad bolt will become loose or bent, and a bad spring will either be broken, or lose its shape and elasticity. Of two carriages of exactly the same appearance, and in precisely the same service, one will last for years, while the other will give signs of dissolution in a month.

In these *hints* to those who would purchase a carriage either ready made or made to order, we would not claim that any one, however experienced, can avoid being cheated if he fall into the hands of a dishonest maker, who has no regard for his reputation. In a hundred things can the purchaser be deceived; the quality of iron and steel—of the wood and leather—of the paint and varnish even—can only be tested by actual use; and the carriage-maker himself has to depend in a great degree on the "brand" or the reputation of the manufacturers, for the quality of many of the materials. Much more, then, must the purchaser of a carriage, which, when it is delivered to him, is covered up with paint and trimmings, depend on the character of the carriage manufacturer or merchant.

To those who would buy a carriage, our advice then is:

First—Make the most diligent investigation into the character of the firm with whom you deal; if possible, obtain the opinion of those who have dealt with them previously, as to their reliability; and when you are satisfied on this point, do not let an undue suspicion prevent your asking and following their advice—obtaining, when you can, a full guarantee for at least one year, against all defects or breakages, accidents excepted. Do not hope to buy a good carriage at a very low price. A dealer who professes to sell at cost is always to be suspected. A well-made carriage is always cheaper than one poorly made, at any difference in price.

Second—Consider well the purpose for which you require a carriage, and the character of the roads on which it will be used, and let your selection be carefully made in reference thereto. The weight of the carriage, the thick-

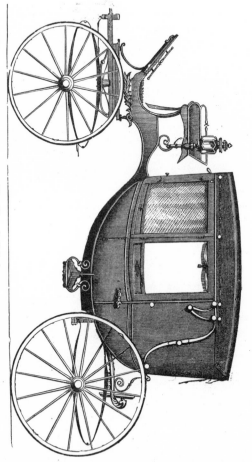

Fig. 56. A Caleche.

ness of the tire and felloes, size of the wheel, strength of the iron work, the stiffness of the springs, materials for the trimmings, the plating, the leather — all should correspond with the intended use. A desire for ornament, or a fine appearance, should never lead you to buy a fine carriage for a vehicle of all work. A "shabby gentility" will be the result after the gloss is worn away. If a nice carriage is required for occasional use, while there is also a necessity for driving during bad weather and on bad roads, it is poor economy to try to make one vehicle answer all purposes. A second, more strongly made, with more durable trimmings, must be provided, or the finer one will soon expose your want of judgment.

VARIETIES OF CARRIAGES.

THE COACH (Figure 55). — All panelled carriages with seats for four persons inside, and an elevated coachman's seat, are designated coaches. The *town coach* proper, has windows in the doors, and one in each end, the quarters being panelled. The most elegant coaches of this kind have a full sweep in the lower line of the body, although the outlines are varied to please individual taste. For many purposes windows in the quarters are deemed desirable. For country use, leather curtains in the quarters, instead of panels, are becoming popular. For cold weather the curtains may be "squabbed" on the inside, and rendered perfectly warm, while, in summer, by rolling up the curtains, the comfort and convenience of an open carriage may be obtained. A full sized town coach weighs about 1500 lbs. Price, $900 to $1200. The one from which our figure is taken* is finished in the best style, and would command the highest price. A curtain-quarter coach, for road use, may weigh 1200 lbs.; price, $750 to $900.

* From the extensive manufactory of Messrs. G. & D. Cook, New Haven

THE CALECHE (Figure 56) is of French origin; a carriage with leather top, and portable glass shutters on the sides, and a panelled front, with sliding window. The whole front may be removed in a few minutes, making it an elegant open Barouche, with a half-top over the back seat. No carriage is so desirable for winter and summer use. They are made for four persons inside. Weight, about 1350 lbs., with the front. Cost, about $75 more than a coach of the same quality.

THE LANDAU is similar to the Calèche, without the portable front and glass sides; the entire top being of leather, supported by folding joints in each quarter. The top may be divided in the centre, the whole falling front and back. These are complex in construction and liable to get out of order, which prevents their popular use. Weight and cost about the same as a calèche.

THE BAROUCHE (Figure 57) is made for four persons inside, and has an elevated coachman's seat; leather half-

FIG. 57.—The Barouche.

top over the back seat, or an extension top, covering the four inside seats. The latter form is desirable for country use, as it affords protection from the sun and rain. The half-top, for morning and evening drives, is much liked: the top being thrown down, the carriage presents an elegant appearance, and affords an opportunity for the display of full dress—hence it is popular with visitors at watering-places and public parks. Weighs about 1100 lbs. Cost, $750.

No. 58. An adjustable Seat Barouche, arranged for two persons.

No. 59. An adjustable Seat Barouche, arranged for four persons.

A smaller Barouche is made to carry four persons, including the driver, of less pretension and much cheaper and lighter, with an extension leather top (covering four seats), which may be thrown back at pleasure. It may be used with one or two horses. Weight, about 600 lbs.; cost, $350 to $400.

A Barouche of the smaller kind is made with a "jump-seat," so that it may be in a few seconds converted into a buggy, with seats for two persons. There are some objections to this *mongrel*, such as its liability to get out of order; and it is not possible to have the springs and other parts of the carriage well adapted to a *buggy* and yet capable of doing double duty when required. It is, however, often convenient, and will be much used. Messrs. G. & D. Cook, of New Haven, have just brought out a new style, shown in Figs. 58 & 59, with an adjustable seat and extension top,—the latter feature being new, and a great addition to the value of this vehicle.

THE COUPE, or BROUGHAM.—A half-coach body (Fig. 60), for two persons inside, and an elevated coachman's seat; very popular in Europe, and now becoming popular here. They are used in Europe with one horse only; here with one or two horses. Weight 800 to 1000 lbs.; price, about $700.

FIG. 60.—Coupé, or Brougham.

THE ROCKAWAY.—A Rockaway proper, has a plain square or straight body, with standing top and leather curtains, to roll up; for either four or six persons; all seats on a level. Of late years, all vehicles with standing top and seats on a level are called Rockaways. Some are made for six persons, with panelled sides and glass windows, which approach nearly to a coach in weight and cost. The following styles of Rockaways are in general use :

The square four-seat Rockaway, for one horse. Weight, about 500 lbs. Cost, from $200 to $300.

The same for six persons and two horses. Weight, about 700 lbs. Price, $350 to $400.

The six-seat Germantown Rockaway has the body slightly curved. Weight, say 800 lbs. Cost, $450.

The Coupé Rockaway, for four persons, with a partition ; having windows to divide the front and back seats; body curved, with windows or curtain in sides. Weight, about 700 lbs. Price, from $350 to $500.

THE BRETT.—A Brett proper, is a French half-top Barouche, with all the lines of the body at right angles. They are generally made with four inside seats, and elevated coachman's seat. Weight, about 800 lbs. Cost, $650.

The form more familiarly known in this country as a Brett, resembles that of the English Barouche, except it has only a half-top. Of this style we give an illustration in Fig. 61.

THE PHÆTON.—There is an infinite variety of Phætons. As originally made, they have seats for four, with a portable half-top, or without a top. Some are hung on platform springs without a perch ; others on two springs with a perch. They are also made with a comfortable front seat, having a leather top, and a smaller seat behind for a servant only. The varieties in use are : The "*Mail Phæton*," the "*Park Phæton*," the "*Sylph Phæton*," the "*Copcut*," the "*Victoria*," and the "*Pony Phæton*." Price, from $350 to $650.

A form of Phæton, very common and popular, has seats for two. The Queen's Phæton (Fig. 62) is a good carriage

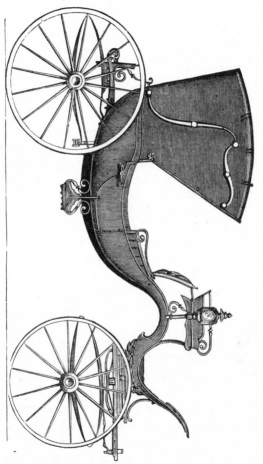

Fig. 61. A Brett.

for old people, or for ladies' use, being wide and roomy, hung low, and the top coming well over the seat. Price, $250 to $300. There is a form of this buggy-phæton, with a close Boston top, well adapted for Physicians' use.

THE BUGGY.—Of this kind there is a great variety. All, however, have four wheels, and seats for two persons. They are made of every conceivable form, both with and without a top; at all prices, varying from $75 to $400.

The Victoria Buggy (Fig. 63) is one of the prettiest styles, showy and of graceful form. As usually finished, it sells for $150 to $175.

Our Figure 64 represents a plainly finished but fine vehicle, costing from $175 to $225.

Figure 65 is what the Messrs. Cook call the World's Fair Buggy, having taken the medal there, and can be made for from $250 to $500.

For buggies without tops we give Fig. 66—a very light trotting wagon of 145 lbs.; Fig. 67, the light Concord

FIG. 68.—Skeleton Wagon.

buggy; and Fig. 68, a skeleton wagon for use upon the track.

THE DOG-CART, is made with two or four wheels. The original English Dog-Cart is on two wheels, Fig. 69, the body being nearly square, and carrying four persons. The back end of the body is made to drop and form a foot-board; the persons on the front and back seats riding back to back. The sides are generally made with blinds or lattice work, to accommodate dogs, when used for sporting pur-

FIG. 69.—Dog Cart.

poses. Two-wheel dog-carts weigh about 450 lbs. Cost about $275. On four wheels they weigh about 600 lbs. Cost about $450.

THE JAGGER WAGON is for two persons. The body is attached to axles without springs. Weight, 200 lbs. Price, $100 to $125.

CONSTRUCTION—THE WHEEL.

THE HUB of the wheel being at once its centre and foundation, mechanically speaking, should be particularly strong and of well-seasoned wood. Red elm, white elm, and particularly the gum, are good timber for this part, as they are not liable to crack in seasoning, or to split by the pressure of the spokes. The modern form of the hub is much shorter than that used even a dozen years ago, and though it may have some advantages in crowded thoroughfares, where, as on Broadway, New York, collisions are frequent, it is undoubtedly a change for the worse, so far as strength is concerned, as it gives a shorter hold to the axle.

Fig. 62. Queen's Phaeton.

THE SPOKES should, for heavy work, be made of white oak of clear grain, and free from checks or knots—for light carriages hickory is preferable—fourteen in the fore wheel and sixteen in the hind wheel, except in vehicles of the lighter kinds, when two less in each wheel will answer. If the tenon or "tang," which is inserted in the felloe, is square instead of round, it will greatly add to the strength, though few makers are found who will take this trouble. Every spoke which is discovered to be defective, in any way, should be scrupulously rejected by the carriage-maker; for one bad spoke will spoil the wheel. In a business wagon, the spokes should be set in the hub in range, or in a straight line, while in a buggy or light carriage, they should be placed alternately, in and out, that the weakness caused by their light construction may be compensated for by the bracing position, which this zig-zag position affords.

THE FELLOES or RIM.—This part of the wheel should be of the best eastern white ash or hickory (the western growth is softer and less tough). Oak is often used for this purpose, but is much more liable to sun checks, and will split more easily, and is more apt to break in at the joints. For pleasure carriages, which are kept well painted, and, for the most part, secure from the weather, the bent rim is better than the short pieces or sawn, felloes; but for business wagons, or those much exposed to the sun and rain, with the paint not always in the best condition, and which require a more frequent resetting of the tire and the consequent cutting of the ends of the felloe-sections, it is better not to be obliged so often to cut the same ends, as is the case when there are only two pieces. There are always, when the felloes are *sawn*, two spokes to each section.

The wheels should, in all cases, be dished, as this adds

much to their strength and durability. A light wheel for
road wagons, 4 feet in diameter, should dish about ⅜ to ½
inch; and coach wheels, 3 ft. 6 in. in diameter, should dish ½
inch, the measurements being taken, in both cases, after the
tire has been set.

THE TIRE.—It is upon this part of the wheel that most
of the wear comes, and if defects exist here, no excellence
in the other parts will be of any avail. The important
points in a good tire are, that it should be made of good
iron, that it should be the size best adapted to the vehicle
on which it is to be used, and that it be "set" well, neither so tight as to draw the wheel out of shape, or so
loose as to allow any racking of the spokes. The tires
should be made of Ulster iron, or the best English re-
fined iron. Ordinary steel tires, though thrice as durable
as iron, are apt to snap in frosty weather. Imported
"homogeneous" steel is now being successfully used in
light vehicles; but its cost (16c. per lb.) precludes its
use on heavy wheels. It is very durable, and remarkably
tough.

Flat tire is the best for all purposes; convex tire is
satisfactorily used on the flat, hard roads of Europe, but
they are not adapted to American use. Heavy tire on
light rimmed wheels is objectionable, for the reason that it
breaks down the felloes. All tires yield, more or less, to
sudden concussions; if heavy, it retains its bent form,
while, if light, it is forced back to its proper position by
the spring of the felloes. Wide tires are desirable on soft
roads, being less likely to cut in (causing the carriage to
run heavily, and injuring the road,) than narrower tires.
All tires should be fastened on with bolts, one between
each two spokes.

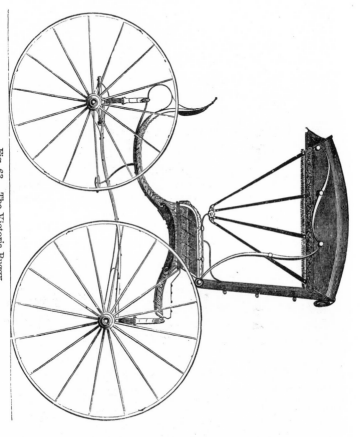

Fig. 63. The Victoria Buggy.

THE AXLE.

Since the general introduction of the iron axle, the wooden axle has gone out of use, except for the heaviest description of wagons for the farm, or other heavy work.

Axles may be either straight, arched, or cranked; the arched form, which is essential for all very light axles, being stronger than straight ones, though a very slight arch answers the purpose. Cranked axles are adopted for the purpose of allowing the body to hang low. Particular care should be given to setting the axles exactly at a right angle to the line of travel. Any deviation from this rule causes undue friction to the arm of the axle and the hub, and places the wheel in a position to receive more injury from concussions, and to be more easily wrenched out of its proper shape than when properly directed.*

THE PATENT AXLE, or as it is sometimes called the *Mail Axle* is represented in Figure 70. *a* is the arm of the axle, around which the hub revolves ; *b* is a shoulder which serves to keep the hub in place ; *c* is a circular iron plate, having through its centre a hole to fit the arm of the axle, behind the shoulder, where it revolves ; it is secured to the inside end of the hub by the long bolts, *e e*, which run through the entire hub and the plate *d*. There is a washer, which should be of hard sole-leather, nicely ad-

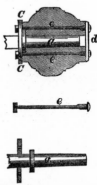

FIG. 70.—The Patent Axle.

---

* These remarks do not refer to the slight "gather" which is frequently given to wheels, to cause them to crowd slightly toward the carriage, rather than to run against the nuts at the end of the axle.

17

justed to the proper thickness, on each side of the shoulder, to prevent the wear of the *boxes* and *plate* against the shoulder. On taking off the wheel, the nuts, before-mentioned, are removed with a wrench, and the hub is drawn off the end of the axle, leaving the plate *c* remaining upon the axle. The leather washers require to be occasionally renewed, if they wear so thin as to give too much lateral motion to the hub.

This form of axle has many advantages, among which are: that it prevents rattling, or the lateral motion of the wheel; it is safer, for if the axle break at any point beyond the shoulder, the wheel is still retained in its place by the plate behind the shoulder; it forms a tight space about the arm of the axle for the lubricating oil, excluding grit or other substances which would cut away the axle. Its great disadvantage for small hubs is, that it is necessary to cut away so much of the hub in boring for the bolts that it is weakened. This is, however, very greatly obviated by the patent of E. M. Stratton, the gentlemanly

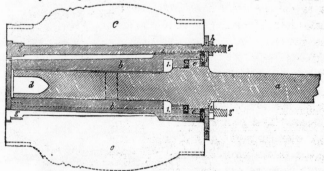

Fig. 71.—A longitudinal section of Stratton's Patent Axle and Box.

a The axle; *b* The box, inserted on the hub *c*; *d*—1 are spaces for holding the oil; *e* The shoulder of the axle; *f* The plate attached to the inner end of the hub; *g* The bolts which pass through the hub and the plate *f*, and are secured by the nuts *h*. 2 & 3 are leather washers on each side of the shoulder.

editor of the *Coach Maker's Magazine*. The form of hub for this axle is given in Fig. 71, and its peculiarity consists in having the bolts run in a groove made in the surface of the *box*, taking in one half the diameter of the bolts. This lessens the amount which is necessary to be cut from the substance of the hub.

THE HALF-PATENT AXLE is similar to the foregoing, but does not retain the bolts and plate. The wheel is secured by a nut upon the end of the axle.

THE SPRINGS.

These are of many kinds. The old C spring (Fig. 72), the cradle spring (Fig. 73), the elliptic spring, (Figs. 74 and 75), the shackle spring (Figs. 76 & 77), and the platform spring. That in most common use, and by far the best for ordinary purposes, is the elliptic spring, of which those shaped like Fig. 74 are better than those like Fig. 75. It is of the first importance that the springs should be of the proper degree of stiffness required by the weight of the carriage, and the number of persons they are intended to bear; if too stiff, they will "ride hard" and cause great discomfort; or if they are not stiff enough they will collapse or break. The stiffness is regulated by the thickness of the steel used, the length of the

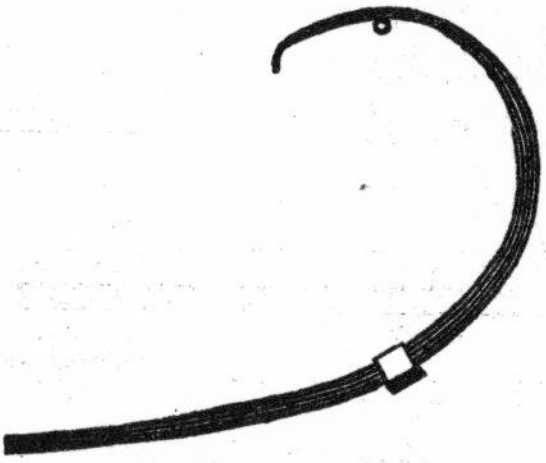

FIG. 72.—C Spring.

FIG. 73.—The Cradle Spring.

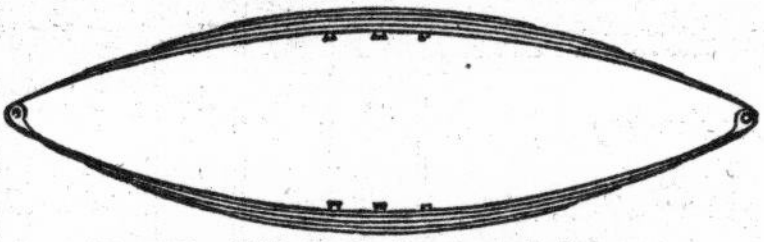

FIG. 74.—Elliptic Spring—good shape.

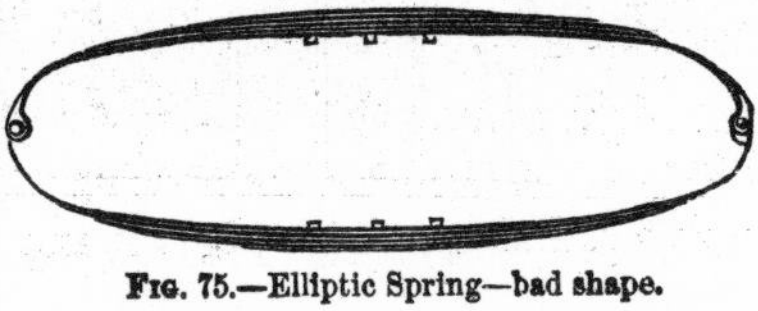

FIG. 75.—Elliptic Spring—bad shape.

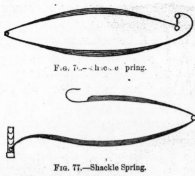

Fig. 76.—Shackle Spring.

Fig. 77.—Shackle Spring.

spring, and the width and number of leaves or plates. The body should be set on the springs a little inclined backwards as the tendency is to "run forward" in use. And in the coach, the forward end of the springs should, for the same reason, be set a little higher than the hind end.

TABLE OF DIMENSIONS OF PARTS OF THE WHEELS OF DIFFERENT VEHICLES.

Kind of Vehicle.	Diameter of Hub at the Centre.	Width of Spoke at the Hub.	Depth of Felloe or Rim.	Size of Tire.	Diameter of Fore Wheels.	Diameter of Hind Wheels.	Number of Spokes.	Diameter of Axle at Arm.	Length of Axle in Hub.
	inch.	inch.							ins.
Coach...........	6½	1⅞	7⅞	½ x 1½	3 ft. 4	4 ft. 2	14 & 16	1½	9
Rockaway........	5½	1⅜	1½	¼ x 1¼	3 ft. 4	4 ft. 2	14 & 16	1¼	8
Buggy	4¼	1⅛	1¼	⅜ x 1	3 ft. 10	4 ft. 2	16	1⅛	6½
Trotting wagon or Light Buggy....	3¼	1 in	1⅛	3⁄16 x ⅞	4 ft.	4 ft. 2	16	⅞	6
Doctor's Gig......	5½	1¼	1⅜	⅜ x 1	3 ft. 4	4 ft. 2	14 & 16	1¼	8
Sulkey...........	4½	1⅛	1⅜	¼ x 1	4 ft. 10		18	1	6½

Fig. 64. A Plain Buggy.

No 65. The World's Fair Buggy.

TABLE OF DIMENSIONS (IN INCHES) OF SPRINGS FOR
DIFFERENT VEHICLES.

Kind of Vehicle.	Length.	Width.	No. of Leaves.	Size of Steel.
Coach............	44 incs.	$2\frac{1}{4}$	6	No. 2 & 4
Rockaway........	40 "	2	5	" 3 & 4
Buggy...........	38 "	$1\frac{1}{2}$	4	" 4
Trotting Wagon or Light Buggy....	36 "	$1\frac{1}{4}$	3	" 4

The bodies of town carriages with low wheels, should be hung low; for country use bodies should be hung high, and high wheels used. The draught is less when so hung. When the diameter of the wheels will permit, the springs are best hung on the under side of the axle, as in this position they keep better in place, having less tendency to pitch forward. The use of springs on even the heavier description of wagons, except where subjected to excessive loads or very rough usage, is desirable, as it lessens the wear on all parts of the vehicle, and makes a lighter draught.

SHAFTS.—The best wood from which to make shafts is hickory. It is, however, more affected by wet than ash or oak. Second growth eastern ash makes very good shafts; but oak, except for heavy work, in which a considerable amount of timber is allowable, will be deficient in stiffness. For such heavy work it is the best, as it is the most durable, wood used in carriage-making. Shafts for light wagons are generally steamed and bent to such form as is required. They should be bowed out widely at the rear, and in front should turn well out, away from the horse's shoulders.

THE POLE for light wagons should be of hickory, steamed and bent; coach poles, of second growth eastern ash,—oak, when made up in this size, being apt to warp But for farm wagons, omnibuses, stages, &c., which admit of more material being used, oak is very much the best.

For the *attachment of the Shafts or Pole to the Axle* there have been very many devices to prevent rattling and accident; but none of them, for simplicity and cheapness, compare with that of Mr. Chapman, of Cincinnati. This is simply a piece of vulcanized india-rubber, (see Figs. 78 and

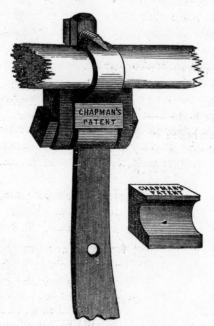

FIGS. 78 & 79.—Chapman's Patent Shaft Fasten.

79,) about 1 inch square, grooved on one side, and intended to be placed between the end of the shaft-iron, and the back part of the clip which is on the axle. The shaft is then forced back into its place and the bolt inserted. The constant pressure prevents all rattling of the jack-bolt, and, even if the nut should be lost off, which is unlikely, the bolt cannot rattle or slip out. It can be applied to carriages of the ordinary construction after they are worn so as to become loose.

THE BODY, PANELS, ROOF, LEATHER, ETC.

FOR COACHES.—The body frame work should be made of soft western ash; the top ribs of hickory, ash, or maple; the panels of white wood; and the roof of pine-wood deal. The ribs should be of ash, maple or cherry, and the frame of ash: hickory rots if much wet. The roof should be covered with canvas, or, which is better, with ordinary bed-ticking of the best quality. Before this is put on, the roof should receive a coat of pure white lead, and the canvas then stretched tightly over it and tacked fast. It should on no account be sized, (as was formerly the custom,) but should be heavily painted with pure lead and oil.

FOR TOPS, FALLS, etc., enamelled leather is now almost universally used, and, though less durable than the old fashioned " oiled top-leather," it looks better, being black and brilliant, and is not so apt to shrink. It works smoother and better than oiled leather. It is sometimes, however, badly enamelled, and then is apt to crack and scale off—especially if moved or rolled up in very cold weather. It will then crack beyond restoration and will look badly. Enamelled leather, which has been tanned with hemlock, is apt to stain the lining of the top, or fall when it gets very wet: the best quality is tanned with oak bark. Enamelled cloth is made to represent leather in appearance, and is used for some purposes advantageously,—say for carriage curtains not intended to be rolled up often. Its chief recommendation is its cheapness compared with leather; it is for no purpose so good.

For the *Dash*, "grain" patent leather is best. Its quality may be determined by its pliability. Hard, stiff leather will crack when exposed to heat and cold. The enamel should be smooth and brilliant, and show no " pitting," or unevenness in polish. Good dash-leather is *jet* black,— not greyish or reddish black.

VARNISH.—For the under coats, to be " rubbed," American varnish answers every purpose, but for finishing coats, English varnish is universally esteemed as the best. There is no way of testing the durability of varnish until it is used on the vehicle. English varnish will not crack, and expose the paint and wood to the action of the weather,—American varnish will do so. Finishing coats are now "flowed" on, not polished, as formerly, and they are, in consequence, more durable.

PLATING.—None but a professional man can determine the quality of plating. The seams of good plating should not show prominently; "two and half quality" silver— its technical term—is the poorest quality that should be used on carriages; "three quality" is the best. Electro plating, when well done, is desirable on hub-bands made of German silver or composition metal, as the bands will not rust when bruised, nor does the silver shell break, as close plate on iron bands will do. Iron cannot be electro-plated with advantage.

TRIMMING AND PAINTING.

TRIMMING.—The most durable material for trimming is cloth; if in high colors, it should be of English manufac-

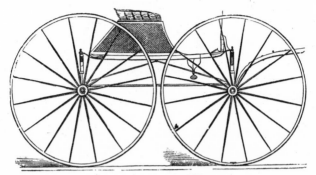

Fig. 66.   A Trotting Wagon.

Fig. 67.   A Light Concord Wagon.

ture, as, in the grade of cloth used for carriages, its colors are more durable than those of French and German man- ufature. High colors in American carriage cloths will not stand the sun.

The most elegant material for coaches is " côteline," a silk and cotton fabric, the best of which is made at Tours, in France. The greater portion of that imported to this country is made at Lyons, and it is inferior in quality to that made at Tours,—the colors being bad, and wearing badly. These goods are well adapted to warm latitudes, as they do not, like cloths, harbor moths. When style and elegance are chiefly desired, these goods are the most satis- factory; and when durability alone is consulted, cloth is best.

For stuffing seats and backs, nothing but the best curled hair should be used. If hair of inferior quality be mixed with it, it will breed vermin, especially in damp situations. Curled hair keeps the seats elastic.

HINTS ON COLORS.

A carriage body painted *green* should never be lined or trimmed with blue,—it produces a disagreeable effect. *Drab, crimson, brown* and *clarets*, harmonize well with green painting.

Blue bodies should never be trimmed with green. Drab and blue, and blue and grey, harmonize with blue bodies.

Claret or Lake bodies may be trimmed with almost any color,—blue being the least desirable.

CARPETS should harmonize in color with the trimmings, —as for instance :

Blue linings require blue and claret, blue and grey, or two shades of blue in the carpet. Red is objectionable.

Drab linings look best with blue crimson or green car- pets.

Green linings harmonize with carpets of crimson, or crimson and green.

Brown linings require brown and blue, brown and green, or green and black carpets.

Claret linings require green and crimson, crimson and black, or crimson and claret.

IN CARRIAGE LACES the same arrangement of colors as has been suggested for the carpet and linings, will be found to produce a pleasing effect.

STRIPING THE RUNNING GEAR.

On Black, stripe with orange, blue, carmine or green.

On Blue, with black, white or grey.

On Green, with black, red or white.

On Orange or Yellow, with black.

On Vermillion, with black.

On Lakes, with black, carmine or green.

HARMONY OF THE COLORS IN THE TRIMMINGS, WITH THE COMPLEXION AND DRESS OF LADIES.

To those who are desirous of doing no violence to the laws of harmony in even the smallest particulars, the following "hints" will be appreciated.

Blue, in the trimmings, harmonizes with the complexion of a *blonde*, while it impairs the beauty of a *brunette;* and with a crimson dress or shawl, blue is decidedly inharmonious.

Crimson, in the trimmings, suits well the complexion of either a blonde or a brunette, but the dress should not have blue as a predominating color.

Brown trimmings are suitable for a brunette, and agree with *green* drapery on the person.

Green, in the carriage, demands warm tints in the dress, and is then harmonious with all complexions.

Drab agrees well with all colors in the dress, and with all complexions.

We would sum up, then, tne following

RULES TO BE OBSERVED IN PURCHASING VEHICLES.

First. Choose for your carriage-maker one who has a character for fair dealing and good work.

Second. Never purchase a vehicle made for two horses with the hope that it will "do" for one horse. Your mistake will be apparent when you find your horse failing from over-work.

Third. Always insist upon "case-hardened," or steel converted axles. If you have any doubts of their quality, try a file on them. If " hard " it will make no impression.

Fourth. Insist upon "tempered" springs, made from English steel. Test your springs by loading the carriage before you buy it, and ascertain what weight they will carry when in use on the road.

Fifth. Examine all iron plates, clips and bolts. If the iron-work is not fitted to the wood with exactness, don't buy the carriage: a poor workman has been spoiling good material.

Sixth. See that the "jacks" or irons connecting the pole or shafts with the axles, are well fitted and sufficiently heavy. If badly fitted they will rattle; if not strong, they will endanger your life, if you use the carriage.

Seventh. See that the axles are "set" with exactness. No carriage will be durable, or run with ease, if the axles are not " set " with mathematical precision.

Eighth. Never select a carriage because it is elaborately finished with silver plate,—it soon looks shabby, and requires a great deal of care to keep it in order. Carriages are often elaborately finished to cover up serious defects in the workmanship.

Ninth. Examine closely the painting: a few years owner ship of a carriage will show a greater outlay in making good original defects in painting, than for any other item If the varnish is dull, it generally argues that the painting has been hurriedly done. The varnish will "strike in " on bad painting, and a little exposure in bad weather will crack the paint to the wood.

Tenth. Never permit, in the cushions or backs, any ma terial but pure curled hair. Moss soon becomes hard.

Eleventh. If you desire cloth linings in high colors always insist upon English cloths. French and German cloths, in high colors, for the qualities used in carriages will soon fade. In drab cloths, the American twilled is the best in use.

Twelfth. See that the cloth on the glass frames has been shrunk before it was put on: if not shrunk, the first rain to which it is exposed will draw it off the frames.

Thirteenth. See that the door locks and handles work with ease, and do not rattle. Nothing is more annoying than bad door locks, or even good locks badly fitted.

Fourteenth. In purchasing a carriage for road use, see that it is made to "track" in the ruts in the district where you intend to use it. There are at least a score of differ ent tracks in different parts of the Union—varying from 4 feet 4 (from centre to centre of the wheels, measured on the ground,) to 5 feet 4½ inches.

THE CARE OF THE CARRIAGE.

Having procured a carriage which has a fine lustre, which runs easily and smoothly, and which is generally well finished, it is desirable to maintain it in this condition as long as possible. This requires it to be properly cleansed, oiled when necessary, kept free from dust in the carriage-house, and to have its bolts tightened whenever they have worked loose.

The appurtenances necessary for this purpose are a pail, a watering-pot, (the water should never be thrown through a hose, as it ruins English varnish, and penetrates all the crevices in the springs, &c., causing rust,) two large soft sponges, free from grit, two full-sized chamois skins, an unlimited supply of water, a wisp-broom, a feather duster, (a cloth one will answer), a sheet for covering the whole carriage, a can of sweet oil, or, which is better, pure sperm oil, and a screw wrench. Soft water is much better than hard, as the latter is injurious to the varnish.

All of the fine carriages now made being varnished with English varnish, it may be well to call to mind that it has these peculiarities: it will become spotted whenever the mud is allowed to remain long upon it, and the more frequently it is washed, the more lustrous will it remain —hence it is necessary, in order that it may be kept in the best condition, that the carriage should be washed every time it comes in, and at least once a month whether it is used or not.

All freshly varnished carriages should be nicely washed, with soft cold water, four or five times before being used; it hardens the varnish and prevents its spotting by mud.

Never place a carriage near a stone or brick wall; the dampness destroys the varnish. Varnish requires a well ventilated room.

Ammonia from the stable will also destroy varnish in a short time.

The washing should be done in the following manner:

1. Supposing the top to be sufficiently clean, the cush-

ions, and whip removed, the inside of the carriage wiped out, and the curtains fastened down, sprinkle water on the body of the carriage with the watering-pot until all of the mud is washed off, by the action of the water alone, without having recourse to rubbing, and until you are sure that no grit remains.

2. Wash the whole body with the sponge which is kept for this purpose, using as much water as possible, and rubbing very lightly, continuing the operation until the water runs from the body perfectly clear.

3. Wet the chamois skin which is used for the body, and wring it out as dry as possible. This will soften it so that it cannot scratch the varnish. Use this to absorb the water which has been left after washing, wringing it out as often as may be necessary. Continue this until the body is dry. Do not *rub* it with the chamois skin, and do not use the skin, nor any substitute for it, when dry and stiff.

4. Pursue the same course with the running gear, (the wheels, springs, etc.,) as has been specified for the body but lay aside the sponge, and the chamois skin which were used for the body, and use for this portion the ones designed for it. Be careful to wash the wheels in such a manner as to throw as little water as possible on the body, and, whenever any does strike it, remove it at once as before directed. Do not apply soap to any part of the carriage, or even a sponge which has been used with soap, as it will destroy your varnish.

5. Having removed all the dirt, and thoroughly dried the carriage, paying particular attention to those parts where iron is likely to rust if any water is left, rub up the plate with a bit of dry chamois skin kept for the purpose, adding a little dry whiting where necessary, though if the plate is never allowed to become much tarnished there will

be little occasion to do more than to rub it with the leather.

6. The top may, when necessary, be washed by the same process as has been recommended for the body, and with the same care.

Having cleaned the carriage in every part, replaced the cushions, and rolled up the curtains, throw a muslin sheet over it to keep dust from it.

If the carriage has not been out since it was washed before, it will only be necessary to wet it thoroughly, and to dry it as directed.

This is the best method for washing the best carriages. It may be, and in most instances it probably will be, modified to suit the purposes of those who do not care to devote so much labor to this work; and in all such questions of object and expense, the judgment of the individual must establish the compromise.

At least once a month place a wrench on every nut on your carriage. You will thus prevent the loss of nuts and bolts, and preserve your carriage; a loose bolt frequently leads to serious breakages.

As often as once a month, and oftener if necessary, the wheels should be taken off, and the axles and boxes should be thoroughly cleaned, by scraping them with a sharp-edged piece of hard wood, covered with flannel or woollen. They should then, if full-patent axles, receive as much sweet oil, or pure sperm oil, as they will retain without allowing it to work out over the wheel. One tablespoonful to each wheel will be a good quantity.

When your leather washers are worn out, replace them with new ones. A patent axle running with worn out washers will soon be good for nothing.

For the half-patent axle, clean lard, or other grease, or any of the patent wagon-greases, will be found as effective as oil, and more permanent.

In lubricating the axle we can use for the heavy wooden or the plain iron axle a mixture of one-third tar and two-thirds lard, or some of the patent wagon-grease now offered for sale everywhere.

If from want of oil, or other cause, the friction of the axle in the box should cause the wheel to "stick" on the road, it will be necessary to stop until the iron becomes entirely cool, and contracts to its proper size; this can be facilitated by pouring cold water on the axle at the rear of the hub. The wheel may then be knocked off, and the axle sufficiently filed to remove the roughness caused by the slight welding which occasioned its sticking. It may then be oiled and the wheel put on again. If you have occasion to use a carriage when it probably needs oiling, you should take the precaution, as often as possible, to feel of the axle near to the wheel. If it is at all warm, it is unsafe to proceed without oiling it.

REPAIRS.

TIRE SETTING is the most important repair which will be necessary in the case of well-kept carriages, unless they become accidentally broken or worn from long use. This operation should, unless rendered necessary by accident, or improper construction, be performed only in the dryest summer weather, when the wood of the wheel is shrunk to its narrowest limits.

Injuries resulting from *Loose Tires* are: they cause the spokes to work loose, (technically, "churn out,") at the hub; they do not properly confine and support the felloes; and they are liable to be broken, or to become bent. The most certain indication of looseness of the tire is, that when struck on the flat with a hammer, it will give a dead, flat sound; a tight tire will give a clear, ringing sound when so struck. A "creaking" noise indicates a loose tire on an inferior wheel.

In every case in which it becomes necessary to revarnish, replate, or otherwise rejuvenate a good carriage, it is best to send it to a competent carriage-maker. Many persons, actuated by penny-wisdom, attempt to make many of these repairs themselves, but they almost invariably leave a permanent "botched" appearance, and lose, in durability and appearance, much more than they save in cost. Even the varnishing and the oiling of leather will be almost as cheaply, and much more satisfactorily performed, by a professional man than by one entirely unacquainted with the business.

In the preparation of this chapter, on the Selection and Care of the Carriage, we most cheerfully acknowledge our indebtedness for valuable aid, to Mr. J. W. BRITTON, of the firm of Brewster & Co., 372 & 374 Broome St., New York, whose tasteful and reliable suggestions have greatly enriched our pages; also, to Mr. E. M. STRATTON, editor of "*The Coachmakers' Magazine*," 106 Elizabeth street, New York, whose well-sustained and elegant journal is indispensable to every member of the "*craft*;" and to Messrs. C. and D. COOK, New Haven, Ct., from whose extensive establishment we have procured most of the drawings of vehicles which illustrate our descriptions; and to W. L. McDonald, Esq., of Beekman street, New York. We can only wish that our readers, in their search for an honorable and reliable firm of whom to purchase, may be so fortunate as to find one like unto these gentlemen whom we have mentioned.

CHAPTER XXIV.

HARNESS.—ITS SELECTION AND CARE.

THE QUALITY OF LEATHER—QUALITY OF WORKMANSHIP—THE COLLAR—THE
TRACES—THE BRIDLE—THE BIT—THE SADDLE—THE GIRTHS—THE CRUPPER
—THE BREECHING—THE HOLDBACKS—THE REINS AND MARTINGALE—THE
MOUNTING—HOW TO HARNESS AND UNHARNESS THE HORSE—THE CARE OF
HARNESS—CLEANING THE PLATING.

ALL who drive are interested in the subject of harness—
not only those who, keeping their own carriages or business wagons, have to procure and maintain one or more
sets of harness, but, in a less degree, those who have to
trust their valuable persons to the fidelity of strap and
buckle. The horse-keeper, from motives of economy,
should acquire such knowledge of the quality of leather
and workmanship, and of the best means of preserving
harness in sound condition, as will enable him to purchase
as wisely, and as seldom as possible. While those who
ride in hired vehicles should be able to assure themselves
of the safety of the harness by which they are drawn.

It is the object of this chapter to give as much information concerning harness, as can be comprised within its
limited space, by general remarks on the quality of materials and workmanship; descriptions of the various parts
of the harness; and directions for keeping the leather,
bits, buckles, &c., in the best possible condition for safety,
durability, and good appearance.

NOTE.—In preparing this chapter we have been greatly aided by Messrs. J. T. Smith
& Co., of 342 and 344 Broadway. The saddles, harness, bits, etc., illustrated in this
work, were mainly selected from their extensive stock.

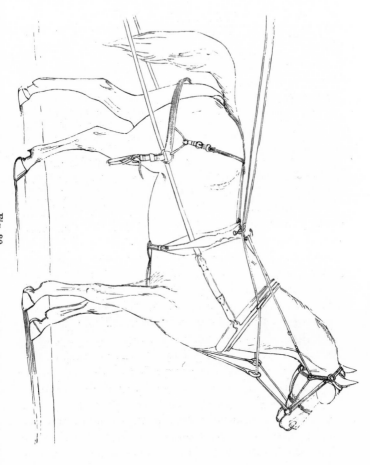

THE QUALITY OF LEATHER.

There can be given no very definite rules for judging of the quality of leather, but the following hints are not without value:—

All harness-leather of good quality is made from the hides of neat cattle, and is tanned either with oak or hemlock bark; that tanned with oak bark being very much the best.

Leather which has been tanned with oak bark alone, has, when cut, a yellowish drab color, without the least tinge of red, while that tanned entirely, or in part, with hemlock bark, has a reddish tinge, more or less decided in proportion to the quantity of hemlock bark which has been used. This reddish tinge is sometimes visible on the "wrong" or *flesh* side of the leather, though it is often disguised by subsequent coloring. By cutting a piece so as to show the inside of the leather, the red hue may be distinguished. If it has this appearance in any considerable degree, it should be discarded as not of the best quality. Leather which has been sufficiently tanned, is of the same color throughout its entire thickness; while, if it has been only imperfectly tanned, the middle will appear darker than the part near the outside. Hence if leather, on being cut across and having its newly cut surface moistened by the tongue, shows a dark streak in the centre, it may be fairly assumed that it has not been properly tanned.

Nearly all harness-leather has, on its black side, a wrinkled appearance. These wrinkles run from the back of the animal around to the belly; and, in this direction, the leather is weaker and more liable to stretch, than in the direction of the length of the animal's body, or *across* the wrinkles. The purchaser should, therefore, see that

every strap of the harness has the wrinkles running *across*
it, and not in the direction in which its strength is to be
tested.   No saddler with a regard for his reputation would
cut his straps in the direction of these wrinkles, and it is
chiefly in purchasing ready made harness, of a cheap
quality, that this caution is necessary.   Poor leather is
sometimes varnished, to give it a bright appearance.   This
can be detected by comparing it with leather known to be
of good quality.   Varnished leather should be rejected
in all cases when good quality is desirable.

The softness and pliability of leather is a pretty good
test of its quality, inasmuch as a skin is never so soft and
pliable when rotten, or half tanned, as when fully tanned
and of good stock.   The fact that the best tanned sole-
leather (English Bend) is very hard, seems to be opposed
to this idea, but this hardness is due, in a great degree, to
compression.

Beyond these, and, possibly, a few other similar indica
tions, there is nothing which can be said on this subject,
which would be of any practical value to those whose
only interest in learning the character and quality of
leather is based on their occasional necessity to purchase
harness.   Important differences between two tannages of
leather appear, to the uninitiated, as subtle as those between two vintages of old wine, and they can be detected
only by men cunning in the craft.

THE QUALITY OF WORKMANSHIP.

Of course the most casual observer will perceive great
differences between the style of manufacture of different
harness.   Aside from ornamental stitching, and scrolled
edges, there is a certain air of neat and dexterous workmanship apparent in the stitching and trimming of well-
made harness.

If the stitches be somewhat wide apart (or long) they are stronger, supposing good thread to have been used, than those which are very close together. Again, if the awl, which is dagger-shaped and not round, has been so inserted as to make the greatest length of its puncture in the direction of the stitching, the work is not nearly so strong as if the holes have their longest diameter extending *diagonally across* the line of the stitching. This difference is a very important one. Especially in cheap harness, the improper style of piercing is frequently adopted, from its greater rapidity. The reason why it is not so well is, that it weakens the leather by a too continuous line of cutting. When the proper plan has been pursued, the ends of the slit-like awl-holes can be seen on either side of the stitches.

PARTS OF THE HARNESS.

THE COLLAR.—The best for heavy work is the *English Collar*, which is shown in figure 80, as it distributes the draught over the whole surface of the breast and shoulders. Its size and weight should be regulated by the nature of the work to be performed. If for light work, too great weight should be avoided, as it increases the heat about the shoulders. For heavy work, it should be broad and full, especially at the point where the most direct strain comes, viz: where the traces are attached.

The proper fitting of the collar is an important matter, and should receive the especial attention of the horse-keeper. If it is too loose, it will gall the shoulders and chafe the neck by its motion; or if too tight, it will obstruct the breath by its pressure upon the windpipe. When in its proper position, snug against the shoulders, there should be space enough between the collar and the windpipe to allow the insertion of the fingers. With horses of stylish carriage, holding their heads high, and having very sloping shoulders, the collar is liable to work too much against the windpipe. This may be obviated by selecting *hames*, with the attachment of the traces very low down, and by the use of a breast strap, or false martingale, passing from the collar, between the fore legs, to the girth. A collar which is open at the top, fastened by straps and buckles, does not afford so firm a resistance to the draught, and for light harness is not so desirable as one solid-made, though it allows the *size* of the collar to be regulated to the neck.

For fine harness, collars are usually made with patent leather on the outside, because this has a more finished appearance, but a strong quality of common leather is more durable. The lining for the collars of fine harness should always be of leather. This is also best for work harness, but woollen cloth is generally used, because it is cheaper. The stuffing in an English collar, for light work, may be soft; but for heavy work it should be hard and perfectly even. It should be of some material which will not become matted together. For a buggy harness it may be of long straw, bound together, and covered with woollen; while for heavy harness there is no material so good as rye straw, cut as short as possible, so that it may be packed away in the collar, like sand. This will always give an even bearing on the shoulder, and will remain dry and cool.

The Breast or Dutch Collar, which is represented in figure 81, is better than the English collar for any light work, (in single harness) and it has the advantage of showing off a fine shoulder, which the other style would only conceal. The construction of the breast-collar is very simple. It should be lined on the inside with a wide, double fold of soft enamelled leather, under the breast-strap

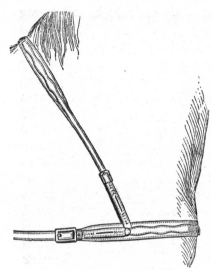

FIG. 81.—The Breast or Dutch Collar.

or plate, as well as under that which passes over the neck. The plate should be so long as to bring the trace buckles over the line of the back part of the fore leg. The plate, in front, should be furnished with a loop, to hold the martingale in its proper position.

THE TRACES should be of a size proportioned to the weight to be drawn. Square traces look unwieldy, and round ones are apt to rip. The best form is oval,—that is, a narrow, flattened trace, thick in the centre, and rounded at the edges. Coach traces are cut seven feet long, and are usually supplied with an arrangement by which they are secured *around* the end of the whiffle-tree, while the traces of buggy harness are six feet three inches long, and are fastered by a slit at the end, to an iron in the end of the whiffle-tree.

THE BRIDLE may be, with propriety, more ornamented or more highly finished than the rest of the harness (except perhaps the saddle); for a neat, plain harness, the bridle should be especially neat, with some slight ornament, as a rosette, or with a very little modest stitching; for a more highly ornamented harness, it may be covered with a profusion of fine work, and have a fair allowance of plated ornaments and buckles. In its general construction, it consists of a head strap, cheek pieces, throat-lash, and bit-

BLINKERS, or BLINDERS, (as they are very appropriately termed,) are, fortunately, growing more and more unpopular. There is no earthly reason why they should be generally used, except that they afford a good field for the display of initial letters and family crests. They are a frequent cause of blindness, resulting from an undue pressure against the eye; they cause horses to be frightened by the sudden appearance before them of objects which, without blinkers, they would have seen slowly approaching; and their use for the mere purpose of ornament is as unfortunate as is the use of green spectacles by fine-eyed men. It is not, of course, to be recommended that they be at once discarded in the case of horses on which they have always been used, though many such would go better without them: it is on young horses that their use is especially to be deprecated.

There are, now and then, to be found cunning horses, who regulate their pace to the indications of danger from behind. They will watch the driver, and go fast or slow, according to the probability of his using the whip. Such animals should wear blinkers, to prevent their looking back to the carriage. Even in these cases it would be better to substitute the "half-blinker," which consists of a narrow piece back of the eye, preventing the horse from looking back, while it allows him to see directly to the side.

Where it is considered necessary to use blinkers of the ordinary form, great care should be paid to their shape, and their position on the bridle. They should be very much hollowed out over the eye, and should be so placed that the greatest concavity will come directly over it. If placed a little too high or too low, their edges are liable to bruise and chafe the parts.

THE CHECK, or BEARING REIN, is another unaccountable mistake in harness invention. While it holds the horse's head in an unnatural, ungraceful, and uncomfortable position, it gives the mouth a callous, horny character, and entirely destroys all chance for fine driving. The check-rein is considered valuable, especially to prevent horses from grazing, or from lowering the head. The same end may be equally attained by substituting a simple bridle rein, to be fastened to the saddle without passing through the loops of the throat-lash.

THE BIT.—The bit is the most important part of the bridle; in fact, the chief use of the latter is to hold the bit in its place in the horse's mouth. Bits are of various devices; that most commonly used is the *snaffle*, figure 27, and for ordinary mouths, it should be large, plain, and easy to the mouth; the smaller it is, the more severe it will

be. The *bar* bit is a simple bar of iron, without a joint; it is easier to the mouth than the snaffle, and is much used for

FIG. 82.—The Bit.

fast trotting horses, which are to be driven with a strong hand. A still easier bit is that represented in figure 82, which is made of leather, covered with India-rubber; it is useful for very tender mouths. All of these bits should be supplied with long branches, or large rings, or with large discs of leather, to prevent their being drawn through the mouth, when either rein is drawn in turning. For carriage teams there is often employed a species of curb bit, called the Hanoverian, which does not differ, in principle, from the Hanoverian bit, shown in figure 28. Its form is somewhat modified by having its branches straight, and supplied with holes for attaching the reins at greater or less distances from the mouth-piece, according to the amount

18

of leverage required. The mouth-piece is usually made plain,—without the port or curve which is used in the Hanoverian bit, for riding.

Whenever a curb-chain is used, particular attention should be given to its length. If too tight, it chafes the horse's chin; if too loose, it does not act with sufficient power. It should be so adjusted that, when the branches are perpendicular, and the horse's head in its proper position, the finger may be easily passed between it and the chin.

THE BODY.—The body part of the harness consists of the saddle, with girths, the back-strap, and crupper, and the breeching and hold-back.

THE SADDLE.—The saddle may be either heavy or light, according to the character of the harness. For buggy harness and for light double harness, it should be very narrow and light, (in all cases, it should be stuffed on either side of the spine), with a piece of heavy felt, or leather plate, of somewhat greater width attached to it, to prevent it from injuring the horse's back,—this is entirely separate from the saddle, and is attached to it by two small straps passing around it, one at either end of the saddle. The terrets are two standing rings at the sides, and a hook in the centre, to which the check-rein is fastened.

THE GIRTHS should be made in the same manner as the shoulder-piece and plate of the breast-collar,—that is, of a piece of ordinary leather, protected on the side next to the horse, by a pad of softer leather of greater width. Single harness has two girths—one to hold the saddle, and one to hold down the "tugs," (through which the shafts are passed,) while double harness has but one girth, the traces being passed through a loop on the lower part of the saddle-straps on either side.

THE BACK-STRAP AND CRUPPER.—The back-strap passes

from a ring at the back of the saddle to the crupper, and has an opening over the horse's hips, through which the strap, supporting the breeching, is passed, and the continuation is divided at its end so as to buckle into either end of the crupper.

The *Crupper* is that part which passes under the horse's tail, and which serves to hold the saddle back to its proper place, and to prevent its yielding to the tension of the check-rein, when one is used. It should be very large (as being less likely to hurt the horse), and filled with some material which will not become hard and stiff; a very large crupper will prevent the horse from holding his tail hard down over the rein, and thus removes a serious difficulty incident to driving.

THE BREECHING.—The breeching is the strap which passes back of the horse's thighs, and which sustains the weight of the carriage in descending hills, and moves it in backing. It is indispensable in single harness, but is not necessary in double harness, except for heavy work or in hilly countries. On tolerably level roads, and with moderately light loads, horses will work equally well and more comfortably without it, while their appearance is very much improved by its absence. The breeching should be made in the same manner as the plate of the breast-collar, having at its ends strong rings instead of buckles. It should not be too long, the rings coming very little forward of the horse's stifle. It is supported by a strap passing over the horse's hips, to the divided ends of which, on either side, it is attached at the ring and at a point further back, which should not be less than six inches from the ring. This supporting strap may be either split up nearly to the back-strap, or it may be connected by a ring with two short straps which pass to the two points of attachment of the breeching.

The *Holdbacks* are the straps which connect the rings at the ends of the breeching with the shafts. In these very essential parts of the harness, strength should never be sacrificed to appearance. They should be made of the best quality of leather, cut straight at the sides, stitched coarsely at the fastening on of the buckle, and be of good size. They will be stronger and more durable if made of one thickness of stout leather, than if made of an equal weight of two strips of thin leather stitched together.

THE REINS should be so strong that, if the traces or whiffle-tree break, the horse may draw his load by the bit;

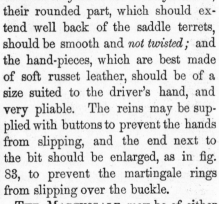

their rounded part, which should extend well back of the saddle terrets, should be smooth and *not twisted;* and the hand-pieces, which are best made of soft russet leather, should be of a size suited to the driver's hand, and very pliable. The reins may be supplied with buttons to prevent the hands from slipping, and the end next to the bit should be enlarged, as in fig. 83, to prevent the martingale rings from slipping over the buckle.

THE MARTINGALE may be of either the standing or ring sort, according to the taste of the purchaser. It is not a very important part of the harness, if the horse has been trained to carry his head in its proper place. If he persist in running out his nose, he will probably be most effectually cured by the use of the standing martingale, while, if he have a trick of tossing his head, a rather short ring-martingale will enable his driver to resist or punish

FIG. 83.

the attempt. The martingale, in its passage from the girth to the reins, should be securely attached to the collar (if the English collar be used); and if there be no martingale, the collar should be connected with the saddle girth by what is called a false martingale. This is very important, especially in double harness without breeching, when fully one-half of the weight of the load, in going down hill, comes upon this false martingale.

THE MOUNTING.—The finest bits are of polished steel; and the terrets and buckles of plated metal, orcovered with leather. The steel bits should be smooth, and entirely free from flaws and dull spots; the brilliancy of the polish is of no consequence. Plating is of two sorts,—electro-plating, and close-plating; the latter is the best, and may be distinguished by breathing on it, and examining it while covered with moisture, when there will be found, on some part of it, the joint where the two edges of the leaf of silver or gold come together. When no such joint can be found, reject the mounting as electro-plated. The plating should be free from little cracks. Covered buckles and terrets are a *vanity*. They look well at first, but they are never strong, and the leather in time wears off and looks shabby. Even plain japanned buckles are to be preferred to covered ones.

HOW TO HARNESS AND UNHARNESS THE HORSE.

Lead the horse out from his stall to where the collar has been conveniently hung, and, with the large end uppermost, put the same carefully over his head, having first widened it by pulling it over the knee. After it has passed his head, turn it (in the direction in which the mane falls) to its proper position. The breast-collar may be passed over the head, of course, without these precautions. Now tie your horse securely, and fit the collar to its place, that it may become warm before work commences. Examine the hames to see that neither the strap at the top nor the connecting links of the traces are twisted; then put them over the collar, and buckle them at the bottom. If fastened by an iron at the bottom, they should not be unfast. ened at the top, but the iron may be put in its place while they are over the horse's neck, and then they may be put in their place on the collar and drawn up at the top. In either case they should be drawn snugly to their place, without being made so tight as to press the collar too tightly against the neck. Take the body of the harness from its peg, hold the saddle in the left hand, and with the right properly adjust the various parts; then, taking hold of the back-strap near the supporting strap of the breeching, place the whole quietly on the horse's back. Standing by the side of the horse's hip, raise the tail with the left hand, and, with the right, put the crupper in its place under the tail, being careful to free it from the hairs of the tail. Buckle the crupper to the back-strap, and then draw the saddle forward to its place; the back-strap should be short enough to keep it well back of the withers. Pass the girth, which holds the saddle, through the loop of the martingale, and fasten it pretty tightly, leaving the other girth buckled to the terret on the off-side of the saddle. Now adjust the parts of the bridle, hang its head-piece over the thumb of the left hand, and remove the horse's halter, slipping the right hand over the top of his head and holding him by the forelock. Take the top of the bridle in the fore finger of the right hand—the others still retaining their hold of the forelock—and with the left insert the bit in his mouth, drawing it quickly to its place, and passing the head-piece over the horse's ears. Now arrange the bridle, drawing the forelock under its front piece, and fitting the bridle about the ears. Buckle the throat-lash long enough to allow it to fall down against the cheeks. If you use a check-rein, pass it over the terret hook of the saddle; see that it is not so short as to unnaturally confine the horse's head.

In putting the horse to the wagon, if you are not sure that he is well trained to stepping into the shafts, either have a second person to hold up the shafts while you back him into them, or stand him before them and raise them up so as to draw them over his hips. Pass the shaft through the near-side tug about 6 or 8 inches, and then go around to the off-side and put the end of the other shaft through the tug and the loop of the second girth, which is buckled through it. Unfold the trace of the off-side and pass it first under the tug, and then through the loop on the shaft, fastening it, without a twist, to the whiffle-tree. Then come back to the near-side and fasten the other trace; after which unfold the holdback and pass it down between the horse and the trace, through the loop under the shaft, and again over the top of the shaft, forward of the loop, then down between the shaft and the trace, up again outside of the shaft, and then between the shaft and the turn which has been made over it, and back to the buckle. Fasten the other holdback in the same manner, and adjust the buckles of both so that when the horse is standing back squarely against the breeching, there shall be a slack of 3 inches in each trace; this will give him room to work. *See that the breeching is high enough,*—not more than 12 or 14 inches below the setting on of the tail. Unfasten the second girth from the terret of the off-side, pass it through the martingale loop, and buckle it around the shaft and through the tug on the near-side. Uncoil the reins, pass them through the martingale rings and the terrets of the collar and saddle, and, carefully avoiding twists, buckle their ends together, and your horse is geared. Be sure that you have every strap only sufficiently tight: do not emulate the example of that distinguished Hibernian who drew taut all of the straps, buckled them in the last hole, and then cut off the ends "to make it look nate."

To *unharness*, pursue the following order:—Unbuckle the reins and coil them to the rings of the bit; let down the check-rein; unbuckle the second girth and fasten it to the terret; unfasten and fold up the holdbacks; unfasten and coil the traces; slip the tugs from the shafts; lead the horse out of the shafts, lowering them easily to the ground; lead the horse to the place of unharnessing and remove the bridle, holding him by the mane until his halter is made fast; unbuckle the crupper and the saddle-girth, slipping the latter free from the martingale loop; take the saddle in the left hand, and the back-strap in the right, drawing the body part off over the hips, and remove the harness,—hanging each part of the harness in its place as taken off. Now unfasten the halter-tie; move the collar to the upper part of the neck, widen it by drawing its sides apart, and turn it upside down (turning in the direction in which the mane falls); stand in front of the horse's head, and draw off the collar, squarely and slowly, holding the sides as much as possible away from the horse's eyes.*

The work of putting on and taking off harness is done as much as possible on the near-side of the horse, and special care should be taken to do everything with the utmost quietness and gentleness.

In harnessing the double team, the same general plan is to be pursued as with the single horse, deviating from the

* If the collar can conveniently be left in its place until the neck is cool, the skin will be less liable to become sore from its pressure than if it be immediately removed.

above described system only so much as is required by the different character of the harness,—and 'earing in mind the remarks on coupling-reins, and occasionally changing sides with the horses, which will be found in chapter XIX., (How to Drive a Horse.)

THE CARE OF HARNESS.

Fine harness should not be kept where it will be constantly surrounded by an atmosphere saturated with ammonia, as in the stable, or so near to it as to be within reach of the fumes of the manure of the horses. The ammonia would be absorbed by the imperceptible film of moisture on it, and would "eat up" the oil of the leather. For the same reason it should not be hung against a whitewashed wall, as the lime would get on the leather, and injure it by the same action.

For each harness there should be two long pegs, five or six feet from the floor. On one, hang the bridle, next to the wall; and the collar, the small end up, outside of the bridle. On the other, hang the body of the harness, by the saddle, letting the back-strap and breeching hang down, and the hames outside of the saddle. Thus arranged they will be in the proper order for putting on to the horse.

When the harness is taken from the horse, take a woollen cloth or chamois skin, kept for the purpose, and wipe off the dust, and all moisture from rain or perspiration; and when the harness is nearly dry, rub its damper parts very thoroughly with a second cloth or skin, until it is quite soft and pliable.

The bits and plated mounting should be cleaned and rubbed with a slightly oiled rag before the harness is

18*

finally hung in its place. It is well to protect the harness from dust by covering it, on its pegs, with a sheet, or, better still, by hanging it in a closet. When the leather of the harness becomes dry and hard, it should be cleaned and oiled. The best published directions for these processes are contained in the following, written to the *N. E. Farmer,* by Mr. J. Hart, of Portsmouth, N. H.:—

First, I take the harness apart, having each strap and piece by itself; then I wash it in warm soapsuds. I used to soak it in cold water for half a day, as others did, but I find that warm water does no harm, and much facilitates the job. When cleaned, I black every part with a harmless black dye which I make thus:—One ounce of extract of logwood, twelve grains bichromate of potash, both pounded fine; upon that I pour two quarts boiling rainwater, stirring until all is dissolved. When cool it may be used. I keep it on hand all the time, in bottles. It may be applied with a shoe brush, or anything else convenient. If any one objects to the use of this blacking, fearing that the bichromate of potash it contains would injure the leather, I would say, that this kind of potash will not injure leather, even when used in a much larger proportion. The blacking generally used contains copperas, sulphate of iron, and it is found that it will eat out the life of leather, unless used with great caution. When the dye had struck in, I go through with the oiling process. Some have a sheet-iron pan to oil in; but I have a sheet of iron nailed to a board; it is about two by three feet square. This I lay upon a table; I lay a piece or part of the harness upon this, and with neat's-foot oil applied with a paint-brush, kept for the purpose, I go over it, oiling every part. The traces, breeching, and such parts as need the most, I oil again. For the last oiling I use one-third castor oil, and two-thirds neat's-foot oil, mixed. A few hours after, or perhaps the next day, I wipe the harness over with a woollen cloth, which gives it a glossy appearance. Why I use some castor oil for the last coat is, because it will stand the effects of the atmosphere and the rain much longer than neat's-foot oil,—consequently the harness does not require oiling so often. One pint of oil is sufficient for one harness.

The common way of oiling a harness is, to apply as much neat's-foot oil containing lamp-black as the leather will take up; then washing off with castile soap and water. This way is not so good as mine, because it makes the harness smutty, and also the soap that is used contains barilla,—a strong alkali,—which cuts up and feeds upon the oil in the leather, and the weather, especially if rainy, soon renders the harness stiff and unyielding as before; the wax in the threads is also destroyed, and the stitching gives way. I have experimented with different kinds of oil, and find that the kind, and the process I now use, is the best.

A French work, "*Le Bourellier et le Sellier*," gives the following recipe for restoring old and stiff leather:

Melt over the fire, in a metallic vessel, eight pounds of very pure beeswax, stirring it until it is all melted; then introduce one pound of litharge, which has been pulverized in water, dried, and passed through a fine sieve. Leave it on the fire, and stir it until all of the soluble part of the litharge is incorporated with the wax; remove the vessel from the fire, and when the mixture shall have lost a portion of its heat, incorporate with it, little by little, one pound and a half of very fine ivory black, of the best quality; replace it on the fire, and stir it incessantly until the wax commences to boil again; then remove it and allow it to get nearly cool. Then add to it spirits of turpentine, until it is of the consistency of a paste. More turpentine may from time to time be added, as may become necessary.

APPLICATION.—If the leather is old and stiff, or covered with gum, wash it with a brush with weak potash-water or soap, and then with pure spring-water; leave it to dry, and then blacken it with ink. When that is well absorbed, wipe it with a cloth, and then grease it abundantly with fish oil of good quality, (neat's-foot oil is probably preferable.) When the grease has been thoroughly imbibed, pass over it a sponge moistened with spirits of turpentine, to remove the grease from the surface; then give it, with a shoe-brush, a layer of the above preparation; finish by polishing with a soft and dry brush.

This process will restore the leather to a soft, pliable condition, and give it a beautiful appearance.

CLEANING PLATE.—If the plated portions of the harness become tarnished, they may be cleaned by rubbing first with whiting and water, and then with whiting alone. Polished steel mountings should be kept clean and imperceptibly oiled, by the use of a cloth which contains *only a suspicion* of sweet oil. Use no acids in cleaning the plate, as it will soon destroy the coating.

INDEX.